Lecture Notes in Computer Science   10429

Commenced Publication in 1973
Founding and Former Series Editors:
Gerhard Goos, Juris Hartmanis, and Jan van Leeuwen

More information about this series at http://www.springer.com/series/7407

Peter Parycek · Yannis Charalabidis
Andrei V. Chugunov · Panos Panagiotopoulos
Theresa A. Pardo · Øystein Sæbø
Efthimios Tambouris (Eds.)

Electronic Participation

9th IFIP WG 8.5 International Conference, ePart 2017
St. Petersburg, Russia, September 4–7, 2017
Proceedings

 Springer

Editors
Peter Parycek 🆔
Donau-Universität Krems
Krems
Austria

Yannis Charalabidis
University of Aegean
Karlovassi
Greece

Andrei V. Chugunov
ITMO University
St. Petersburg
Russia

Panos Panagiotopoulos
Queen Mary University of London
London
UK

Theresa A. Pardo
University at Albany
Albany, NY
USA

Øystein Sæbø
University of Agder
Kristiansand
Norway

Efthimios Tambouris
University of Macedonia
Thessaloniki
Greece

ISSN 0302-9743   ISSN 1611-3349   (electronic)
Lecture Notes in Computer Science
ISBN 978-3-319-64321-2   ISBN 978-3-319-64322-9   (eBook)
DOI 10.1007/978-3-319-64322-9

Library of Congress Control Number: 2017947799

LNCS Sublibrary: SL1 – Theoretical Computer Science and General Issues

Printed on acid-free paper

This Springer imprint is published by Springer Nature
The registered company is Springer International Publishing AG
The registered company address is: Gewerbestrasse 11, 6330 Cham, Switzerland

Preface

The International Federation for Information Processing (IFIP) Working Group 8.5 (Information Systems in Public Administration) is very pleased that the dual IFIP EGOV-EPART 2017 Conference was hosted this year in St. Petersburg – the second largest city and the cultural capital of Russia – at the State University of Information Technologies, Mechanics and Optics (ITMO University). Университет ИТМО (ITMO University in Russian) is one of Russia's National Research Universities and one of the Russian universities selected to participate in the "Russian Academic Excellence Project 5-100" by the government of the Russian Federation so as to improve its international competitiveness among the world's leading research and educational centers. It specializes in information technology, optical design, and engineering and has 11,200 students, of whom 1,500 are foreign students from 71 countries. This made it an ideal place for the 2017 IFIP EGOV-EPART Conference.

The IFIP EGOV-EPART Conference presents an opportunity for researchers and experts from all over the world to meet and exchange current ideas and research on a range of issues addressed in the tracks on e-government, e-participation, open government, open and big data, policy modeling and informatics, and smart governance, government, cities, and regions. The papers submitted contain current research findings, implementations, ongoing research, methodological and theoretical issues, as well as critical reflections. Authors also cover emerging and special topics, provide models, and help visualize the data and results obtained. A PhD Colloquium offers students the opportunity to present their work; they benefit not only from the feedback and guidance given by senior scholars, but also from other researchers' experiences, cross-disciplinary inspiration, and the networking opportunities.

This volume of the IFIP EGOV-EPART proceedings contains the full papers from the "eParticipation" track and the "Policy Modeling and Policy Informatics" track. Following a double-blind peer-review process, the papers from these two tracks were finally accepted for this volume.

eParticipation is the use of information and communication technologies (ICT) to enhance political participation and citizen engagement, but is by definition a multidisciplinary field of study, and the papers from the "eParticipation" track present recent developments drawn from several technical, political, and social areas. The authors who submitted to this track describe new and innovative developments in this expanding discipline, and focus on research topics such as citizen engagement in public affairs and public participation facilitated by information and communication technologies. The "Policy Modeling and Policy Informatics" track focuses on supporting public policy making using innovative ICT and involving relevant stakeholders. The papers accepted to the "Policy Modeling and Policy Informatics" track look at public policy-making with innovative ICT that involves the relevant stakeholders, policy analysis, programming, conceptual modeling, and visualization of simulation models. While both these tracks highlight the importance of theoretical foundations, critical reflections, and implementations, they address in particular the importance of inter-disciplinary research and the use of existing concepts and approaches combined in innovative ways to achieve powerful, transparent, participative, data-driven, and collaborative solutions. Thus the research made available in these tracks is not just multidisciplinary, it is also complex, as it considers different political, economic, social, human, and technical aspects.

Several authors focus on methodological issues. Amizan Omar, Vishanth Weerakkody, and Uthayasankar Sivarajah consider the performance metrics necessary for evaluating participatory budgeting based on multiple channels. Such participatory platforms are important as they foster citizen engagement and aim to have sociopolitical impact, but determining the success of such an initiative and platform requires the development of criteria to evaluate it accordingly. Other authors, such as Magnus Adenskog and his colleagues, consider both the potential and the risks of using the living lab approach to evaluate mobile participation by focusing on a Täsä, a new mobile application that enables interaction between citizens and city authorities in Turku, Finland. Kevin Klamert and Sander Münster look at gamified tools and methods for fostering public participation in urban planning. They suggest that playful formats as well as gamification and serious gaming may improve public participation, and provide insights for the design of participatory platforms.

In terms of practical implementations of eParticipation, Uwe Serdült and Thomas Milic consider e-voting in Switzerland for citizens living at home or abroad. Using structural equation modeling, they analyze a survey on e-voting recently conducted in Switzerland to consider the important issues of digital divide and trust associated with e-voting. Using the concept of crystallization, a metaphor borrowed from chemical engineering where the aim is to produce highly purified and ordered crystal lattices from raw materials, Guoray Cai, Feng Sun, and Jessica Kropczynski look at how local (political) knowledge can be "crystallized" to support informed public participation. Using a case study (a community issue about inflationary tax indexing), they show how community-level, panel-based deliberation can be "crystallized" into knowledge to be extracted and used for decision-making in the public domain. Just as important is the presentation of ongoing work, such as that by Lyudmila Vidiasova, Dmitrii Trutnev, and Evgenii Vidiasov, who analyze the factors that impact the development of e-participation in Russia, or by Aggeliki Androutsopoulou, Yannis Charalabidis, and Euripidis Loukis, who consider how ICTs and social media help the transfer and exchange of knowledge as well as interaction for the development of effective public policies in a democracy.

Focusing on data-driven policy making and modeling, Anne Fleur van Veenstra and Bas Kotterink consider the policy lab methodology to support data-driven policy-making, that is, the collaboration between citizens and public administrations so as to co-create policy. They first identify innovations in data-driven policy-making, then map them to the stages of the policy cycle, and find that most innovations focus on the use of new data sources and that methodologies to capture the benefits are still "under development." Cesar Renteria and Ramon Gil-Garcia study the concept of policy analysis and find that it is associated with many different terms and meanings. This has led to conceptual ambiguity, and they use the Min-Max strategy of concept formation to provide conceptual clarity to help future research in this area. Bernhard

Waltl and his colleagues consider to what extent the outcome of appeal decisions based on the German tax law can be predicted. Predicting the outcome or the probability of winning a legal case has always been highly attractive in legal sciences and practice, and they present their research based on a machine-learning classifier to predict the outcome of cases.

Critical approaches and reflections are always important. Wouter Bronsgeest, Rex Arendsen, and Jan van Dijk study a selection of evaluation reports of e-government projects, and point out that such projects are not only often poorly evaluated but also poorly governed, thus do not achieve the aim of participatory e-government. They highlight the importance of the evaluation of projects, but also the need for co-creation in such projects and the involvement of stakeholders. Co-creation is certainly an important aspect of e-participation and policy-making, but Mila Gasco-Hernandez, Rodrigo Sandoval-Almazán, and Ramon Gil-Garcia also consider the role of the intermediaries involved in innovation and innovative processes. In particular large e-participation initiatives need to be considered carefully, and Alessio Braccini, Tommaso Federici, and Øystein Sæbø investigate the Movimento 5 Stelle, which has gained huge momentum and has become an important dimension of the Italian political sphere.

We hope you enjoy reading these papers! The editors would like to take the opportunity to thank not only the authors who contributed their work, but also those who helped to make this year's conference successful: the participants, the organizing team, and, of course, the hosts Dimitrii Trutnev and Andrei Chugunov from ITMO University.

July 2017

Noella Edelmann
Peter Parycek
Yannis Charalabidis
Andrei V. Chugunov
Panos Panagiotopoulos
Theresa A. Pardo
Øystein Sæbø
Efthimios Tambouris

Organization

Electronic Participation

9th IFIP WG 8.5 International Conference, ePart 2017
Russia, St. Petersburg, September 4–7, 2017
Proceedings
Part of the *Lecture Notes in Computer Science* book series (LNCS, volume 10429)

Editors

Peter Parycek	Danube University Krems, Austria
Yannis Charalabidis	University of the Aegean, Greece
Andrei V. Chugunov	ITMO University, Russia
Panos Panagiotopoulos	Queen Mary University of London, UK
Theresa A. Pardo	Center for Technology in Government, University at Albany, SUNY, USA
Øystein Sæbø	Agder University, Norway
Efthimios Tambouris	University of Macedonia, Greece

Organization

IFIP Working Group 8.5 Elected Officers

Chair

Hans Jochen Scholl   University of Washington, USA

Vice Chair

Marijn Janssen   Delft University of Technology, The Netherlands

Secretary

Olivier Glassey   University of Lausanne, Switzerland

Conference Chairs

The General E-Government Track

Hans Jochen Scholl   University of Washington, USA
Marijn Janssen   Technical University Delft, The Netherlands

The General eParticipation Track

Efthimios Tambouris	University of Macedonia, Greece
Øystein Sæbø	Agder University, Norway
Panos Panagiotopoulos	Queen Mary University of London, UK

The Open Government and Open and Big Data Track

Ida Lindgren	Linköping University, Sweden
Bram Klievink	Technical University of Delft, The Netherlands
Robert Krimmer	Tallinn University of Technology, Estonia

The Policy Modeling and Policy Informatics Track

Theresa A. Pardo	Center for Technology in Government, University at Albany, SUNY, USA
Yannis Charalabidis	University of Aegean, Greece

The Smart Governance, Smart Government, Smart Cities, and Smart Regions Track

Peter Parycek	Danube University Krems, Austria
Olivier Glassey	University of Lausanne, Switzerland
Karin Axelsson	Linköping University, Sweden

PhD Colloquium

Anneke Zuiderwijk-van Eijk	Delft University of Technology, The Netherlands

Local Hosts

Dimitrii Trutnev	ITMO University, Russia
Andrei V. Chugunov	ITMO University, Russia

Program Committee

Renata Araujo	UNIRIO, Brazil
Peter Cruickshank	Edinburgh Napier University, UK
Todd Davies	Stanford University, USA
Fiorella de Cindio	Università di Milano, Italy
Annelie Ekelin	Linneaus University, Sweden
Elsa Estevez	United Nations University, Macao, SAR China
Sabrina Franceschini	Regione Emilia-Romagna, Italy
Andreas Gabor	Corvinno Technology Transfer Center Nonprofit Public Ltd., Hungary
Katarina Gidlund	Midsweden University, Sweden
Olivier Glassey	University of Lausanne, Switzerland

Contents

Critical Reflections

Methodological Issues in eParticipation

Developing Criteria for Evaluating a Multi-channel Digitally Enabled Participatory Budgeting Platform

Amizan Omar[1($\boxtimes$)] (ID), Vishanth Weerakkody[2] (ID), and Uthayasankar Sivarajah[1] (ID)

[1] Brunel University London, Uxbridge, UB8 3PH, UK
amizan.mohamedomar@brunel.ac.uk
[2] University of Bradford, Emm Lane, Bradford, BD9 4JL, UK

Abstract. "Enabling Multichannel Participation through ICT Adaptations for Participatory Budgeting ICT-enabled platform" (EMPATIA) is a multi-channel participatory budgeting (PB) platform that represents a significant social innovation process of democratic deliberation and decision-making, involving citizens within complex public-institution structures. EMPATIA was targeted to deliver socio-economic and political benefits, such as enhancing citizen-government engagement, increasing public value through PB process, promoting 'inclusiveness' among the marginalized groups of citizens, and impeding political discontent that underpins distrust and scepticism towards the government. The attainment of these benefits will be driven by the EMPATIA's performance. Hence, a performance measurement tools is needed to enable assessment of EMPATIA, empirically. With an aim to propose an integrated performance evaluation metrics, this study presents a set of assessment criteria for multi-channel digitally enabled PB service platforms – especially EMPATIA. Findings from a qualitative, multi-strategies research approach suggest that the metrics should include five key technical and non-technical performance indicators, to be used as the basis for the development of future evaluation instruments. Of major signposts, the metrics would inform key performance aspects to be considered during the PB platform development, and evaluated to indicate the PB platform performance.

Keywords: Digitally enabled services · Participatory budgeting · e-government · Public sector · Evaluation

1 Introduction

The emergence of Participatory Budgeting (PB) programs in the public institutions were often linked to the increasing pressures imposed by the stakeholders including the governments, citizens and non-governmental organizations (NGOs). The central target is to provide opportunities for citizens to deliberately negotiate over the utilization and allocation of public money [1]. Besides fostering citizens'-government engagement and increasing transparency in public service delivery, subliminally PB has potentials to educate and empower the citizens, especially those niches. Traditionally, low-income and low-level of formal education citizens refrained

© IFIP International Federation for Information Processing 2017
Published by Springer International Publishing AG 2017. All Rights Reserved
P. Parycek et al. (Eds.): ePart 2017, LNCS 10429, pp. 3–11, 2017.
DOI: 10.1007/978-3-319-64322-9_1

themselves from involving in the government-related decision-making activities. By empowering them, the government could expand outreach and enhance the quality of democracy [1]. Acknowledging these potentials, PB could be a tool for more inclusive and accountable governance, contributing towards a higher public value [2, 3]. Many public institutions use social media (e.g. Facebook, Twitter) to engage with their citizens [4, 5]. Nevertheless, such alternatives constraint the citizens' empowerment process [6, 7] due to the absence of real-time process and the "virtuous circles" [8, 9]. Hence, the need for a digitally-enabled PB platform triggers, leading to the development of EMPATIA (Enabling Multichannel Participation through ICT Adaptations for Participatory Budgeting ICT-enabled platform).

EMPATIA was developed under the framework of European Union's innovation and research programme i.e. Horizon 2020. Its ultimate aim is to benefit global society and democracy [10]. The platform integrates the existing e-government platforms, and adds new features such as auto generation of data and visualization, voting systems and opinion mining to accommodate the desired PB function and enhance performance. It was hoped that these features would entice its adoptions, thus help to achieve the policy objective. However, the failure of past e-government platforms due to the scarcity of adoptions had triggered a risk to EMPATIA. To mitigate such risk, the critical performance indicators need to be identified. Hence, an objective and a cohesive evaluation metrics is needed to facilitate such action – which is what this study attempts to propose. The rest of this paper is organised as follows. Following this introduction, the paper presents the conceptual background discussing the significance of digitally enabled platform and participatory budgeting. Then, a description of the methodological approach was outlined, entailed by the discussion on the EMPATIA's evaluation metrics. Finally, the paper concludes by highlighting the expected impact of the EMPTIA platform and way to move forward.

2   Conceptual Background

Digitally enabled service transformations offers vast potentials to create self-sustaining change in a broad range of connected technology, universal culture, and closely-linked communities [11, 12]. Explicit growth of digitally enabled services in public institutions was flourished by the expectancies to enhance governance process, increase citizens' participations, and break the siloes between public institutions [12]. Such trend is also affiliated to the impact of communication technology advancements [3]. Many do not realized that the phenomenon partly caused by the New Public Management (NPM) movement [12]. NPM had redefined public services and government-citizens' relationship, raising expectations on service standard and quality [13]. The scenario increases adoption of private sectors' practices, including computer-aided services that subliminally deter democratic values by treating a citizen as a customer and imposing charges for rendered services. Next, the focus was shifted towards the quality of governance, where the concept of "participation" was introduced [14]. Such concept urged revitalization of the public sector's roles through "partnerships" between government-citizens to improve social well-being and the quality of public administration, leading to the emergence of the participatory budgeting (PB) concept [13]. Meanwhile, the evolution of technology, increasing demands/expectations of the civil societies and complex political inferences prospers the growth of digitally-enabled services in public institutions [15]. The growth was also due to the over-arching economy pressures, which has channelled the focus of service delivery from public value (PV) creation (evaluated against services, outcome and trust) to cost feasibility [16]. Along the same line, the PV concept was argued as mimicking the definition of 'perceived value' in the marketing discipline. As such, it was claimed that the PV theory was unfit to evaluate the actual 'value' created by the digitally-enabled services – as the value was partly attributed to the information quality, system quality and service quality. In this perspective, the value is an antecedent determining satisfaction and trust among the users that will lead to re-use intention and increases usage level that characterized the IS success [16].

The e-voting feature in EMPATIA is claim as the main PV determinant. Besides promoting citizens' empowerment, such feature facilitates political inclusiveness, while reducing contentment. Scholars have different views on how the introduction of an online platform for participation will affect the citizens, politically. Evidence shows that the introduction of an online platform for participation will encourage citizens' participations [17]. Nevertheless, the digital divide advocators suggest that due to unequal access to the internet, the online PB platform will increase the involvement number of "economically advantaged groups" (i.e. people from the middle class to high-income groups) – who are already politically active, hence has a null effect on the politically-excluded group [18]. Instead, it will further empower the groups who are already resourceful and determined to participate. As the effect varies, this aspect worth an assessment. To enable the strategy development for the 'politically excluded' groups, citizens' demographics information (e.g. income group, age, education level) and their motivation underpinning the system usage need to be retrieved. On top of the "inclusion" issue, the rising tide of discontentment in the global political landscape has aroused anti-politics orientation among the citizens [19]. This scenario creates the feeling of unrepresented in politic, unheard by the politicians, excluded due to social class and constrained opportunity to influence political decisions [20]. These feelings are often expressed in negative sentiments towards politicians, political institutions or politic per se, creating a gap between citizens and politically linked process, institutions or individuals [21]. Noting its ability to facilitate transparency and efficient execution of institutional roles, hypothetically, such issue can be reduced by PB implementation [22] – hence, should also be included in the metrics for evaluation.

3 Methodology

The overall methodological approach adopted to develop the EMPATIA's evaluation metric was based on qualitative approach. It was stated the use of a single strategy limits data richness about certain phenomenon, and therefore the combination of strategies in a single research allows the weaknesses of certain strategy to be complemented by others [23]. Thus, a combined strategy of state-of-the-art literature review (secondary research), expert views mining and focus groups were used to collect data on the potential key performance indicators that will allow objective assessment of the online PB platform from the users' point of view. Besides rich in data, such combination also facilitates the data triangulation process, which underpins the rigorousness of research [24].

The process started with a comprehensive state-of-the-art literature review (SOTA LR) and archival research on the relevant public sector - technology adoption and diffusion reports and publications. Using the thematic analysis approach, the investigation's results were classified into two types of indicators - i.e. technical and non-technical, followed by an evaluation on its context-suitability against PB platform (i.e. EMPATIA). Next, a group of 20 experts dominating various roles across public and private sectors in several European countries were identified and invited to present their views towards PB platform in the two series of online 'expert mining sessions'. They include the renown IS/IT/e-Government/Public Administration scholars, public sector employees (i.e. council staff and policy makers) and private sector practitioners (e.g. IS/IT consultants/contractors/consortiums) who have vast experience and specialities related to the PB platform. The findings from SOTA LR were used to stimulate the experts' discussions and help to clarify certain issues. The outputs from the two sessions were used to structure an agenda for the subsequent focus group. Although it is not necessarily required [25], it was acknowledged that the agenda had elucidated themes for probing during the focus group sessions, which were held in three countries. Each session involves ten participants consisting the municipality staff, consortium members and public representatives (i.e. citizens). Finally, the findings were analyzed and triangulated to form a list of KPIs (and sub-indicators) that could facilitate an objective assessment of the PB platform's performance.

4   Proposed Evaluation Metric

The process of making decisions pertaining budget allocations is part of the government's primary role. Hence, the implementation of a multi-channel digitally enabled PB platform, or in this context EMPATIA - implied that such role is about to be heavily determined by the citizens. In this case, the proposed evaluation metric for the platform should be more incline towards the citizens' interests. As stated in the earlier section, the platform was aimed to define a new form of democracy for the 21st-century nations and will be available freely for everyone to use. For such purpose, EMPATIA will be piloted in three different countries – each with unique requirements, scenarios, and users. Ideally, the platform should be assessed differently (i.e. according to their specific context). Nevertheless, the development of a generic evaluation metric is required as a performance baseline. Hence, this section presents the evaluation metric for EMPATIA's performance assessment, developed based on the synthesis of findings derived from data collection strategies that were described in Sect. 2. The metric is displayed in Table 1. While the technical indicator focuses on the operation and performance of the platform's "network" and "architecture", the non-technical indicator evaluates the social-economy, behavioral, political and process aspects of the platform.

Table 1. KPIs for EMPATIA platform

Aspects	KPIs	Descriptions
Technical	Technical	To measure the network and architectural service performance of the platform
Non-Technical	Behavioral	To measure the citizens' acceptance and satisfactions derived from the platform usage
	Socio-Economic	To identify the socio-economy factors influencing citizens' decision to use the platform
	Political	To indicate the level of 'inclusiveness' (who participate in the PB process) and political alienation (unhappy or dissatisfy with certain aspects of society) from the platform use
	Process	To identify the 'process' factors influencing citizens' decisions to use the platform

4.1 Technical KPIs

Data syntheses suggest that 'technical indicator' is highly important for the measurement of the platform's technical-related performance. It is particularly critical, since the platform will be implemented across various contexts. Besides enabling the troubleshooting process, the indicator helps to determine the root of discrepancies in four dimensions: performance, usability, maintenance, and monitoring – adapted from the "Systems and software engineering - Systems and software Quality Requirements and Evaluation (SQuaRE) - System and software quality models", as outlined in ISO/IEC 25010:2011. Although SQuaRE proposes the assessment of all characteristics its two models of "quality in use" (focus on the outcome of interaction) and "product quality" (focus on the software's static properties and system's dynamic properties), findings suggest that only five characteristics (from the "product quality" model) are relevant to the research context [26]. The technical KPIs for EMPATIA are listed in Table 2.

Table 2. Technical KPIs selected for EMPATIA

Characteristics	Sub-characteristics
Performance Efficiency	Time behavior; Resource utilization
Usability	Accessibility
Reliability	Maturity; Fault tolerance; Availability; Recoverability
Security	Confidentiality; Non-repudiation; Integrity; Accountability
Maintainability	Modularity; Adaptability; Reusability; Install-ability; Modifiability

4.2 Non-technical Indicator: Behavioral

The behavioral indicator is one of the non-technical KPIs selected to indicate the PB platform's performance. The sub-indicators under the behavioral indicator category are proposed based on the findings of the literature review. It was discovered that various models/theories were introduced to facilitate investigations on the reasons underpinning technology acceptance among the users. Nevertheless, user satisfaction remains as a central focus in all approaches. Against this backdrop, a theory known as 'Unified Theory of Acceptance and Use of Technology (UTAUT) was developed to integrate eight 'technology acceptance and use' theories such as Theory of Reasoned Action (TRA) and Technology Acceptance Model (TAM), and used to explain the relationship between users' intentions and their subsequent usage behavior [27].

Although many argue that the IS design, implementation strategy, and usage level are the important determinants for IS success, Bailey and Pearson [28] suggest that 'user satisfaction' is the key driver for the IS usage, which leads to its success. Next, Technology Acceptance Model (TAM) that encapsulates 'user involvement concept' was introduced [29]. TAM demonstrates how perceived usefulness and ease of use; as well as attitudes and behavioral intentions resulted into IS adoption. This indicates that user involvement is key to IS success. Such insight was incorporated in the Information System Success Model (ISSM), where success was attributable to the information quality, system quality, use, user satisfaction, individual impact and organizational impact [30]. According to 'perceptions regarding information privacy' theory, system security and information privacy are two other critical factors affecting users satisfaction on IS usage, thus worth evaluation [31]. Hence, it is proposed that the PB platform behavioral model to include concepts from UTAUT, ISSM and 'perceptions regarding information privacy' theory, and used these concepts as sub-indicators for evaluation purpose.

4.3   Non-technical Indicator: Socio-Economy

In a study that investigates citizens' perspective toward digitally enabled public service, three indicators i.e. technical, social and economy were combined to assess the socio-economy impact [see 32]. As this evaluation metric will be used in the same context of digitally-enabled service, the same indicators will be used to evaluate the PB platform performance from the socio-economy perspective. However, since the technical evaluation will be conducted separately, the metric for socio-economy impact will be limited to social and economy indicators, as outlined in Table 3.

Table 3.   Proposed KPIs for EMPATIA's socio-economy assessment

Sub-indicators	Components of assessments	Focus of assessment
Social	Openness	Transparency
	Trust	Trust in the internet; Trust in the government's organization
Economy	Cost saving	Money saving; Time saving

4.4   Non-technical Indicator: Political

Political indicator is important to enable the evaluation of the PB platform's impact on the evolution of internal and external efficacy of users and overall trust in democratic institutions. Such evaluation can be performed by assessing the "inclusiveness" (i.e. to investigate participants' profiles), and "Political Alienation" (i.e. to investigate participants' "incapability" and "discontentment") [32]. Two types of political alienation are identified as incapability and discontentment [33]. Incapability refers to efficacy (either internal efficacy i.e. citizens' self-assessments of their own political judgments, or external efficacy i.e. citizens' perceptions on how they influence the political decisions), and discontentment (i.e. negative affectation towards political objects, explaining why people believed that certain government policies are biased, or why they distrust political authorities). Restoration of trust towards government's integrity in the decision-making processes is vital to remedy these situations [33]. As a platform that encourages transparency in public-budgeting processes, PB is advocated as a tool to fix the integrity issues, and subsequently enhance trust towards the government. Thus, a metric to evaluate such political aspects of PB platform performance, should consist of two main types of indicators – (1) internal and external efficacy and (2) anti-politics (measures of trust), where comparison of the users' attitudes post PB platform usage with the baseline attitude of the random population in the same region is required to allow an objective assessment.

4.5 Non-technical Indicator: Process

Process indicator is a required to assess the level of process standardization during the pilot implementation. It was proposed that the process indicator should outline the basic requirements for the pilot implementation (i.e. to start the pilot), and criteria to exit the pilot (i.e. to stop the pilot) against user and process perspectives. Hence, the aspects to be considered in the evaluation metric under this indicator are listed in Table 4.

Table 4. Proposed indicators for EMPATIA's process assessment

Perspectives	Focus of assessment
User	Usability; Satisfaction; Reliability
Process	Anonymity of sensitive data; Encryption of Sensitive data and communication; Data storage in a physically secured location; Data Security; System development cost; Time for decision making process; Local government resources committed for the new system; Learning time for new system use; Time-to-staffs: Meeting the staff and starting the examination; Waiting time for decision; Number of staff/ public involved in the pilot; Conformance to decision

5 Conclusions

The 'participatory budgeting' (PB) concept was introduced against the backdrop of a contemporary public administration to provide a platform for citizens to involve in the public budgeting process. In general, PB was targeted to improve the quality of public services and social well-being. With the emergence of new technology, the digitally enabled PB platform has sheds new lights in fostering better citizens-government engagement and broadening social-political impacts (e.g. improve economy conditions, enhance education level and flourish democracies). Nevertheless, the attainment of these desires is conditioned by the platform's success – measured by its level of usage. Usage is determined by series of the cause-effect relationship. The process started with gaining value from the services, which raises satisfaction level among the users, producing the 're-use intentions'. Hence, value creation (often linked to the service performance) is essential to ensure the PB platform's success. To do so, the KPIs representing the PB platform's performance need to be identified, followed by the metric for evaluation. Since the existing models or theories offer limited scope of evaluation, this study proposes a new evaluation metric for the PB platform, outlining the technical and non-technical KPIs, developed against the context of EMPATIA. The metric served as a basis for the evaluation's instruments development in a near future, where the platform's performance result will be obtained. Besides signposting numerous potential practical and theoretical insights, the evaluation's outcomes will assist interventions, thus help to promote the success of the digitally enabled PB platform.

References

1. Wampler, B.: A Guide to Participatory Budgeting Public Sector Government Accounting Service - Participation Budgeting, pp. 21–52. The World Bank, Washington, D.C. (2007)
2. Cabannes, Y.: The impact of participatory budgeting on basic services: municipal practices and evidence from the field. Environ. Urban 27, 257–284 (2015)
3. Sintomer, Y., Herzberg, C., Röcke, A., Allegretti, G.: Transnational Models of citizen participation: the case of participatory budgeting. J. Public Deliberation 8(9) (2012)
4. Kamal, M.M., Sivarajah, U., Allegretti, G., Secchi, M., Autunes, S.: Enabling multichannel participation through ICT adaptations for participatory budgeting, pp. 1–9 (2016)
5. Agostino, D.: Using social media to engage citizens: a study of Italian municipalities. Public Relat. Rev. 39, 232–234 (2013)
6. Nitzsche, P., Pistoia, A., Elsavier, M.: Development of an evaluation tool for participative e-government services: a case study of electronic participatory budgeting projects in Germany. Revista Administratie si Management Public 18, 6–25 (2012)
7. Pateman, C.: Participatory democracy revisited. Perspect. Politics 10, 7–19 (2012)
8. OECD, The case for e-government: excerpts from the OECD report the e-government imperative. OECD J. Budgeting 3, 61–96 (2003)
9. Wampler, B.: Participatory budgeting: core principles and key impacts. J. Public Deliberation 8, 1–13 (2012)
10. Cordis, H2020-EU.2.1.1. - Industrial leadership - Leadership in enabling and industrial technologies - Information and Communication Technologies (ICT), European Commisson. http://cordis.europa.eu/programme/rcn/664147_en.html. Accessed 10 Feb 2017
11. Omar, A., Weerakkody, V., Millard, J.: Digital-enabled service transformation in public sector: institutionalization as a product of interplay between actors and structures during organisational change. In: 9th International Conference of Theory Practice in Electronic Government, pp. 305–312 (2016)
12. Weerakkody, V., Omar, A., El-Haddadeh, R., Al-Busaidy, M.: Digitally-enabled service transformation in the public sector: the lure of institutional pressure and strategic response towards change. Gov. Inf. Q. 33(4), 658–668 (2016)

13. Džinić, J., Svidroňová, M.M., Markowska-Bzducha, E.: Participatory budgeting: a comparative study of Croatia, Poland and Slovakia. NISPAcee J. Public Adm. Policy **9**, 31–56 (2016)
14. Loeffler, E., Power, G., Bovaird, T., Hine-Hughes, F.: Co-production of Health and Wellbeing in Scotland. Governance International, Edinburgh (2013)
15. Omar, A., El-Haddadeh, R.: Structuring institutionalization of digitally enabled service transformation in public sector: does actor or structure matters? Full paper. In: Twenty-second America Conference of Information. System, San Diego, pp. 1–7 (2016)
16. Osmani, M.: Examining the Antecedents of Public Value in E-Government Services. Brunel University London (2015)
17. Spada, P., Mellon, J., Peixoto, T., Sjoberg, F.M.: Effects of the internet on participation: study of a public policy referendum in Brazil. In: World Bank Policy Research Work Paper (2015)
18. Roberson, Q.M.: Disentangling the meanings of diversity and inclusion in organizations. Group and Organisation Management **31**, 212–236 (2006)
19. Jennings, W., Stoker, G., Twyman, J.: The dimensions and impact of political discontent in Britain. Parliament Affliation **69**, 876–900 (2016)
20. Rooduijn, M., Van der Brug, W., De Lange, S.L.: Expressing or fuelling discontent? The relationship between populist voting and political discontent. Electoral. Stud. **43**, 32–40 (2016)
21. Brandtzæg, P.B., Heim, J., Karahasanović, A.: Understanding the new digital divide—a typology of internet users in Europe. Int. J. Hum. Comput. Stud. **69**, 123–138 (2011)
22. Clarke, N., Jennings, W., Moss, J., Stoker, G.: Anti-politics and the left. J. Labour Politics **24**, 9–26 (2016)
23. Yin, R.K.: Mixed methods research: are the methods genuinely integrated or merely parallel? Res. Sch. **13**, 41–48 (2006)
24. Yin, R.K.: Qualitative research from start to finish (2011). doi:10.1007/s13398-014-0173-7.2
25. Morse, J.M.: Critical analysis of strategies for determining rigor in qualitative inquiry. Qual. Health Res. **25**, 1212–1222 (2015)
26. ISO, IEC25010: Systems and software engineering–Systems and software Quality Requirements and Evaluation (SQuaRE) – system and software quality models. Int. Organ. Stand. **34**(2011), 2910 (2011)
27. Venkatesh, V., Thong, J.Y.L., Xu, X.: Consumer acceptance and use of information technology: extending the unified theory of acceptance and use of technology. Manage. Inf. Syst. Q. **36**, 157–178 (2012)
28. Bailey, J.E., Pearson, S.W.: Development of a tool for measuring and analyzing computer user satisfaction. Manage. Sci. **29**, 530–545 (1983)
29. Pang, M., Lee, G., Delone, W.H.: IT resources, organizational capabilities, and value creation in public sector organisations: a public-value management perspective. J. Inf. Technol. **29**, 187–205 (2014)
30. DeLone, W.H., Mclean, E.R.: The DeLone and McLean model of information systems success: a ten-year update. J. Manage. Inf. Syst. **19**, 9–30 (2003)
31. Dinev, T., Hart, P.: Privacy concerns and levels of information exchange: an empirical investigation of intended e-services use. e-Service J. **4**, 25–60 (2006)
32. Olson, M.E.: Two categories of political alienation. Soc. Forces **47**, 288–299 (1969)
33. Olson, M.E.: Rapid growth as a destablizing force. J. Econ. Hist. **23**, 529–552 (1963)

Balancing Potential and Risk: The Living Lab Approach in Mobile Participation Research

Magnus Adenskog[1](✉), Joachim Åström[1], Titiana Ertiö[2], Martin Karlsson[1],
Sampo Ruoppila[2], and Sarah-Kristin Thiel[3]

[1] Urban Studies, Örebro University, Örebro, Sweden
`magnus.adenskog@hkr.se`, {`joachim.astrom,martin.karlsson`}`@oru.se`
[2] Department of Social Research, University of Turku, Turku, Finland
{`titiana.ertio,sampo.ruoppila`}`@utu.fi`
[3] Austrian Institute of Technology, Vienna, Austria
`sarah-kristin.thiel@ait.ac.at`

Abstract. Living labs as a research approach have been said to hold
many promises regarding the evaluation of state-of-the art technologies
in real-world contexts, for instance by allowing close cooperation with
various stakeholders. At the same time, a living lab approach is connected
with substantial complexity and increased risk. This paper elaborates
on a conducted living lab with the objective to explore challenges and
opportunities of mobile participation. For this purpose, a novel mobile
application enabling interaction between citizens and city authorities was
tested over a period of five months in Turku, Finland. In this paper, we
describe identified risks associated with a living lab approach to mobile
participation research. We conclude with an overall evaluation regarding
the appropriateness of the living lab approach within the e-participation
research field and provide recommendations on how to balance potential
and risk in future projects.

Keywords: Mobile participation · Citizen participation · Urban
planning · Living lab · Trust

1 Introduction

Governments around Europe are trying to improve ways to integrate citizens
in public decision-making processes [15]. Hopes have been placed especially in
information and communications technologies to broaden the scope of involved
citizens [21]. Most recently, great expectations have evolved around smartphones
as platforms to achieve these aims. Always carried along, they offer affordances
to participate wherever and whenever, including reflecting on a topic in situ [12].
Besides written comments, phones also enable the supply of sensor data such as
GPS. Nonetheless, the urban governance and planning applications have yet to
exploit this potential [7,9].

Published by Springer International Publishing AG 2017. All Rights Reserved
P. Parycek et al. (Eds.): ePart 2017, LNCS 10429, pp. 12–23, 2017.
DOI: 10.1007/978-3-319-64322-9_2

To take a step further in exploring advanced mobile participation, our research group set the task to define the pre-requisites (e.g. [8]), build a working prototype, and test it in a living lab. The Täsä app (here in local dialect) was tested in real-world circumstances in Turku, Finland, from May to October 2015.

'Living lab' is a research and innovation methodology that entails involving end users in an early stage of the research process as well as conducting experimentation in real-world contexts rather than in a controlled setting [1]. As a research approach, living labs suggest a lucrative opportunity for studying the impact of state-of-the-art technologies in real-world contexts. Optimally they may provide great potential for scientific discoveries as well as the development of applications and practices. This opportunity stands in contrast to much of the existing research on e-participation and democratic innovations, which concentrates either on experimental research conducted in controlled environments, and addressing specific research questions (e.g. mini publics, deliberative polls, online discussion experiments), or research on real world e-participation cases, but based on broad evaluative frameworks (e.g. studies of e-petitioning websites, everyday talk etc.). While the first category might have access to state-of-the-art technologies, it tends to lack applicability [17]. The latter category, on the other hand, suffers from a reactive approach to the current practices, limiting its perspective on real-world complexities to a frame based on previous knowledge, and lacking access both to the most promising technologies and to the most challenging forms of participatory governance.

Against this backdrop, it is evident that a living lab approach offers important advantages for e-participation research, combining state-of-the-art technology, collaborative project design between practitioners and researchers, and implementation in real-world context [3]. However, living labs are also associated with increased risk. Emerging technologies might cause usability problems, and real-world circumstances might have more complex settings than expected, both causing vulnerabilities. Hence, implementing a living lab entails a balancing act between potential and risk.

In this paper, we reflect on our living lab experience in studying the implications of the newly introduced mobile participation app Täsä. The project produced valuable insights on how a mobile setting can enrich participatory planning. In this paper, we focus on the identified risks of a living lab approach, which constitute an important part of our overall results. We conclude with recommendations to future developers of mobile participation processes.

2   Running the Living Lab

In this chapter, we outline the main features of Täsä, who used it and the collaboration with the municipality.

2.1 Täsä Application

The mobile participation application Täsä, developed and tested in the Building Pervasive Participation project (b-Part, 2013-16), allowed citizens to become involved in urban planning and place-based development in various ways. User-generated geo-referenced pieces of content were central to the applications concept. In contrast to traditional reporting apps, Täsä allowed for a further differentiation of posts into the contribution types: Issue, Idea, Opinion, and Poll. With those, citizens could make their intentions clear. All contributions could be supplemented by adding a photo, a point of interest and an icon that corresponded to the persons perception of the addressed situation. Other citizens were able to browse contributions on a map and as a list, express their support by liking and leave textual comments to spark discussions. In order to achieve a two-way communication between a city and its citizens, city officials were encouraged to respond to citizens input. As an additional element, city representatives could create *missions* (e.g. asking for feedback or calling for ideas) that citizens could respond to by tagging their contributions with the corresponding mission identifier. To further encourage citizens, several game elements were incorporated in Täsä [20]. In general, the system served as a crowdsourcing tool and indicator for hot topics, providing planners an overview of citizens concerns and opinions.

2.2 Usage Results

The results on who participated self-selectively in the living lab, what kind of topics they addressed through the mobile app, and what was the spatial pattern of participation, have been reported at length in other papers, but are only summarized here to give more information about the living lab. The analysis draws from usage data stored in the backend and user surveys – one sent to the users immediately after registration (pre-survey hereafter) and another at the end of the trial (post-survey). The first survey was designed to collect various sorts of background information, whereas the second focused on experiences related to the application and the trial in general.

Altogether 780 citizens downloaded Täsä, and one third (32%) of them produced one or several kinds of content - contributions, comments, likes, or votes. Similarly to many ambitious e-participation initiatives previously, most of the Täsä-users were younger and had higher level of education than Turku inhabitants on average. Regarding ownership of the most recent devices as well as motivation and skills required to use them, mobile participation sets apart as a typical novelty along the expected lines of a 'digital divide', which is partly age-related. Yet, it showed potential in involving a group notoriously absent from face-to-face forms of citizen participation: the young to middle aged citizens [10]. Further, an analysis taking into account attitudinal predispositions such as an interest in politics and satisfaction with democracy revealed, importantly, that mobile participation can contribute to a constructive re-engagement with 'critical citizens' interested in politics but dissatisfied with democracy [2]. All in all, the results showed that groups who cared about politics are more interested in participating - whether they are satisfied or dissatisfied with the current state of affairs. Citizens who are not interested in politics are less likely to participate, even with new tools.

The qualitative analysis of the content produced showed that most (81%) of the citizens postings were about the urban environment (e.g. infrastructure, green areas), transportation planning, or various recreational activities. Thematically participation focused on 'common good' issues, which is an important finding. The protectionist NIMBY (Not In My Backyard) attitude, often associated with citizen participation by the skeptics (see Sect. 3.2), was totally absent [18].

The spatial analysis revealed more usage in the city center than in the suburbs. This logically matches the 'common good' topics: the most frequented public spaces or green areas and the most intense transportation planning conflicts, for instance, are found in the city center (see [18]).

In contrast to our expectations, the majority of Täsä-users were primarily interested in bringing their own issue to the attention of the municipality, and showed little interest in interactive features, especially discussing other citizens' postings [10]. The usage was thus characteristically individualist, and almost resembled a typical use of reporting apps. Moreover, the incorporated game elements were considered meaningless in supporting motivation to engage [19]. The respondents of our end-survey were critical of the usability of the prototype (see Sect. 3.1), but highly supportive of developing the mobile participation concept. The affordances of mobile participation, such as not being restricted by temporal and spatial constraints, and the ability to reflect 'on site', were considered valuable [10].

2.3   Collaboration with the Municipality

Implementing the living lab required active collaboration with the City of Turku. Their attitude towards becoming a platform for mobile participation trial was straight-forward, or even enthusiastic. In practice, the research team hosted several workshops with the city officials to prepare them in advance to think about potential benefits of the app, asking them to propose topics for missions (i.e. participatory tasks given by the municipality), and helping them with communications once the application went live. The City of Turku granted the Täsä-app an official participation platform status during the trial, and actively marketed it through their communication channels online as well as via printed and social media. The research team also did its share of marketing through social media, appearances in the local newspapers and radio, citizen workshops, and other efforts.

While the collaboration with the municipality ran quite smoothly all in all, there were three challenging occasions, which reflect how the new ideas of citizen participation, represented by the trial, did not easily match with the current governance culture regarding citizen participation, and hence were not optimal for the trial.

First, as we were encouraging the planners to suggest missions that could be implemented during the trial, they tended to come up with only light-weight and uncontroversial tasks, indicating an interest in harmless participation theater rather than serious discussions and significant citizen insights on urban development policies. We needed to return to the issue a few times to get them to suggest at least some potentially more controversial tasks. On one occasion, we agreed with an urban planner to include a mission in which citizens could suggest potential new uses to an old power station owned by the city and soon to be vacated. However, once the real estate department found out about this plan, they insisted on withdrawing it, because they "did not want public participation anymore than was absolutely necessary" (excerpt from e-mail). This illustrates general skepticism on the benefits of planning, presented by many local politicians and planners, discussed in Sect. 3.2.

Secondly, our aim was to develop an interactive application, meaning that we wanted to encourage discussions among citizens, but also between citizens and city authorities. Responding to this, the city insisted on synchronizing the use of the application with their permanent electronic participation system, a web-based (at the time of the trial) rather clumsy model, which people use predominantly to report problems and concerns, but which can also be used to transmit new ideas. For that service, the municipality has in place a follow-up system, in which more than 100 city officials from different departments are involved to give an answer to each message within a few days. Instead of getting people to discuss in Täsä, we were obliged to transfer the input generated in Täsä to the other system, and the answers given back to Täsä. The main problem here was the way the city officials responded. Characteristically, they did not participate in discussion, were not eager to learn more, but gave 'the answer' that almost every time killed the discussion going on in Täsä instead of encouraging it. Instead of being able to harness a new participation culture, the new tool was forced to integrate into an existing but unfitting form of communication.

Thirdly, how and to what extent citizen feedback was taken into consideration, basically depended on the judgment of each city official who engaged with the feedback. There is no way to follow up on this type of engagement. Most likely, individual actors viewpoints in this matter, and therefore their implementation, differ substantially. The unclear status of citizen input is, however, the single most obvious problem in the Finnish system of participatory planning [4] - not only in this trial.

3   Challenges Encountered in the Living Lab

In this section, we develop the two challenges we identified during the Täsä trial.

3.1   Challenges of the New Participation Application

Testing a novel kind of participation application brought about a number of challenges, mainly related to its usage. Although we communicated that it was a prototype produced within a research project and not a polished product, the users did not seem to be lenient towards any shortcomings. The user experience expectations are set high by social media apps, for instance, and delays or crashes experienced - inevitable in a prototype - increase the risk of losing users. Admittedly, it took quite long, for instance, to load the map and display all the contribution and missions icons on it, and some shortcuts between displays could have been added. Based on the feedback we received during the trial, and actively collected, we elaborated on the user experience.

Among the people who registered as Täsä-users, 68% did not produce any content with the app. In order to understand this behavior, we approached a random group of such users (during the trial, via e-mail) to conduct interviews. It turned out that some had in fact taken a passive onlookers role, while others had stopped using Täsä altogether. The previous group included many who felt they did not have anything to contribute on the topic (but were interested in what others did), while the latter group comprised many who had abandoned the app for the usability issues, e.g. feeling the app was "clumsy and hard to use". It also turned out that one big challenge was communicating to the citizens what they could do with the app. We assumed that users were familiar with the use of apps from other activities such as entertainment, social media or work. But as one informant pointed out, the concept of missions (i.e. tasks given by the city administration) was difficult to grasp. Similarly, many of the game elements included in Täsä were not even recognized by number of users, as it turned out in the post-survey.

Among other questions, the post-survey asked participants how the app worked. 45% of respondents answered that it worked fairly or very poorly, 37% satisfactorily (value 3 on a 5-point Likert scale) and 19% fairly well. Surprisingly, many respondents gave minute feedback by answering the open questions. While the respondents were generally supportive of developing the mobile participation further and recognized the project as a "good start" - they were very critical of the usability of the app. Some of the feedback was highly general, e.g. "the app was slow and crashed", "it should have worked properly", "difficult to use, it reduced my participation" or "the app was badly designed", which indicates that for some users, the usability challenges made them abandon the app altogether. On the other hand, many other users, who did indeed spend some time with the app, provided more specific comments, which can be quite helpful for refining the application. Examples include "when I wanted to add a location, it showed strange places nearby", "faster loading map", "it was hard to add the picture", "the registration process annoyed me" or "it would have been nice to see some visual summaries in the app". The amount of feedback received from the users signals their interest in a better functioning application in the future and hence encourages developing mobile participation further.

More generally, participants reported to be indifferent towards the game elements we introduced in Täsä [19]. Points that were awarded for in-app activities (e.g. commenting) also did not raise participants' interest. These incentives should have been linked to rewards that provide meaning and thus make the incentives more attractive [16]. Some of the (game) elements were not even recognized as such. Altogether, they did not serve as the motivators we had anticipated. As somebody put it, "the game elements brought no pleasure since the app worked poorly". Interestingly enough, when asked to evaluate how the app worked, more than half of participants indicated that Täsä worked satisfactorily (37%) and only 13% indicated that it worked very poorly.

In retrospect, not only the usability of the app was considered troublesome, but the entire idea of having only the app. During the trial, several participants expressed a wish for a possibility to participate using a personal computer. Some more knowledgeable participants stated that they would have preferred an open, mobile-optimized web page, which could have been accessed across many types of devices. In fact, the respondents ranked a web-based platform (83%) as a more important channel for interacting with the local government than a mobile application (65%), although both ranked higher than other alternatives. While the preference for (any, not only our) mobile application was not found to depend on age ($rs = -.211$, $p = .142$), it was positively influenced by perceived mobile skills ($rs = .315$, $p = .026$). Those favoring web-based applications were not only less experienced in using mobile devices, but were also older ($rs = -.294$, $p = .038$). These insights are in line with the finding that older generations feel less invited by mobile technologies in the context of public participation, which might be a reason for them having been less active. Moreover, those rating mobile interaction channels as important were also more active participants than those who did not ($rs = .218$, $p = .017$).

In the Täsä-trial, the basic access barriers, such as owning a relatively good smartphone, being motivated to participate in urban planning and having the skills to do so, also played a role in who could participate in the first place. Although smartphone ownership is relatively high in Finland, a suitable device running a rather recent operating system was needed for the Täsä-application to work well. This was due to having employed a framework that allowed for cross-platform development, making it possible to have the exact same app for all major operating systems (i.e. iOS, Android, and Windows). This in turn, contributed to the self-selection of active, working age participants, with a good socio-economic status, and good skills in using a mobile phone [10].

In summary, participants encountered a number of technology-related obstacles that negatively influenced their participation behavior. While some aspects were specific to the implementation of our application, others apply more to the individual attitudes towards adopting novel technologies.

3.2 Political Distrust and Skepticism on Citizen Participation

The relationship between trust and citizen participation is both intricate and multifaceted. Substantial trust between actors is required for constructive and cooperative processes of citizen participation. In order for citizens to devote time and effort to participatory procedures, with uncertain impact on policy, they must trust the intentions and compliance of planners and policy makers. Oppositely, both policy makers and planners must trust the capacity, intentions and knowledge of citizens' engagement and input in the participatory procedure in order to be willing to delegate power to implement their suggestions [11].

Yet, at the same time, citizen participation in general and democratic innovations in particular are often hailed as a means to restore trust between citizens and elites in situations of mutual and wide-spread distrust [22]. Citizen participation is thought to strengthen trust through consensus building [6], fostering an increased understanding of the 'other' [5] and strengthened problem solving capacity through knowledge sharing and cooperation [14].

To map the political context in Turku, we conducted a round of interviews among local politicians and civil servants between 2014 and 2015. Through the interviews we identified a wide-spread skepticism regarding the potential of citizen participation to inform policy-making and planning in Turku. The most common concern raised in the interviews relating to the opinions, knowledge and ideas generated by the citizens in participatory initiatives was that the citizens were unable to see, or take interest in, 'the big picture' or the 'universal interests' of the city. Instead, the interviewees found that citizens through participatory processes again and again represented and communicated their particular self-interest. One such example is that NIMBY (Not In My Backyard) issues, according to civil servants and politicians, were a common theme among citizens. Similar observations were made among civil servants, indicating that citizens tend to become more interested in issues close to their neighborhood rather than general or large scale issues. Interestingly enough, however, the participatory input in Täsä was free from NIMBY content, as it was used mostly to indicate 'common good' topics (see Sect. 2.2). All in all, the attitudes and perceptions of the policy makers and planners indicate a distrust in the ability and intention of citizens to represent or advocate the general interest in participatory processes. Citizens are perceived to advocate their particular interest as well as abstain from participation unless they are directly affected by the issue at hand.

Another recurring theme in the interviews was that the politicians and planners perceived the citizens of Turku to resist all or most changes in the urban area. Hence, there is a widespread perception of skepticism to change in urban planning in the modus operandi of the engaged citizen. For instance, several interviewees stated that when a public meeting is called for, it is primarily citizens who are critical towards the project at hand that show up. Hence, citizens were viewed as neither constructive nor cooperating with the policy makers and planners, but rather as opponents creating obstacles in the process. Taken together, these experiences and attitudes suggest that the input of the citizens is seen as overtly critical. This, in turn, legitimizes the view that the knowledge provided by the citizens is not considered salient and that the politicians therefore many times make their decisions without considering the opinions provided by the citizens in the participation initiatives.

So far, we have focused on describing the lack of trust in citizens among policy makers and planners. Yet, an equally important part of the equation is understanding the citizens' and particularly the participating citizens' attitudes and dispositions towards the political institutions and actors. Based on the surveys conducted among registered Täsä-users, we could analyze their level of trust in political institutions.

Many of the Täsä-users (living lab participants) shared a relatively low level of trust in politicians, parties, and the local government of Turku. More than four out of ten participants expressed distrust in the local government as they scored on the lower half of the ten-point trust scale. Five out of ten participants distrust politicians in general and six out of ten distrust political parties. Further, there seemed to be a discrepancy between the participation level of general satisfaction with how democracy works in Finland and their level of trust for local political institutions and actors. More than a third (36%) of the participants, who in general were satisfied with how democracy works in Finland, still lacked trust in the local government of Turku. Hence, there seems to be evidence of a reciprocal distrust between citizens and local city officials.

Moreover, it also seems that the citizens' distrust is stronger regarding the local level, and hence is connected to the local context rather than an expression of a general discontent with the Finnish democracy. On the whole, the context of the living lab must be described as contentious as we find evidence of a reciprocal distrust between local city authorities (i.e. politicians and planners) and citizens. Implementing an experimental and progressive mobile participation experiment in such a contentious context was challenging as neither planners, policy makers, nor citizens were ready to trust the genuine engagement and willingness to cooperate of the other.

4   Conclusions and Discussion

Living labs are projects in which the high potential is correlated with high risk, and vice versa. By raising the degree of novelty, and the complexity of the project one also increases the risk levels. As the Täsä living lab explored how novel technology could be applied in a real urban planning context, this project ought to be categorized a high risk project. In this paper, we identified two major challenges that correspond to potential risks with living lab projects: (1) challenges of introducing novel and emerging technologies and (2) conflict dimensions in the political context. We believe that an understanding and anticipation of these identified risks are of importance for the fields of mobile participation as well as for future living lab projects within the field of political participation in general. Based on these identified risks, we recommend future projects to reflect on the following potential counter measures.

Cross-platform e-participation solutions to serve diverse participants. The introduction of innovative participatory tools creates new divides when it comes to usage. Anticipating the changes is hard and often leads to unreasonable expectations. Our living lab trial with Täsä confirmed again that new tools or applications are most likely used by 'early adopters'. Even more so, some citizens prefer only to be informed (than actively participate) or even choose to 'rationally ignore' invitations to participate [13].

In order to avoid generational divides and achieve a more inclusive participation process, we recommend – at least for the time being – to provide a solution accessible with both mobile and personal devices, phones and computers. The setting of our project specifically sought to investigate a novel pervasive participatory tool. For near future use, we recommend as a workable solution to aligning mobile apps with a web-based participation alternative. Interestingly enough, our trial showed that the digital divide is no longer placed at the intersection of online and offline, but between mobile phone vs. PC and app vs. webpage. Overall, while designing an inclusive participation process should be the top priority for any participatory trial, the pre-conditions should be fulfilled as well: citizens need to be aware of (a) the opportunity to participate and (b) the benefits active participation entail.

Designing participatory processes to act as a mediating institution between political actors. The lack of trust in institutions among citizens is well documented, but the distrust of politicians and planners in the citizens' competencies and intentions is often disregarded [23]. This project identified a prominent reciprocal distrust between citizens and public officials that challenged the implementation of the living lab. Wide-spread distrust within the context of the living lab may have hindered broader engagement among citizens as well as stronger commitment from public officials. Future projects ought to strive to design participatory processes to act as mediating institutions. Such designs could include third party actors with a mediating role between citizens and public officials as well as introducing a participants' ombudsman within the institutional structure that can strengthen the position of citizens in the participatory process.

Lifting our eyes from the specific challenges of mobile participation to the potential of the living lab approach in e-participation research in general, we found that it lends itself well to the type of exploratory research that testing new technologies entails. It offers a tough test of novel technologies that is effective in identifying challenges and risks as experimentation is conducted among users rather than test subjects, and in the context of intended implementation rather than a lab. In the context of our project, the living lab format made possible the discovery of challenges and issues that would not have been identified in a strictly experimental test of Täsä. A strictly experimental test of the Täsä application would not have been able to identify the usability challenges connected to introducing a novel participation technology in a real world setting. Further, under strictly experimental conditions we would not have been able to identify the challenges of implementing an e-participation process in a context characterized by wide-spread distrust. Hence, in the balancing act between potential and risk – as conducting a living lab might be described – we ultimately opted for raising the stakes rather than playing it safe.

Acknowledgements. The research project Building Pervasive Participation (b-Part) was funded by JPI Urban Europe. The authors would like to thank the City of Turku for their collaboration.

References

1. Almirall, E., Wareham, J.: Living labs and open innovation: roles and applicability. eJOV: Electron. J. Virtual Organ. Networks **10**, 21–46 (2008)
2. Åström, J., Karlsson, M.: Will e-participation bring critical citizens back in? In: Tambouris, E., Panagiotopoulos, P., Sæbø, Ø., Wimmer, M.A., Pardo, T.A., Charalabidis, Y., Soares, D.S., Janowski, T. (eds.) ePart 2016. LNCS, vol. 9821, pp. 83–93. Springer, Cham (2016). doi:10.1007/978-3-319-45074-2_7
3. Åström, J., Ruoppila, S., Ertiö, T., Karlsson, M., Thiel, S.K.: Potentials and challenges of a living lab approach in research on mobile participation. In: Adjunct Proceedings of the 2015 ACM International Joint Conference on Pervasive and Ubiquitous Computing and Proceedings of the 2015 ACM International Symposium on Wearable Computers, pp. 795–800. ACM (2015)
4. Bäcklund, P., Mäntysalo, R.: Agonism and institutional ambiguity: ideas on democracy and the role of participation in the development of planning theory and practice-the case of Finland. Planning Theory **9**(4), 333–350 (2010)
5. Carr, D.S., Halvorsen, K.: An evaluation of three democratic, community-based approaches to citizen participation: surveys, conversations with community groups, and community dinners. Soc. Nat. Resour. **14**(2), 107–126 (2001)
6. Cheryl, K., Stivers, C.: Government is us: Public administration in an anti-government era (1998)
7. Desouza, K.C., Bhagwatwar, A.: Citizen apps to solve complex urban problems. J. Urban Technol. **19**(3), 107–136 (2012)
8. Ertiö, T., Ruoppila, S.: Supporting 'participation' in mobile participation. In: Proceedings of the ePart 2014 Conference, Dublin, Ireland, pp. 3–10 (2014)
9. Ertiö, T.P.: Participatory apps for urban planning - space for improvement. Planning Pract. Res. **30**(3), 303–321 (2015)
10. Ertiö, T.P., Ruoppila, S., Thiel, S.-K.: Motivations to use a mobile participation application. In: Tambouris, E., Panagiotopoulos, P., Sæbø, Ø., Wimmer, M.A., Pardo, T.A., Charalabidis, Y., Soares, D.S., Janowski, T. (eds.) ePart 2016. LNCS, vol. 9821, pp. 138–150. Springer, Cham (2016). doi:10.1007/978-3-319-45074-2_11
11. Harding, M., Knowles, B., Davies, N., Rouncefield, M.: HCI, civic engagement & trust. In: Proceedings of the 33rd Annual ACM Conference on Human Factors in Computing Systems, pp. 2833–2842. ACM (2015)
12. Korn, M.: Situating engagement: Ubiquitous infrastructures for in-situ civic engagement. Ph.D. thesis, Aarhus Universitet, Science and Technology, Department of Computer Science (2013)
13. Krek, A.: Rational ignorance of the citizens in public participatory planning. In: 10th symposium on Information-and communication technologies (ICT) in urban planning and spatial development and impacts of ICT on physical space, CORP, vol. 5, p. 420 (2005)
14. Lawrence, L., Debbie, A., Deagen, R.: Choosing public participation methods for natural resources: a context-specific guide. Soc. Nat. Resour. **14**(10), 857–872 (2001)
15. Michels, A.: Innovations in democratic governance: how does citizen participation contribute to a better democracy? Int. Rev. Admin. Sci. **77**(2), 275–293 (2011)
16. Nicholson, S.: A user-centered theoretical framework for meaningful gamification. Games+Learning+Society **8**, 1 (2012)
17. Parkinson, J., Mansbridge, J.: Deliberative Systems: Deliberative Democracy at the Large Scale. Cambridge University Press, New York (2012)

18. Ruoppila, S., Åström, J., Lybeck, R., Karlsson, M.: Putting citizen participation in place: will mobile phones change the spatiality of participatory planning? Article manuscript (2017)

19. Thiel, S.K., Ertiö, T.P.: Play it to plan it? The impact of game elements on usage of a urban planning app. In: Saqib Saeed, T.R., Mahmood, Z. (eds.) User-Centric E-Government - Challenges and Opportunities, vol. 1. Springer, Heidelberg (2017, forthcoming)

20. Thiel, S.K., Lehner, U.: Exploring the effects of game elements in m-participation. In: Proceedings of the 2015 British HCI Conference, British HCI 2015, pp. 65–73. ACM, New York (2015)

21. Vogt, M., Fröhlich, P.: Understanding cities and citizens: developing novel participatory development methods and public service concepts. In: Real Corp. 16: 21st International Conference on Urban Planning and Regional Development in the Information Society GeoMultimedia 2016, pp. 263–272 (2016)

22. Wang, X., Wan Wart, M.: When public participation in administration leads to trust: an empirical assessment of managers perceptions. Public Adm. Rev. **67**(2), 265–278 (2007)

23. Yang, K.: Public administrators trust in citizens: a missing link in citizen involvement efforts. Public Adm. Rev. **65**(3), 273–285 (2005)

Child's Play - A Literature-Based Survey on Gamified Tools and Methods for Fostering Public Participation in Urban Planning

Kevin Klamert[✉] and Sander Münster[✉]

Media Center, Technische Universität Dresden, 01062 Dresden, Germany
{kevin.klamert,sander.muenster}@tu-dresden.de

Abstract. As urban planning processes are often complex and protracted, fostering public participation in this sector has to be seen as a major challenge. Nevertheless, previous research on that topic offers various solutions that aim to tackle that problem, either by focusing on playful formats or on gamification and serious gaming. Often examined separately, these approaches deliver promising strengths to improve public participation in the urban sphere. Hence, a synopsis of those strategies seems to be worthwhile and is therefore further investigated in this paper. In order to analyze current works on that issue systematically, the paper is structured via a literature-based classification of different stages of public participation that distinguish whether citizens are being *informed*, *consulted* or *collaborated with* during the planning process. By giving an insight on innovative participation tools and methods in this field, the pursued outcome of this article are impulses for designing an advanced participatory platform which is part of the research project U_CODE (Urban Collective Design Environment).

Keywords: Public participation · Urban planning · Mobile participation · Gamification · Playfulness · Serious gaming · Augmented reality

1 Introduction

At first glance, fostering a citizen's interest in the field of urban planning seems to be challenging. But, due to the technological progress and innovative research approaches, the field is actually given a wide range of possibilities for increasing civic engagement and effectively tackling signs of political apathy. Imagine a smartphone app that demands users to explore neighborhoods in order to find nearby planning projects: After receiving a GPS-based notification, the person uses their smartphone for displaying first design proposals of the future building right at the spot. The user also receives additional information about the project which automatically pops up on the screen. Additionally, the person gets the possibility to comment, rate and share the project proposal and is able to answer project-related requests for feedback. By doing so, every single user action is tracked by a gamified design that not only incorporates user input in the decision-making process but also stimulates engagement, rewarding dedicated users with invitations to collaboratively work with involved professionals.

© IFIP International Federation for Information Processing 2017
Published by Springer International Publishing AG 2017. All Rights Reserved
P. Parycek et al. (Eds.): ePart 2017, LNCS 10429, pp. 24–33, 2017.
DOI: 10.1007/978-3-319-64322-9_3

That single sequence demonstrates only one of (possibly) many ideas for increasing public participation in urban planning. Starting with this example, the intention of this paper is to evaluate how public participation can be designed in an exciting way for efficiently raising civic engagement and, ultimately, improving mutually accepted decisions in the field of urban planning. It approaches this question by investigating new technologies as well as recent scientific knowledge. Based on literature concerning different stages of public participation, the goal of this paper is to deliver a systematic overview of recent developments that distinguish between the levels of citizen influence in the process of public participation.

One of the major hurdles for participative planning processes we investigated in another study [1] is that especially publically initialized participative activities often lack a sufficient number of users. This may be caused by lacking information on the process [e.g. 2, 3], barriers in culture, understanding or accessibility [e.g. 4] or even weak motivation to participate [e.g. 5]. Therefore, motivational strategies such as gamification as well as the implementation of playful approaches through innovative technologies are in the scope of this investigation, each of them providing valuable impressions for designing a well performing prototype of a participatory system which is the goal of the U_CODE (Urban Collective Design Environment) research project.

2 Gamification, Playfulness and Mobile Participation

Game and play open innovative ways for making public participation more exciting, which is why research in this field serves as a theoretical framework of this paper. As shown in the introductory scenario, formats of mobile participation are an important aspect of this work, too, as they expand the range of possibilities for the implementation of gamification or playfulness in matters of urban planning as well as being promising to overcome the mentioned obstacles. Mobile participation "covers all initiatives, actions and methods that result from mobile end devices (e.g. mobile phones, smartphones and tablets) via wireless communication technology in order to expand the participation of citizens and other stakeholders in urban planning processes" [6]. Because mobile enabled tools can be used everywhere and anytime, the participation process no longer depends on time and space. Also, the mobile participation approach increases the chance to reach an audience who is normally missing in the participation process [7].

When it comes to motivating people to engage in public affairs, the research area on gamification offers solutions. In literature, several understandings of the term exist (for an overview [8, 9]). A widely accepted definition of gamification describes it as the "use of game design elements in non-game contexts" [10]. Zichermann and Cunningham focus on gamification as "the process of game-thinking and game mechanics to engage users and solve problems" [11]. Gamification is "usually intended to create gameful and playful user experiences, motivate desired user behaviors, and generally, increase joy of use" [12]. So, it can be stated that the goal of gamification is to engage users to take desired actions and to solve real-world problems - by using game elements. In the case of urban planning, solving real-world problems would mean tackling the deficit of participation that normally requires citizens to engage for a long period of time in order to give a constant input to a generally tedious decision-making process. Well-known game elements are e.g. point systems, badges or leaderboards, progress bars and quests. The diversity in understanding gamification makes it difficult to compare findings, and recent studies on the motivational impact of gamification elements partly lack scientific accuracy [9]. Yet, positive effects of gamification on user behavior are attested [13, 14].

Deterding et al. distinguish gamification from two other aspects: playful design that in contrast to gamification contains no rules or specific goals, and serious games that are rather defined as full-fledged games for non-entertainment purposes [10]. But clearly allocating a format in either gamification, playful design or serious gaming sometimes can be difficult and is not the intention of this paper. In order to present lines of development on promising public participation formats, it seems rather beneficial to not only explore gamification in the field of urban planning but also to include approaches that more likely refer to the field of playfulness or serious games. Following the idea of immersive planning, diverse ways should be able to bring citizens into an experience during the public participation process, e.g. by using 3D environments or by GIS-based technologies [15]. In terms of public participation, settings that are generally considered to be inefficient such as forms of play do not have to be at a disadvantage but can instead facilitate the evolvement of meaningful civic actions [16].

3   Methodology

Since there was recently much research on gamification for both conceptual and practical implementation, the methodical approach was to review and classify that literature. From a methodical point of view, a literature review is "a systematic search of published work to find out what is already known about the intended research topic" [17], to provide "an informed evaluation of that literature" [18]. A literature review is a relatively low standardized method and relies on stages of data search and critical evaluation [19]. Since this investigation provides a basis for a future development of a gamified platform for citizen engagement in urban planning, a purpose of this study is to "familiarize the researcher with the latest developments in the area of research" and „study the definitions used in previous works as well as the characteristics of the populations investigated, with the aim of adopting them for the new research" [20]. Therefore, the outcome of this paper is a descriptive and structured overview of recent gamified or playful participation tools that can be used for urban planning processes.

In order to retrieve information on that subject, a literature review on innovative public participation formats especially in the field of urban planning was performed. It focused on the aspects of gamification, playfulness and mobile participation, using the search items "gamification", "gamif*", "playful", "mobile participation" and "urban planning", including the databases EBSCOHost, ACM Digital Library and Scopus. Besides, by using the snowball principle, additional scientific works were found that were not covered by the database-driven keyword search. Due to the rapid development in this research field, an additional internet research went beyond scientific contributions and included current participation services in urban planning. In total 188 publications were retrieved and assessed.

The final selection of the findings was based on whether the participation tool exemplarily represents a new facet to the topic of public participation in urban planning. As such, it can not only represent characteristics of gamification but also of playfulness or serious gaming. By uncovering the diversity of tools and methods that are currently available, the obtained results present an overview of the state of the art and offer impulses for shaping the future design of an innovative and well performing participation system.

For clustering the results of this investigation, literature on public participation provides a categorization that distinguishes different stages of public influence on final decisions. Most commonly, actively sharing information with the public or giving them the possibility to *inform* themselves is declared as a first step of citizen participation [21–24]. On this informational level, citizens usually are not able to reply to the professional's input, which is why it is described as one-way communication [21] or one-way relationship [23]. A broader form of public participation is achieved when the public is *consulted* in an urban planning process, which means that public feedback is collected and taken into consideration in the decision-making [22]. However, at this stage, it still depends on the planner's decision whether to include that feedback. In contrast, a farther-reaching dimension of participation named collaboration stresses a partnership between the public and the planners in which citizen's advice is being implemented "to the maximum extent possible" [22]. On that stage, citizens directly contribute to the process of urban planning by discussing ideas, developing solutions and creating alternatives in deep interaction with other stakeholders.

Despite the fact that literature mentions even higher stages of public participation, the following structure is considered to be best suitable for classifying participation tools and methods for the purpose of this paper (Table 1).

Table 1. Stages of citizen participation

Category	Information	Consultation	Collaboration
Description	Citizens inform themselves or are being informed of current plans, decisions and actions	Citizens are asked to give input and feedback (e.g. opinions, solutions)	Citizens and other stakeholders actively work together in decision-making
Relation	*One-way*	*Limited two-way*	*Advanced two-way*

4   Results

4.1   Information

When it comes to informing the public in urban planning processes, visualization techniques such as augmented reality (AR) offer a variety of innovative solutions to effectively support informational purposes. For instance, mobile devices can be used in order to display designs of urban planning projects in existing landscapes [6, 25]. By that, citizens can playfully evaluate a proposal from different perspectives and are able to explore the planner's intention at an early stage of a project. This approach can be carried forward, allowing users to edit 3D visualizations or to vote for favored project proposals [26], which would of course go beyond the stage of public informing. With AR technology, transforming a 2D development plan into 3D for a better understanding among non-professionals or improving ordinary city walks by displaying additional information of buildings is also possible [27]. In addition, environment-centric applications which are often initiated by local governments such as "Metropulse" enable a one-way flow of information from those responsible to the citizens [28]. An example for visualizing future districts and allowing users to virtually explore future public places illustrates the 3D app "Dundee Waterfront 2018" [29].

Moreover, virtual worlds such as the online platform "Second Life" offer playful environments in which citizens can familiarize themselves with urban issues, exploring future public spaces by controlling an avatar [30]. This kind of immersive experience shows potential to inspire people to engage in urban planning projects. The approach can easily be gamified, e.g. by implementing tasks and high scores into the design. Besides informing citizens, it would also be possible to request public feedback for urban planning projects: In the case of the tool "Participatory Chinatown", it can even form a coherent game [15] that facilitates a process of deliberation among stakeholders.

4.2 Consultation

In terms of consulting the public in matters of urban planning, the online platform "Nextsuisse" gathers concepts on the future of Switzerland by asking users to propose text-based ideas and to play a web-based scenario game. Participants can playfully create 2D scenarios of their hometown by placing urban elements such as houses, trees and shopping malls on a virtual city framework. Adding elements to the setting influences the displayed overall satisfaction level of the city, and doing so in a sustainable way is being rewarded with positive feedback [31]. In that way, the citizen gets a feeling for the needs of their hometown. The created scenarios are published on the platform and can there be viewed and rated by others. Beyond consultation, the platform also arranges real-life collaborative workshops.

Other consulting formats focus on citizens as local experts and strive to collect neighborhood knowledge by using mobile data collection tools. For instance, the mobile application "Maplocal" asks users for feedback about their residential environment by letting them post photos or commentaries. The design seeks to improve public engagement in the early phase of planning processes [32] and offers playful options to contribute to the planning process by simply wandering around a familiar district. Moreover, valuable data for planners can be aggregated passively by mobile apps [6]: "Stereopublic" and "Widenoise" capture noise levels and display them on a map [33]. By identifying silent and noisy areas in cities, those apps deliver useful input for the urban planner's decision-making. Moreover, these environmental monitoring formats can be gamified [34] for improving the user's motivation to contribute.

The online platform "MetroQuest", whose design is inspired by a game called "Sim City", educates the public about urban projects through a series of informative screens and offers options to rank priorities, rate scenarios or allocate budgets, whereas professionals can use the platform e.g. by initiating surveys. By offering a variety of screen-based participation formats, the tool is adaptable for many urban planning projects, supporting options for different levels of civic engagement. Similar to "MetroQuest", the data-based platform "mySidewalk", formerly known as "MindMixer", allows civic decision makers to engage with their residents by letting citizens post ideas, give feedback or support and vote on urban planning ideas. The platform uses a gamified design that rewards user activities with digital coins and also implements high score lists for raising user motivation [31].

4.3   Collaboration

Initiating an intense process of collaboration between the public and professionals is the intention of a gamified mobile app called "Community Circles". It stimulates user interactions and contributions that refer to local urban planning issues with digital points [31]. Similar to "Maplocal", the app demands participants to explore their location in order to participate. Additionally, in-app crowd-sourced user contributions will gradually disappear from screen after a certain period if community feedback is lacking - in that way, high amounts of user input is managed. The platform not only allows citizens to contribute opinions and ideas, but also offers city authorities the chance to give constructive feedback or to raise urban issues [35]. By initiating intense interaction, this design approach aims to facilitate a mutual collaboration process between users and the local government [36].

The mobile participation tool "Love your City" takes a similar approach such as "Community Circles", seeking intense collaboration among all stakeholders in the urban planning process, but it thereby focusses on AR visualization technology. By introducing an AR-based interface that accomplishes participation activities between users and local governments at a user's current location, the tool aims to facilitate co-creation processes between stakeholders [37]. Depending on the situation and complexity of tasks, either citizens or city administrations can perform actions within the participation process, starting with the initiation of an issue, leading to a stage of co-creating and decision-making and finally ending in the display of visible results. User actions are rewarded with points and are tracked within a user profile [38].

Finally, the web-based online platform "Community PlanIt" is designed for assisting urban planning meetings, transforming an urban instance into a "mission" that contains game elements such as challenges, leaderboards and in-game rewards. By completing those missions, the citizen contributes to the planning process, earning virtual coins which can be spent to support urban concepts that frame the topic [31]. Additionally, the platform seeks to integrate as many stakeholders as possible and strives to initiate a mutual learning process. Besides online activities, the game final is facilitated by an offline workshop that is also open for non-members [39]. Similar to "Community PlanIt", the platform "Play the City" creates game scenarios that engage multiple stakeholders to meet physically and to collaboratively resolve complex urban challenges.

5   Conclusions

Considering the stages of the public participation process, the findings of this paper reveal a diversity of approaches in the field of urban planning, each offering impulses for creating a sustainable system for public participation.

First of all, the growing number of mobile devices in use obviously lowers barriers for participation and raises the chance for addressing a wider range of participants. In matters of urban planning, mobile tools can playfully facilitate the collection of public feedback as well as the communication between citizens and experts. Moreover, they allow displaying urban design proposals right at the spot, which might foster interest in public participation. The findings also reveal that urban planning projects can even be designed as full-fledged games in which citizens interact with other stakeholders in a playful manner. Furthermore, gamification strategies show potential not only to arouse curiosity for participation formats but also to improve long-term user motivation to participate. Commenting and rating design proposals, sharing own ideas or playing goal-related project missions can be rewarded with points or badges, while formats of discovery motivate people to explore their district in order to find urban issues of public interest.

Conceptualizing a platform that facilitates participation in every stage of the urban planning process is challenging. A gamified crowdsourcing service that effectively collects contributions and ensures in-depth communication and feedback at an early stage covers only one aspect of the process. At later stages, visualization techniques such as 3D environments and augmented reality sketches of future buildings show potential to make urban projects more exciting and tangible. For this, the concept of "Metropulse" provides a solution as it offers a toolbox of participation formats that are adaptable for every stage of a project. Following this approach, different levels of citizen involvement during the urban planning process can be considered, having a flexibility to offer several participation modules a project owner is willing to accept. But in order to foster intense collaboration processes, the examples of "Community PlanIt" and "Nextsuisse" advise that online technologies cannot replace the necessity of real-world meetings that include all stakeholders, which is why real-world workshops also remain important for the process.

Since participation processes as well as related challenges have been in focus of research for long [cf. 1], the employment of gamification strategies and principles within these contexts would add novel opportunities as well as raise novel questions for future investigations. To provide two examples: As figured out in many studies, people willing to participate in urban planning processes rarely represent a majority of inhabitants or involve (potential) opinion leaders [e.g. 40, 41]. A related question would be whether gamified approaches could help to overcome these challenges, e.g. by motivating these opinion leaders to actively mobilize followers. Especially when using digital tools, the digital readiness, accessibility and communication channels have to be considered and thoroughly analyzed. It would be of interest to investigate if and how digitized and gamified approaches would maybe exclude stakeholder groups.

The results of this paper only give an introductory overview of the field of current participation formats in urban planning and have no claim to being complete. They are primarily used to provide impulses for the design of an advanced participation platform. However, to reasonably implement such tools and methods within an overall concept is challenging, which is why future research on how to effectively implement gamification into a participation environment as well as on how to coordinate innovative service modules into an overall design remains a major task of the project.

Acknowledgements. The research upon which this paper is based was part of the project U_CODE (Urban Collective Design Environment) which has received funding from the European Union's Horizon 2020 research and innovation program under grant agreement No 688873.

References

1. Münster, S., Georgi, C., Heijne, K., Klamert, K., Nönnig, J.R., Pump, M., Stelzle, B.: How to involve inhabitants in urban design planning? An overview on a state of the art, key challenges and promising approaches. In: KES 2017 (accepted paper)
2. Brabham, D.C.: Crowdsourcing the public participation process for planning projects. Plan. Theory **8**, 242–262 (2009)
3. Nabatchi, T.: A Manager's Guide to fostering Transparency and Democracy. IBM Center for The Business of Government (2012)
4. Deyle, R., Schively Slotterback, C.: Group learning in participatory planning processes. J. Plan. Educ. Res. **29**, 23–38 (2009)
5. Giering, S.: Public Participation Strategies for Transit. Howard/Stein-Hudson Associates, New York (2011)
6. Höffken, S.: Mobile Partizipation: Wie Bürger mit dem Smartphone Stadtplanung mitgestalten. Rohn, Lemgo (2015)
7. Ertiö, T.-P.: M-participation: the emergence of participatory planning applications: Research Briefings 6b (2013)
8. Kim, B.: Understanding Gamification. Library Technology Reports, vol. 51, no. 2. American Library Association, Chicago (2015)
9. Seaborn, K., Fels, D.I.: Gamification in theory and action: a survey. Int. J. Hum Comput Stud. **74**, 14–31 (2015)
10. Deterding, S., Dixon, D., Khaled, R., Nacke, L.: From game design elements to gamefulness: defining "gamification". In: Proceedings of the 15th International Academic MindTrek Conference Envisioning Future Media Environments, pp. 9–15. ACM, New York (2011)
11. Zichermann, G., Cunningham, C.: Gamification by Design: Implementing Game Mechanics in Web and Mobile Apps. O'Reilly, Sebastopol (2011)
12. Deterding, S., Björk, S., Nacke, L., Dixon, D., Lawley, E.: Designing gamification: creating gameful and playful experiences. In: Mackay, W.E. (ed.) CHI'13 Extended Abstracts on Human Factors in Computing Systems, pp. 3263–3266. ACM, New York (2013)
13. Hamari, J., Koivisto, J., Sarsa, H.: Does gamification work? A literature review of empirical studies on gamification. In: 47th Annual Hawaii International Conference on System Sciences, pp. 3025–3034. IEEE, Piscataway (2014)
14. Morschheuser, B., Hamari, J., Koivisto, J.: Gamification in crowdsourcing: a review. In: Bui, T.X., Sprague, R.H. (eds.) Proceedings of the 49th Annual Hawaii International Conference on System Sciences, pp. 4375–4384. IEEE, Piscataway (2016)
15. Gordon, E., Schirra, S., Hollander, J.: Immersive planning: a conceptual model for designing public participation with new technologies. Environ. Plan. B Plan. Des. **38**(3), 505–519 (2011)

16. Gordon, E., Walter, S.: Meaningful inefficiencies: resisting the logic of technological efficiency in the design of civic systems. In: Gordon, E., Mihailidis, P. (eds.) Civic Media: Technology, Design, Practice, pp. 243–266. The MIT Press, Cambridge (2016)

17. Robinson, D., Reed, V.: The A-Z of Social Research Jargon. Ashgate Publishing Limited, London (1998)

18. Power, T.: Guidelines for a literature survey and an annotated bibliography. http://www.trinity.utoronto.ca/library_archives/theological_resources/Theological_guides/literature_survey_bibliography.html

19. Bortz, J., Döring, N.: Forschungsmethoden und Evaluation für Human- und Sozialwissenschaftler. Springer, Heidelberg (2009)

20. Bless, C., Higson-Smith, C.: Fundamentals of Social Research Methods: An African Perspective. Juta Education, Lusaka (2000)

21. Arnstein, S.R.: A ladder of citizen participation. J. Am. Inst. Plan. 35(4), 216–224 (1969)

22. IAP2. IAP2 public participation spectrum. Louisville. IAP2 (2013). http://c.ymcdn.com/sites/www.iap2.org/resource/resmgr/files/iap-006_brochure_a3_internat.pdf

23. OECD: Citizens as Partners: OECD Handbook on Information, Consultation and Public Participation in Policy-Making. OECD Publishing, Paris (2001)

24. Tufte, T., Mefalopulos, P.: Participatory Communication. The World Bank (2009)

25. Broschart, D., Zeile, P.: Augmented reality in Architektur und Stadtplanung – Techniken und Einsatzfelder. In: Strobl, J., Blaschke, T., Griesebner, G., Zagel, B. (eds.) Angewandte Geoinformatik 2014. Beiträge zum 26. AGIT-Symposium Salzburg, pp. 638–647. Wichmann, Berlin (2014)

26. Gnat, M., Leszek, K., Olszewski, R.: The use of geoinformation technology, augmented reality and gamification in the urban modeling process. In: Gervasi, O., et al. (eds.) ICCSA 2016. LNCS, vol. 9787, pp. 484–496. Springer, Cham (2016). doi:10.1007/978-3-319-42108-7_37

27. Broschart, D., Zeile, P.: Architecture: augmented reality in architecture and urban planning. In: Buhmann, E. (ed.) Peer Reviewed Proceedings of Digital Landscape Architecture 2015 at Anhalt University of Applied Sciences, pp. 111–118, Wichmann, Berlin (2015)

28. Ertiö, T.-P.: Participatory apps for urban planning - space for improvement. Plan. Pract. Res. 30(3), 303–321 (2015)

29. Evans-Cowley, J.: The best planning apps for 2016 (2016). http://www.planetizen.com/node/82996/best-planning-apps-2016

30. Mallan, K., Foth, M., Greenaway, R., Young, G.T.: Serious playground: using second life to engage high school students in urban planning. Learn. Media Technol. 35(2), 203–225 (2010)

31. Thiel, S.-K., Lehner, U.: Exploring the effects of game elements in m-participation. In: Lawson, S., Dickinson, P. (eds.) Proceedings of the 2015 British HCI Conference, pp. 65–73. ACM, New York (2015)

32. Jones, P., Layarad, A., Speed, C., Lorne, C.: Maplocal: use of smartphones for crowdsourced planning. Plan. Pract. Res. 30(3), 322–336 (2015)

33. Evans-Cowley, J.: The best planning apps for 2014 (2014). http://www.planetizen.com/node/66853

34. Martí, I.G., Rodríguez, L.E., Benedito, M., Trilles, S., Beltrán, A., Díaz, L., Huerta, J.: Mobile application for noise pollution monitoring through gamification techniques. In: Herrlich, M., Malaka, R., Masuch, M. (eds.) ICEC 2012. LNCS, vol. 7522, pp. 562–571. Springer, Heidelberg (2012). doi:10.1007/978-3-642-33542-6_74

35. Thiel, S.-K., Lehner, U., Stürmer, T., Gospodarek, J.: Insights from a m-participation prototype in the wild. In: IEEE International Conference on Pervasive Computing and Communication Workshops, pp. 166–171. IEEE, Piscataway (2015)

36. Thiel, S.-K., Fröhlich, P., Sackl, A.: Experiences from a living lab trialling a mobile participation platform. In: Schrenk, M., Popovich, V.V., Zeile, P., Elisei, P., Beyer, C. (eds.) REAL CORP 2016, Proceedings of 21st International Conference on Urban Planning, Regional Development and Information, pp. 263–272. CORP - Competence Center of Urban and Regional Planning, Wien (2016)
37. Stembert, N., Mulder, I.J.: Love your city! An interactive platform empowering citizens to turn the public domain into a participatory domain. In: International Conference Using ICT, Social Media and Mobile Technologies to Foster Self-Organisation in Urban and Neighbourhood Governance (2013)
38. Thiel, S.-K.: A review of introducing game elements to e-participation. In: Conference for E-Democracy and Open Government (CeDEM), pp. 3–9 (2016)
39. Gordon, E., Baldwin-Philippi, J.: Playful civic learning: enabling reflection and lateral trust in game-based public participation. Int. J. Commun. 8, 759–786 (2014)
40. Fung, A.: Varieties of participation in complex governance. Publ. Admin. Rev. 66, 66–75 (2006)
41. Renn, O., Webler, T., Rakel, H., Dienel, P., Johnson, B.: Public participation in decision making: a three-step procedure. Pol. Sci. 26, 189–214 (1993)

eParticipation Implementations

Disentangling Digital Divide and Trust
Internet Voting Affinity in Switzerland

Uwe Serdült[1,2(✉)] and Thomas Milic[1]

[1] Centre for Democracy Studies Aarau (ZDA),
University of Zurich, Aarau, Switzerland
uwe.serdult@zda.uzh.ch
[2] College of Information Science and Engineering,
Ritsumeikan University, Kusatsu, Japan

Abstract. In Switzerland internet voting is currently being introduced in a piecemeal fashion. Since the first trials in 2003 an increasing number of Swiss cantons is offering the digital voting channel to its citizens either living in Switzerland or abroad. So far the question whether the introduction of internet voting in Switzerland would increase the digital divide, favoring the well educated, economically better off citizens could not be answered in a conclusive way. As yet bi- and multi-variate regression analyses of survey data showed that general trust in the internet and in internet voting in particular outweigh the effect of the typical digital divide variables. There is, however, so far no study trying to disentangle the two types of variables by applying structural equation modeling. In the present study we test whether digital divide variables have a direct effect on general support of internet voting in the Swiss population or whether they should rather be treated as exogenous variables of general trust in the Internet and of internet voting in particular. We therefore put forward a structural equation model which helps us to disentangle direct and indirect effects on internet voting affinity. In order to test our model we are using the first Swiss population survey exclusively conducted on the topic of internet voting in April 2016.

Keywords: Internet voting · e-voting · Digital divide · Online participation · Digital democracy · Trust in technology

1 Introduction

As in other federalist countries such as Australia and Canada internet voting in Switzerland is currently being introduced in a piecemeal fashion. Since the first trial in 2003 an increasing number of cantons is offering the digital voting channel to its citizens either living in Switzerland or abroad. So far the question whether the introduction of internet voting in Switzerland would increase the digital divide, favoring the well educated, economically better off citizens could not be answered in a conclusive way. As yet bi- and multi-variate regression

© IFIP International Federation for Information Processing 2017
Published by Springer International Publishing AG 2017. All Rights Reserved
P. Parycek et al. (Eds.): ePart 2017, LNCS 10429, pp. 37–52, 2017.
DOI: 10.1007/978-3-319-64322-9_4

analyses of survey data showed that general trust in the internet as well as trust in internet voting in particular outweigh the effect of the typical digital divide variables. However, so far no study has tried to disentangle the two types of variables by applying structural equation modeling (SEM). In the present study we are trying to fill this gap by testing whether digital divide variables have a direct effect on general support of internet voting or whether they should rather be treated as antecedent variables of trust factors.

First, we set up the stage by describing a bit more in detail the context of Swiss internet voting and then review the current state of empirical studies in the next section. In the theoretical part we briefly discuss the issue of digital divide, the calculus of voting and the technology acceptance model (TAM) which we are using to draw up the hypotheses for our structural equation model. In the methodological part we present the survey data from 2016 and the method of partial least squares (PLS) modeling. In the empirical part we are reporting the measurement model and the results from the analysis. We conclude by a discussion of our main findings and suggestions for further research.

2   The Context of Swiss Internet Voting

In Switzerland the implementation of elections and referendums are a subnational matter. It is therefore the cantons and local executives who maintain vote registries, organise elections and determine voting results. Each canton maintains an Electoral Management Board (EMB) in charge of organising and administering elections as well as referendums on all three state levels. Smaller variants of the cantonal EMBs can be found in all of the approximately 2,350 Swiss municipalities. However, it is important to note that the cantonal political rights legislation is subject to federal approval [8] such that only the Federal Council (highest national executive power in Switzerland) has the authority to approve internet voting trials and to formulate the specific conditions under which the new digital channel can be implemented. There are detailed provisions on prerequisites for internet voting trials put forward in a federal ordinance. Cantons are, however, completely free whether they want to offer internet voting or not. As a general principle, and unlike on the local level in Canada, all other voting channels, i.e. ballot box and postal voting, remain open.

Remote voting is already very much the norm in Switzerland. In the bigger cities more than 90% of citizens are postal voters. Given Switzerland's success in establishing postal voting over the past 30 years as a preferred method of voting [11,14,21], there was hope that the internet as a new channel would be quickly adopted by the Swiss electorate in general and in particular by the young voters - a group usually displaying low participation rates. Due to the frequency of voting in Switzerland's referendum democracy [32], further arguments supporting the introduction of internet voting put forward in the debate were that it will speed up the vote counting process and reduce the number of invalid votes. In the early 2000s, with the federal administration providing financial support, the decentralised implementation of internet voting models began first in Geneva and soon thereafter also in Neuchâtel and Zurich. Three distinct models were developed, with the biggest difference between Zurich and Geneva being that the first is operated by a private company for a very decentralised local government system and the second one for a strongly centralised system developed and maintained mainly by the canton itself. Internet voting in Neuchâtel is different in that it is part of a cantonal e-government portal for which citizens have to register in person and can also be used for various other administrative transactions such as filing tax statements [34].

The first internet voting[1] trial for a binding referendum vote was held in 2003 in the Geneva based municipality of Anières. Zurich and Neuchâtel held their own trials in the following two years. The success of the trials in the three pilot cantons led the Swiss Federal Council to officially give the green light in May 2006 to the step-by-step rollout of internet voting; not only across the whole country, but importantly also for Swiss residents living abroad [8, 23], due in particular to the difficulties that they encounter with postal voting [5, 20]. In 2015, Swiss residents living abroad from roughly half of the 26 cantons were given the option to vote online. Rather than develop their own internet voting systems, the non-pilot cantons have chosen to adopt one of the existing models specifically either that of Zurich or Geneva. Neuchâtels specialised model was originally not easily transferable to other cantons. Trials were then put on hold in Zurich in 2011 [4]. In the meantime, the Canton Aargau took on the role of administrator for the consortium using the Zurich internet voting model. However, in the fall 2015, two months before the national elections this consortium comprising nine cantons did not get permission to use its system due to some flaws discovered on the occasion of an external security audit. Thereafter the Zurich-Aargau consortium dissolved. More recently, the Swiss Post joined forces with the canton of Neuchâtel and so far was able to bring the cantons of Fribourg and Basel City on board. Several other cantons are still in the process of choosing one of the two remaining systems so that the current situation is quite dynamic.

3   Current State of Research

There are several solid empirical studies analysing the socio-demographic profile of internet voters, eg. for Canada [15,16], Estonia [1,37,38], Norway [29] as well as the USA [3,36] just to cite a few of them. They are all documented in a comprehensive meta study [33]. For this paper, however, we limit our discussion to the directly relevant studies drawing on Switzerland.

The pioneer of Swiss internet voting, the Canton of Geneva, was also the first one to commission several studies. Combining online survey data for the municipalities of Carouge and Meyrin with the respective vote registry data [5] found that internet voters tended to be younger and male. 30 to 50 years

---

[1] It would be more precise to speak of internet or online voting. The term e-voting can also entail, for example touchscreen voting devices, which are used in voting booths. However, in Switzerland the term e-voting is commonly used, also by the authorities as a synonym for internet voting.

old men seemed to be specially prone to this new voting channel. In addition, results from the online survey suggested that a higher degree of education and, not surprisingly, the availability of a computer and internet access are further crucial factors explaining the preference for the online voting channel. Similar conclusions could be drawn from [35] presenting survey data from the Canton of Zurich. On the occasion of the national and cantonal referendum votes in fall 2004 a more thorough telephone survey among 1'014 voters as well as non-voters in four Geneva pilot municipalities showed that young, male voters with high income and educational level are over-represented among internet voters [6]. Nevertheless, the global multivariate model revealed that neither demographic nor political variables are good predictors in order to explain the choice of the voting channel. All these variables turn insignificant in the multivariate ICT model. Regarding the variables included in the ICT model such as IT skills, type of internet connection, trust in the internet and trust in the internet voting mechanism remain significant, the last one being the strongest predictor.

In 2009, when the first Swiss cantons such as Neuchâtel, Geneva and Basle City started to offer internet voting to Swiss citizens living abroad, further studies were conducted. According to an analysis drawing on official vote registry data as well as two online surveys for Swiss abroad internet voters registered in the canton of Geneva, the profile of Swiss abroad internet voters and postal voters were compared [31]. Young (the 30–39 as well as the 40–49 cohort using this channel more often than the 18–29) and male Swiss abroad were the most likely users of the online channel. Thirdly, the more distant the country of residence the more likely the person is to vote online. Further studies based on the 2011 election survey data from SELECTS corroborated these findings. Voters whose country of residence does not boarder Switzerland, with high IT skills and good political knowledge are more likely to use the online channel [12].

The hitherto most comprehensive study on the Geneva based internet voting trials [30] best illustrates the interaction of socio-demographic and ICT-related moderator variables. The authors compared traditional voters (ballot box and mail) with e-voters using survey data of a sample of the whole electorate of Geneva (partly telephone survey, partly online survey) as well as of an online poll of internet voters only. Their findings suggest that although male and young voters with a high level of education, high household income, high political and computing knowledge are indeed overrepresented among e-voters, all these variables turn insignificant in a multivariate model which includes the variables frequency of internet use and trust in internet transactions and communication.

Summing up, after more than a decade of internet voting practice in Switzerland studies seem to suggest that digital divide issues are not related to the new voting channel. However, there remains a puzzle to resolve. It might very well be the case that digital divide variables do not affect internet voting affinity directly but in an indirect way if they were to influence the variables most closely linked to internet voting such as ease of use and trust in the internet. Previous studies did not address this option properly. Simple descriptive statistics, bivariate correlations and even multivariate regression analyses do not provide enough discretionary power to disentangle the respective effects of digital divide variables, factors of convenience, worries about security issues and trust in the internet. Inspired by more recent studies such as [24, 26] we aim at making a further contribution in this respect, in a first instance by testing more elaborate causal modelling on very recent survey data for the Swiss case.

4 Theoretical Considerations

4.1 Digital Divide

Not on internet voting in particular but rather on the access and use of the Internet in general, there is the well-known argument that the new technological options favor the better off and well educated strata of society. This phenomenon is usually described as the digital divide. The digital divide [19] is at the same time techno-logical (lack of access in remote areas, the global South), economic (lack of access to a computer at home) and cognitive (lack of skills to use ICTs)[9]. According to [25] the most worrying characteristic of the digital divide is the fact that it follows existing cleavages in society and might increase inequalities further. Other authors, however, point out that such a socio-economic distortion will most likely fade away over time as mobile ICTs are becoming widely available also in more remote places and equipment is getting more affordable [2].

4.2 Technology Acceptance Model (TAM)

In addition to theoretical arguments along the digital divide track we consider the Technology Acceptance Model (TAM) to be of particular relevance for this study. The TAM [7] posits that user's perceived usefulness and effort are major explanatory factors for the acceptance of a technology. Applications in line with ours but with slightly different foci of research such as [24, 26] are demonstrations of the relevance of TAM in the realms of internet voting.

4.3 The Calculus of Voting

According to the calculus of voting [27] one of the major factors affecting an individual voter's decision to turn out for an election is the cost of voting. Many voting reforms hence are trying to facilitate the voting procedure, for example by allowing for remote voting, advance voting periods and finally also by introducing internet voting. Empirical studies showed that convenience reforms of voting can indeed have a tangible effect on participation rates. Postal voting increased participation in Switzerland [21] and the United States [17] by three to four percentage points. Whether internet voting can add to the further reduction of the cost of voting on top of postal voting is still an open debate and might depend on the context. In Switzerland where internet voting is being introduced on top of generalized postal voting, the extra convenience reform does not seem to make a difference [13]. However, irrespective of an eventual effect of internet voting on aggregate turnout in a constituency it can still have an effect on the perception of potential voters on internet voting and should therefore be taken into account.

4.4   Hypotheses

In this contribution we aim at bringing the debate on the question whether internet voting should be regarded as a digital divide issue to a higher level by trying to disentangle relevant variables and concepts which have proven to be of relevance in previous research. From such previous research on internet voting in Switzerland but also from elsewhere we know that trust in the internet in general as well as trust in internet voting in particular do have a strong effect on the actual use, the intent to use and approval rates for internet voting. However, discarding digital divide factors to be at play because they cancel out in multiple regressions would be premature. In case the very same digital divide variables cancel out as direct causes of internet voting affinity are affecting the respective trust variables, and those in return do load on our dependent variable, we would be back to square one. We argue that such an indirect effect of digital divide via the trust components was not properly tested in empirical studies before. We suggest this task can be achieved by applying better statistical techniques, namely by using structural equation modeling.

As depicted in Fig. 1 further below, our structural path model with internet voting affinity as the dependent variable is defined by a group of exogenous variables such as gender, education, age and income as well as of further endogenous components. In addition to being directly linked with the endogenous components convenience, political integration, use and trust of the internet and safety concerns, the exogenous variables can have both a direct or indirect effect on internet voting affinity.

H1 - Direct Effects of Socio-Economic Variables: In the light of detailed meta studies [33] direct effects of exogenous digital divide variables such as age, gender, income and education on the affinity to internet voting as our dependent variable are unlikely. We therefore expect those variables not to have a significant effect or at best a very minor one. Refuting hypothesis H1 would thus lead us to conclude that there is no major digital divide among the Swiss population regarding support for the new voting channel.

H2 - Direct Effect of Intermediate Variables: Following our discussion of the current state of research and theory we suspect certain intermediate components to affect Swiss citizen's degree of affinity towards internet voting.

The **first component** in our path dependency model summarizes items evaluating the convenience aspect of internet voting (comp1). Do respondents of the survey think that internet voting is more convenient (argu2) and simpler (argu5) to handle than postal voting? Do they think it is about time (argu3) to introduce internet voting because they realize there is a gap between all the things they do in their daily lives with the help of the Internet such as online-shopping, booking all kinds of leisure activities and using it in their respective work environment but not for voting (egov2).

The **second component** brings together items measuring how strongly a citizen is integrated in political activities(comp2). Foremost we can measure the degree of political involvement by asking about the interest in political matters in general (polint) as well as the frequency of participation in formal political events (part) such as referendum votes and elections.

The **third component** comprises core aspects of TAM, namely internet use and trust (comp3). Survey participants were asked how much they trust transactions over the Internet (trustint) and how often they are using it (useint).

The **fourth component** groups items about security concerns (comp4). Do respondents think that a vote via the Internet is easier to manipulate than a postal vote (argu4)? Do they even think there is a danger of foreign secret services monitoring the vote and thus breaching vote secrecy (argu6)?

H3 - Indirect Effect of Socio-Economic Variables: Previous research suggests that the internet use and trust component is taking out all direct effects of digital divide variables on internet voting affinity. However, an indirect effect could still be at play and been overlooked so far. In case digital divide variables have a direct effect on the internet use and trust component (c3) and if that same component is having a substantial effect on internet affinity we should conclude that digital divide is playing a role. We are thus looking for strong, statistically significant paths leading from socio-economic variables to the dependent variable via c3.

5   Data and Methods

5.1   The Swiss Internet Voting Survey 2016

To test our hypotheses[2] we are drawing on the data of a recently conducted population survey [22] with the exclusive aim to gain more detailed insights to internet voting affinity in Switzerland. The poll was carried out by the agency LINK between the 11th and the 21th April 2016 using computer-assisted telephone interviewing (CATI). The target population is composed by all Swiss citizens eligible to vote between 18 and 79 years of age. The sample consists of 1'228 respondents. Switzerland has three main linguistic regions: Population-wise, the German speaking part is the largest one, comprising 70% of the whole Swiss population. The French speaking part is making up around 20 and the Italian speaking part around 5% of the whole population. Thus, a dispropor-tionated stratified sampling design was chosen in order to over-sample the two linguistic minorities. In turn, specific design weights were used to compensate for this disproportionate stratification.

---

[2] In a further step the data collected in studies such as [31,35] should be re-analysed in a similar fashion.

All the questions and answer categories used in the analysis are summarized in Table 4 in the Appendix. Most items were measured on a 5-point Likert scale, where "Don't know" answers were included into the middle category. This is certainly true for the arguments which were tested within the survey. These arguments represent statements about internet voting, with which the respondents could agree or disagree with.

We are fully aware of the limitations we are facing with survey data asking about internet voting affinity. Using internet voting affinity as our main dependent variable is one major step away from explaining actual behaviour. Supporting the generalisation of internet voting and actually choosing that particular voting channel are of course two separate matters.

5.2   Partial Least Squares Modelling

We analysed our hypotheses with the help of partial least squares path modelling (PLS-PM). PLS-PM analysis has become an established tool in many fields of research, particularly when there are more than just a few, highly collinear factors explaining the response variable. Generally speaking, PLS-PM belongs to the family of structural equation models (SEM) which in turn, are a blend of different statistical techniques such as confirmatory factor analysis, path analysis, causal modelling with latent variables, and multiple regression. Especially when dealing with latent constructs, SEM is the most preferred methodology of choice. Additionally, our goal is to disentangle factors of internet voting affinity which are situated at different levels of explanation. To estimate such a complex multi-step cause-effect relationship, multiple regression analysis is not a suitable approach. Instead, path modelling in general and PLS-PM in particular are preferable for this sort of research problem.

As we pointed out before, PLS-PM can be thought of a robust structural equation modelling approach. In contrast to covariance-based SEM, the PLS approach does not reproduce a sample covariance matrix, but rather seeks to maximize the explained variance of the endogenous variables by iteratively estimating partial model relationships with OLS regressions [18]. Another distinctive feature of PLS is the fact that in PLS the latent variable scores are estimated and treated as error-free substitutes of the corresponding indicators. In contrast, CBSEM always includes an error term either for the indicators. Additionally, PLS has much less rigid distributional assumptions than covariance-based SEM techniques (CBSEM). For example, it does not require the normality assumption. In contrast, most CBSEM techniques require hard distributional assumptions [23]. Finally, PLS-PM does not have rigid demands on sample size making it suitable for a variety of models and purposes. Because of these advantages, PLS-PM was chosen as method of analysis. PLS analysis was performed with the SmartPLS software [28] using the PLS algorithm [20].

6   Empirical Analysis

6.1   The Measurement Model

In a first step, we tested our measurement model. In Table 1 we present the results of a principal component analysis (PCA) for all latent variables in use.

Table 1. Rotated component matrix of the independent variables (PCA)

Variables	comp1	comp2	comp3	comp4
More comfortable than postal voting	**.40**	−.15	−.23	.24
It is about time to introduce e-voting	**.45**	−.06	−.29	.08
Simpler than postal voting	**.44**	−.04	−.24	−.02
Demand for e-voting	**.43**	.07	−.20	−.02
Political interest	−.01	**.67**	−.15	.15
Participation frequency	−.01	**.68**	−.07	.15
Trust in the Internet	.35	.07	**.56**	−.03
Internet use	.31	.09	**.64**	.18
E-Voting can easily be manipulated	−.05	−.14	.06	**.72**
Secret services might hack the system	−.21	−.12	−.06	**.58**

As we can see, the factor loadings on the second (political integration), third (internet use and trust) and fourth (security concerns) component (comp2–4) are rather strong (above .55), while the loadings on the first component (convenience) are only fairly strong (between .4 and .45). Clearly, the convenience and the trust-usage component have a lot in common. Both indicators of the third component (trust in the Internet and Internet use) load rather strongly on the first component, too. Thus, the discriminant validity of both factors is closer to the lower than to the upper limit of acceptability. This makes also sense from a theoretical point of view. In order to gauge superior convenience of internet voting over postal voting, one has to be familiar with and trustful of the Internet in general. Respondents lacking any experience with the Internet or deeply distrusting it are extremely unlikely to having a preference of internet voting over postal voting. The second factor, however, is overwhelmingly independent of other indicators. In other words, political involvement is indeed independent from internet use, internet trust, internet voting affinity and general safety concerns. The same applies to the fourth component, although to a somewhat lesser degree.

As we can see in Table 2 construct validity is on a fairly good level: The average variance extracted amounts between .56 and .77, the composite reliability between .68 and .87 and Cronbach's alpha between .41 and .79.

Keeping certain limitations of our measurement model such as the border line discriminant power between the convenience and the trust component in mind we have prepared the grounds for the estimation of a PLS model.

Table 2. Construct validity and reliability

Components	AVE	Composite reliability	Cronbach's alpha	R^2
E-voting affinity				.531
Component 1	.613	.864	.790	.071
Component 2	.774	.873	.710	.118
Component 3	.684	.812	.543	.242
Component 4	.563	.682	.411	.017

AVE = Average variance extracted

6.2 Results

Our path model contains four exogenous variables and five endogenous variables (including the main dependent variable internet voting affinity). The model is reflective, i.e. the manifest variables of one block are considered to reflect their corresponding latent variable. For the sake of better visibility Fig. 1 only shows significant paths between latent variables for standardized regression coefficients higher than 0.1. The full results of the model test with bootstrapping are shown in Table 3 further below. Note that regression coefficients in Table 3 differ somewhat from the ones displayed in Fig. 1 since the latter is a representation of a model re-estimating only the paths which proved to be statistically significant in the full model as displayed in Fig. 1. Missing cases were replaced by the mean of the remaining observations.

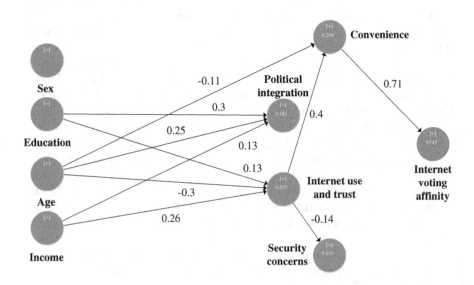

Fig. 1. PLS model estimates for all significant paths greater than .1

The first important point we can notice is the complete absence of direct and statistically significant paths from our exogenous variables to the phenomenon to explain, internet voting affinity. H1 can thus safely be refuted en bloc.

Regarding direct effects between the endogenous components 1–4 we can see that there is only one significant and strong path from the convenience component (c1) to internet voting affinity. All other components link to the dependent variable to such a minor degree that we do not take them into account. With a β of .71 the relationship between a positive evaluation of internet voting as being a convenient channel for voting and internet voting affinity is very strong. While the strength of this relationship is not surprising as such it is rather the absence of any strong connection between the other components and the dependent variable which is surprising.

The relatively strong path between the internet use and trust component (c3) and the convenience component (c1) can make sense intuitively but is probably owed to a large degree to some internal cohesion between the two which already became apparent when testing for discrimination between the components in Table 1. Furthermore, respondents with higher internet use and trust in internet transactions tend to be less concerned about security issues. However, with a β of only −.14 this relation does not seem to be particularly strong.

Looking at each of our exogenous variables in turn, we note that there is no significant partial regression path stemming from gender to any other variable in our model. There is a relatively strong relation between education and the degree of political integration (β = .3 in Fig. 1) and only a minor one towards the internet use and trust component. In that sense our model displays reassuring results. It is common knowledge in political and educational science that a higher degree of political integration corresponds with a better education, a higher economic status as well as higher age. The political integration component is actually not the most relevant for us but it was necessary to have it in the model as a control variable. In order to refute H3 we particularly focus on the internet use and trust component (c3) and check whether strong paths from digital divide variables continue to our dependent variable. However, this is not the case. Although education and income are somewhat or moderately related to the internet use and trust component we do not find the continuation further on to the dependent variable. We find the same pattern with age. The negative link (β = −.3 in Fig. 1) from age to the internet use and trust component is quite strong though.

7   Discussion

The results of the PLS model estimates suggest we can safely disregard a strong direct correlation between digital divide variables such as sex, education, age and income on the affinity to internet voting (H1). From the endogenous components we only find the convenience aspects to having a strong direct effect on internet voting affinity. The fact that the degree of political integration is almost unrelated to our dependent variable is a first hint pointing at the fact that digital

Table 3. Rotated component matrix of the independent variables (PCA)

Path	β	SE	p
age → c1	−.058	.03	.018
age → c2	**.183**	.02	.000
age → c3	**−.320**	.02	.000
age → c4	−.002	.03	.940
sex → c1	.014	.02	.541
sex → c2	−.087	−.03	.000
sex → c3	−.019	−.02	.388
sex → c4	.005	.03	.856
education → c1	.032	.03	.201
education → c2	**.216**	.02	.000
education → c3	**.168**	.02	.000
education → c4	−.064	.03	.001
income → c1	.007	.03	.782
income → c2	**.125**	.03	.000
income → c3	**.226**	.02	.000
income → c4	−.011	.03	.697
c1 → e-voting affinity	**.690**	.02	.000
c2 → c1	**.418**	.03	.000
c2 → c4	**−.166**	.03	.000
c2 → e-voting affinity	.050	.02	.025
c3 → e-voting affinity	.044	.03	.096
c4 → e-voting affinity	−.031	.02	.139
age → e-voting affinity	−.013	.02	.475
sex → e-voting affinity	.024	.02	.193
education → e-voting affinity	.007	.02	.734
income → e-voting affinity	.006	.02	.749

Fit-values: RMSEA = .036, CFI = .98, TLI = .97; SRMR = .027; Estimation: ML; all values are linear regression coefficients. In bold: significant paths higher than .1

divide might not be at play here either. Since a higher degree of education and a higher income do seem to have a moderately positive effect on political participation, a continuation of a strong path from this component to internet voting affinity would have meant that internet voting mostly finds support among the politically active strata of Swiss citizens. But this is not the case. We find the same pattern for the use and trust of the internet component. We would have expected this component to being related to digital divide factors and to also have an impact on internet voting affinity. This is clearly not the case either. The component that moderated almost all digital divide factors out of the equation in previous regression analyses is largely unrelated to our dependent variable. The security concerns component seems to be largely unrelated to the core concepts in the model either. Except for the strong convenience component effect on internet voting affinity we can thus also refute direct effects of the endogenous part of the model (H2). Regarding potential expected indirect effect of digital divide via one of our four endogenous components - in particular the one via the use and trust in the internet component - we only find one via the convenience component which in return is unrelated to digital divide variables. We should therefore also refute major indirect effects (H3).

The current PLS model, however, shows an aspect we so far have rather neglected. Age seems to exert a stronger influence on endogenous components than expected. Focusing on the main digital divide variables such as sex, education and income in this study we might have neglected another phenomenon. The strongest partial regression coefficient pointing to the internet use and trust component is actually the age. For the moment we can only speculate. However, further studies should eventually focus on the question whether the digital divide is not rather an generational gap rather than one of economic and cognitive resources (see [10, 26]).

More geared towards the substantive part of our model a word of caution is at order regarding the quality of some of the endogenous components of our model. In particular, there is a doubt whether the separation of the components convenience and trust in the internet can be upheld. The PCA as well as the relatively strong path link between the two suggests that they might have more in common than what we display in the model. In case the respective endogenous components ought to be regarded as one, and in light of the presence of the very strong link from the convenience component to our dependent variable as well as some of the digital divide variables moderately linking to it, an indirect effect would have to be reconsidered. In a nutshell, in order to gain a clearer insight on potential effects of digital divide variables operating in an indirect way as put forward in H3, there is some further conceptual work at order. In addition, a data set designed for that particular purpose could also help to improve the situation.

Last but not least, we should address some of the further pitfalls we might face with the present study. Firstly, our dependent variable is internet voting affinity and not the use of internet voting per se. Further Swiss data should be re-analysed in order to remedy this shortcoming. Furthermore, the Swiss case might be a peculiar one and not extend easily to other countries. This problem can only be overcome by comparative studies.

Appendix

Table 4. Items used in the analysis

Variable	Label	Wording and answer categories
E-voting affinity	evote	Generally speaking, are you in favour or against the introduction of e-voting? 1: "totally against"; 2: "rather against"; 3: "rather in favor"; 4: "totally in favor"
Participation frequency	part	Usually less than half of the electorate participates in referendums. How is it with you? Lets say there were ten in a given year. In how many would you have participated? Answers from 0–10
Interest in politics	polint	In general, how strongly are you interested in politics? 1: "very much interested"; 2: "rather interested"; 3: "rather not interested"; 4: "not interested at all"
E-voting convenience	argu2	When voting electronically it is possible to vote with a simple mouse click from ones home. This is more comfortable than postal voting. 1: "completely agree"; 2: "rather agree"; 3: "don't know"; 4: "rather disagree"; 5: "completely disagree"
Zeitgeist	argu3	Nowadays nearly everything can be done via the Internet. Hence it is time for e-voting to be universally available. 1: "compl. agree"; 2: "rather agree"; 3: "dont know"; 4: "rather disagree"; 5: "compl. disagree"
Postal voting easier	argu5	The postal vote is so simple, that e-voting is not needed. 1: "completely disagree"; 2: "rather disagree"; 3: "dont know"; 4: "rather agree"; 5: "completely agree"
Trust in the internet	trustint	much do you trust in internet transactions? 1: "not at all"; 2: "rather not"; 3: "depends on the transaction"; 4: "rather"; 5: "completely"
Internet usage	useint	How often do you use the Internet? 1: "never"; 2: "less than several times a month"; 3: "several times a month"; 4: "once per week"; 5: "several times per week"; 6: "once per day"; 7: "several times per day"
Demand for e-voting	egov2	Demand for services by government agencies: the possibility to cast ones ballot online. Scale from 0 (unnecessary) to 10 (very necessary)
Easier to manipulate	argu4	Its easier to manipulate a vote via the Internet than via postal vote. 1: "completely agree"; 2: "rather agree"; 3: "dont know"; 4: "rather disagree"; 5: "completely disagree"
Worries about security	argu6	With e-voting there is a danger of foreign secret services monitoring the vote. 1: "completely agree"; 2: "rather agree"; 3: "dont know"; 4: "rather disagree"; 5: "completely disagree"

References

1. Alvarez, R.M., Hall, T.E., Trechsel, A.H.: Internet voting in comparative perspective: the case of Estonia. PS. Polit. Sci. Polit. **42**(3), 497–505 (2009)
2. Alvarez, R.M., Hall, T.E.: Point, Click, and Vote: The Future of Internet Voting. Brookings Institution Press, Washington, D.C (2004)
3. Alvarez, R.M., Nagler, J.: The likely consequences of internet voting for political representation. Loyola of Los Angeles Law Rev. **34**(3), 1115–1152 (2001)
4. Beroggi, G.E.: Internet voting: an empirical evaluation. Computer **47**(4), 44–50 (2014)
5. Christin, T., Trechsel, A.H.: Qui vote par Internet ? Une approche scientifique des scrutins de Carouge et Meyrin (2004). http://tinyurl.com/l9442g7
6. Christin, T., Trechsel, A.H.: Analyse du scrutin du 26 septembre 2004 dans quatre communes genevoises (Anières, Carouge, Cologny et Meyrin) (2005). http://tinyurl.com/lx6qcux
7. Davis, F.D., Bagozzi, R.P., Warshaw, P.R.: User acceptance of computer technology: a comparison of two theoretical models. Manage. Sci. **35**(8), 982–1003 (1989). http://dx.doi.org/10.1287/mnsc.35.8.982
8. Driza Maurer, A.: Internet voting and federalism: the Swiss case. Revista General de Derecho Público Comparado **13**, 1–33 (2013)
9. Ferro, E., Helbig, N.C., Gil-Garcia, J.R.: The role of IT literacy in defining digital divide policy needs. Gov. Inf. Q. **28**(1), 3–10 (2011)
10. Friemel, T.N.: The digital divide has grown old: determinants of a digital divide among seniors. New Media Soc. **18**(2), 313–331 (2016). http://dx.doi.org/10.1177/1461444814538648
11. Gasser, U., Gerlach, J.: Electronic voting: approaches, strategies, and policy issues– a report from Switzerland. In: van der Hof, S., Groothuis, M.M. (eds.) Innovating Government, Information Technology and Law Series, vol. 20, pp. 101–128. T.M.C. Asser Press, The Hague (2011)
12. Germann, M., Serdült, U.: Internet voting for expatriates: the Swiss case. JeDEM - eJournal of eDemocracy Open Gov. **6**(2), 197–215 (2014)
13. Germann, M., Serdült, U.: Internet voting and turnout: evidence from Switzerland. Electoral. Stud. **47**, 1–12 (2017)
14. Geser, H.: Electronic voting in Switzerland. In: Kersting, N., Baldersheim, H. (eds.) Electronic Voting and Democracy: A Comparative Analysis, pp. 75–96. Palgrave Macmillan (2004)
15. Goodman, N.J.: Internet voting in a local election in Canada. In: Grofman, B., Trechsel, A.H., Franklin, M. (eds.) The Internet and Democracy in Global Perspective. SPC, vol. 31, pp. 7–24. Springer, Cham (2014). doi:10.1007/978-3-319-04352-4_2
16. Goodman, N., Pammett, J.: The patchwork of internet voting in Canada. In: Krimmer, R., Volkamer, M. (eds.) EVOTE 2014, pp. 13–18. TUT Press, Tallinn (2014)
17. Gronke, P., Galanes-Rosenbaum, E., Miller, P.A., Toffey, D.: Convenience voting. Annu. Rev. Polit. Sci. **11**, 437–455 (2008)
18. Hair, J.F., Ringle, C.M., Sarstedt, M.: PLS-SEM: indeed a silver bullet. J. Mark.Theory Pract. **19**(2), 139–152 (2011)
19. Hargittai, E., Hsieh, Y.P.: Digital inequality. In: Dutton, W.H. (ed.) Oxford Handbook of Internet Studies, pp. 129–150. Oxford University Press, Oxford (2013)

20. Lohmöller, J.B.: Latent Variable Path Modeling with Partial Least Squares. Physica, Heidelberg (1989)
21. Luechinger, S., Rosinger, M., Stutzer, A.: The impact of postal voting on participation: evidence for Switzerland. Swiss Polit. Sci. Rev. **13**(2), 167–202 (2007)
22. Milic, T., McArdle, M., Serdült, U.: Attitudes of Swiss citizens towards the generalisation of e-voting (2016). https://doi.org/10.5167/uzh-127938
23. Monecke, A., Leisch, F.: semPLS: structural equation modeling using partial least squares (2012)
24. Nemeslaki, A., Aranyossy, M., Sasvári, P.: Could on-line voting boost desire to vote? Technology acceptance perceptions of young Hungarian citizens. Gov. Inf. Q. **33**(4), 705–714 (2016)
25. Norris, P.: Digital Divide: Civic Engagement, Information Poverty, and the Internet Worldwide. Cambridge University Press, Cambridge (2001)
26. Powell, A., Williams, C.K., Bock, D.B., Doellman, T., Allen, J.: e-Voting intent: a comparison of young and elderly voters. Gov. Inf. Q. **29**(3), 361–372 (2012)
27. Riker, W.H., Ordeshook, P.C.: A theory of the calculus of voting. Am. Polit. Sci. Rev. **62**(1), 25–42 (1968)
28. Ringle, C.M., Wende, S., Becker, J.M.: SmartPLS 3. Boenningstedt: SmartPLS GmbH (2015) http://www.smartpls.com
29. Saglie, J., Segaard, S.B.: Internet voting and the secret ballot in Norway: principles and popular understandings. J. Elections, Public Opin. Parties **26**(2), 155–169 (2016)
30. Sciarini, P., Cappelletti, F., Goldberg, A., Nai, A., Tawfik, A.: Etude du vote par internet dans le canton de Genève: Rapport final à l'intention de la Commission externe d'évaluation des politiques publiques. Geneva: University of Geneva (2013). http://tinyurl.com/k3685ps
31. Serdült, U.: Internet voting for the Swiss Abroad of Geneva: first online survey results. In: Chappelet, J.L. (ed.) Electronic Government and Electronic Participation: Joint Proceedings of Ongoing Research and Projects of IFIP EGOV and ePart 2010, pp. 319–325. Trauner (2010)
32. Serdült, U.: Referendums in Switzerland. In: Qvortrup, M. (ed.) Referendums Around the World, pp. 65–121. Palgrave Macmillan, Basingstoke (2014)
33. Serdült, U., Germann, M., Harris, M., Portenier, A.: Who are the internet voters. In: Janssen, M., Bannister, F., Glassey, O., Scholl, H.J., Tambouris, E., Wimmer, M.A., Macintosh, A. (eds.) Electronic Government and Electronic Participation, pp. 27–41. IOS Press, Amsterdam (2015)
34. Serdült, U., Germann, M., Mendez, F., Portenier, A., Wellig, C.: Fifteen years of internet voting in Switzerland: history, governance and use. In: Téran, L., Meier, A. (eds.) ICEDEG 2015: Second International Conference on eDemocracy & eGovernment, pp. 149–156. IEEE, New York (2015)
35. Serdült, U., Trechsel, A.H.: Umfrage bei Stimmberechtigten der Zürcher Gemeinden Bertschikon, Bülach und Schlieren anlässlich des Pilotversuchs zum Vote électronique vom 27 November 2005 (2006). https://doi.org/10.5167/uzh-135593
36. Solop, F.I.: Digital democracy comes of age: internet voting and the 2000 Arizona democratic primary election. Polit. Sci. Polit. **34**(2), 289–293 (2001)
37. Solvak, M., Vassil, K.: E-voting in Estonia: technological diffusion and other developments over ten years (2005–2015). Johan Skytte Institute of Political Studies, Tartu (2016). http://tinyurl.com/kagtxos
38. Trechsel, A.H.: E-voting and electoral participation. In: de Vreese, C.H. (ed.) Dynamics of Referendum Campaigns, pp. 159–183. Palgrave, London (2007)

Crystallizing Local Political Knowledge for Informed Public Participation

Guoray Cai[✉], Feng Sun, and Jessica Kropczynski

College of Information Sciences and Technology,
Penn State University, University Park, PA, USA
{cai,fzs122,jkropczynski}@ist.psu.edu

Abstract. Municipal governments often struggle to inform and engage citizens around local issues. Due to complexities of local politics and the diverse expressions in public and private spheres, citizens face a huge information barrier towards meaningful participation. To overcome such barrier, we explore a solution to provide citizens with clear, useful, and trustworthy information. We describe a framework for accomplishing this goal through issue-based knowledge crystallization. In order to put this framework into test, we devised *Community Issue Review* (CIR) as a concrete process for crystallizing local political knowledge. CIR is a structured deliberative process that use a citizen panel to conduct analysis of data relevant to a pending issue. We describe CIR in three aspects of its functions: *institutional design, deliberative process*, and *productive outcome*. Three special characteristics of CIR are emphasized: (1) fully embedded within local decision-making context; (2) hybrid (face-to-face and online) deliberation; (3) facilitation on collaborative decision-analysis. We present the iterative design of the CIR process and the lessons learned from field practices in a local community.

Keywords: Civic engagement · eParticipation · Online deliberation

1 Introduction

Democracy empowers the public through their influence on political decisions [7]. Policy issues in local governments are complex and contentious. While electronic government applications provide opportunities for broad participation, meaningful participation of public decision-making requires the ability of the participants to produce reasonable, well-informed opinion in light of discussion, new information, and claims made by fellow participants [2]. Such ability is often hindered by the lack of exposure to a diverse marketplace of ideas [16]. Since most citizens are not experts on public issues, their ability to contribute to public decision making is vitally based on comprehending the necessary information from media and others [15]. Informing the public with adequate knowledge about policy issues is hard for many reasons. Understanding complex policy issues requires synthesizing three types of knowledge. *First*, the public needs to be informed by

© IFIP International Federation for Information Processing 2017
Published by Springer International Publishing AG 2017. All Rights Reserved
P. Parycek et al. (Eds.): ePart 2017, LNCS 10429, pp. 53–64, 2017.
DOI: 10.1007/978-3-319-64322-9_5

good science that characterizes the potential consequences (benefits and risks) of any policy option [3]. *Second*, it must give all stakeholders an opportunity to express their social, economic, and ethical concerns. *Third*, it must be informed by understanding the institutional, political, legal, and operational contexts of decision-making. These knowledge can be buried in a plethora of on-line and off-line information sources.

Recent proliferation of on-line participation platforms have significantly enriched the channels of expressing opinions on public matters [6], but at the same time, it creates information glut to citizens' use. Typically, information about a policy issue is buried in new media, community forums, government web pages, documents, and reports, community meeting notes, as well as in the minds of experts, residents, and other stakeholders. Messages in these data are poorly framed, piece-wise, difficult to connect, redundant, and inconsistent. Unfortunately, interpreting and synthesizing such data are challenging tasks that few citizens are prepared to deal with. This problem has by far received little attention, and no practical solution has been proposed. This problem is well recognized in the literature of deliberative democracy [9] and policy communication studies [18]. Elliman et al. [5] emphasized that the most fundamental barrier in public deliberations is the large amount of heterogeneous knowledge that needs to be made explicit in different formats at different stages of public opinion formation.

To address this problem of the wide dispersion of local knowledge, various computer-mediated systems and data mining techniques have been developed to automatically discover and aggregate diverse sources. Kavanaugh et al. [11] developed a *Virtual Town Square (VTS)*, a local news aggregator, that affords civic interaction through tagging, commenting, and sharing insights. However, even data are aggregated, they may still be too large for the public to make sense of them. Automated textual analysis tools have been used to detect important messages and alert analysts. Hagen et al. [10] automatically analyzed thousands of petitions to generate more concise reports for decision makers. Topic modeling methods [20] are useful here because it summarizes the most popular topics that appear news articles and blogs and representing them together in an intuitive way. Automated methods (as mentioned above) can improve the accessibility of community information sources. However, they are far from providing actionable knowledge to citizens. Useful knowledge has to be discovered from the data and be contextualized for certain tasks [19]. It is cognitively difficult and time-consuming for a person to make sense of large and complex data.

This paper argues for the need to communicate policy relevant knowledge more effectively to the public in order to maximize the chance of their meaningful participation with the constraints of the limited cognitive capacity and attentional resources. This need can be met by incorporating an explicit phase of "knowledge crystallization" before engaging the broader public to elicit their policy preferences. We present a conceptual framework for structuring knowledge crystallization tasks (Sect. 2). Following this framework, we propose a concrete process, *community issue review* (CIR), that can be practiced as a policy knowledge co-creation tool in a variety of policy-decision contexts (Sect. 3). We implemented and used CIR in evaluating a real community proposal and observed the positive impact to the level of engagement (Sects. 4 and 5). In the same time, we received feedback on how the CIR process and the supporting technology can be improved and be made more flexible to support best practices (Sect. 6).

2 Issue-Based Knowledge Crystallization for Democratic Deliberation

Our research addresses the need of crystallizing knowledge to overcome the information glut experienced by local communities when residents are called for participating public deliberation on a pending policy issue or proposal for action. Instead of pouring a large amount of messy data to all the members of a local community, our solution is to crystallize the knowledge about the policy issue into a set of clearly stated findings, called Citizen's Statements, that is amenable to human mental processing [17] by the lay public.

We define knowledge crystallization as a process that aims to produce a most insightful and compact description of the relevant content of a data set for a given task without removing crucial information. Examples of knowledge crystallization tasks include writing a business intelligence newsletter, reporting on the analysis of a business strategic management practice, or a scientist writing a literature review article [1]. Issue-based Knowledge crystallization (IBKC) takes all the data that we can collect about a particular public issue, and puts them through a systematic process of distilling relevant nuggets, purifying, abstracting, and compacting to create a best and most accessible "form" of knowledge for human consumption.

Crystallization is a metaphor borrowed from chemical engineering, where the goal of crystallization is to produce a highly purified and ordered crystal lattice from raw materials through the processes of purification and condensation. We use the concept of *knowledge crystals* to represent a form of knowledge that is highly purified, compact, succinct, structured, and solid.

An overview of the knowledge crystallization process is shown in Fig. 1. The rectangular boxes represent entities involved in the process. The arrows represent flow relationships among them. This process has four small loops and has one set of loops that cycle around knowledge evaporation and another that cycles around knowledge condensation, with plenty of interaction between these. This process is guided by a knowledge schema that reflects the structure of inquiries used by the decision-makers. A bigger rectangular task wraps the entire process and serves as the context.

3 Community Issue Review

Community Issue Review (CIR) is a community-level panel-based deliberation process for crystallizing knowledge about a pending community issue [12].

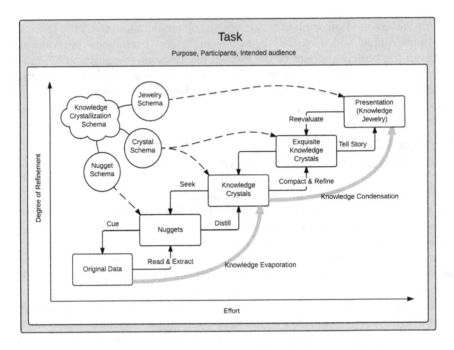

Fig. 1. The framework for issue-based knowledge crystallization

It is specially tailored to the need of informing the public on local policy issues. CIR guides a group of panelists to review an issue relevant to the community in-depth through a multi-day public review process. Panelists are either randomly or strategically selected from a community. As representatives of a community, panelists are given access to a large amount of data from various sources concerning a given issue. CIR aims to generate an informative briefing of the issue, called *Citizens' Statements*, to provide the community with insights concerning the issue so that everyone in the community is able to form opinions effectively and efficiently.

CIR can be conducted in a purely face to face environment. However, citizens have their daily work and can only allocate limited time (especially daytime) and effort for CIR. In our experimental studies we choose to blend online and face-to-face activities. There are two face-to-face meetings on the first and last days respectively, and the panel works online during the time in between. The whole process may last about ten days to two weeks depending on the complexity of the issue. The expected outcome of CIR is a set of Citizens' Statements, including 10 findings, 5 pros, and 5 cons. The slots associated with the 20 statements are allocated in advance and can be assigned with customized labels for easier reference. Each category is equipped with a progress bar that shows the current working process of categorization.

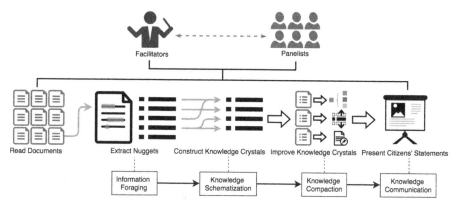

Fig. 2. The overview of community issue review as a knowledge crystallization implementation

In the rest of the section, we describe the phases and relevant activities in a CIR process. We will also identify the challenges users may face and show how technical support can contribute.

3.1   Preparation

Recruiting Citizen Panel. One important design question is: *who should be the part of the CIR panel for crystallizing the community knowledge?* We choose to use a small group of citizens as the panel. By bringing in diverse perspectives and skills, we can expect CIR to perform an in-depth analysis in a deliberative manner. Since the outcome of the CIR is to be used by citizens in a community, using peer citizens in CIR ensures a degree of trust by other citizens. We follow the work of a small group deliberative democracy process [8], which selects panelist from the relevant population through stratified random sampling as representatives.

Assemble information package for a pending issue. In an ideal world, input to CIR should be all the information that can be found about a community issue. In reality, we use a team of undergraduate researchers to collect documents from government websites, public media, experts and senior citizen advisors to compile an information package to be distributed to each panelist. We also identify and invite subject matter experts and government officials to review and supplement the package to ensure completeness. The contents usually include neutral descriptions of proposals/ordinances and evidences for/against a policy proposal. Other than published reports, websites, and news articles, the document collection also contains interviews with subject matter experts and their written statements. During the CIR process, panelists are allowed to add more materials through a request.

Issue Briefing. Before moving to the first phase, the panelists will get together and learn about the community issue through a face-to-face meeting. During this meeting, the CIR panel members are charged with investigating a policy issue that is usually complex and controversial. In the same time, they will pick up an information package with all the details about CIR process, data to be analyzed and the intended outcome. They will have a chance to get to know each other as collaborators. Panelists will also receive a training on how to use the online deliberation system, GeoDeliberator. They can also communicate with experts directly to resolve quick questions.

3.2   Phase I: Extract Information Nugget

Nugget Extraction in CIR is aimed at reliably recognizing and collecting all data segments (or nuggets) relevant to the pending issue. Doing a good job in this phase is the prerequisite for subsequent tasks of knowledge crystal formation, refinement, and compaction. During this first phase of CIR, panelists work asynchronously online to gather information nuggets relevant to a policy issue. The document view contains a collection of documents, plus a table of contents for easy navigation. These documents are identical to those included in the information package. When a panelist recognizes a nugget in a document, and he/she can extract nuggets by selecting a piece of text judged as relevant to one or more theme. Once a segment of text is selected, it will be highlighted with yellow color and be prompted to assign this information nugget to a theme. All the themes are listed on the top and a detailed explanation will be provided when placing cursor over each theme icon.

All the extracted nuggets are collected into the *nugget list*. Nugget List view is actively linked to the Document View, allowing panelists to trace back to where a nugget originates in the document. Capturing the relationship between nugget and its origin in documents effectively makes it possible to replay and review the analytical process later on [14].

3.3   Phase II: Assemble and Improve Claims

The purpose of *Claim Assembly* in CIR is to transform collected information nuggets into claims, which should be relatively well-written, self-contained, and based on facts and evidence. There are two kinds of claims: findings (objective facts) and opinions (facts with implicit position). The opinions can be further decomposed into two categories: substantiate and refute, depending on the position. A claim is informed by one or more information nuggets. Claims can be further elaborated and improved through adding more information nuggets, removing irrelevant or unimportant contents, rewording, merging several claims or splitting a claim.

A new claim can be created by clicking + button on the top of the claim list. Once a new claim is created, the view automatically switches to the claim workspace where one can write the claim text and cite any nuggets (by clicking the "adopt" button next to a nugget) that contribute to the claim. By adopting nuggets to a claim, a semantic link is established between the selected nuggets and the current claim. In addition to editing the claim directly, panelists are also encouraged to leave comments to others and discuss the claim.

3.4   Phase III: Generate Statements

Phase III is to refine the statements by making them more compact, defensible, and understandable. This involves two types of interface operations: categorization and refinement. Categorization is to decide whether a claim is a *finding* statement, or a *substantiate* statement or a *refute* statement. The categorization is performed by dragging and dropping claims from claim list to a category slot.

3.5   Phase IV: Communicate Statements

In this phase, the claims are compiled into a set of statements of manageable length. These statements must be presented in a way that is easily understood by local citizens. Special care is given to the use of language that state expert and professional knowledge in a form usable by the general public. The final Citizens' statements contain ten statements of *Findings* that summarize the issue and why it is important to the community. Another ten statements are allocated to the five strongest arguments in favor of the issue and five strongest arguments against the issue (Fig. 3).

3.6   Facilitative Moderation

CIR requires expert facilitators to be coupled with system support. Facilitators serve on a number of roles. Firstly, they mediate the conflicts among views on issue-relevant information, and manage different understandings, values, and knowledge [13]. Second, facilitators coordinate with the panelists and experts.

The facilitator practices its function through a control panel in the online system. From this control panel, the facilitator can monitor panelists' activities, control the process through a sequence of phases, manage schema, and manage documents.

3.7   Supporting Collaboration

In addition to entity-eccentric discussion and editing, collaboration among panelists is supported mainly through a chat room. Communications among panelists and subject matter experts are supported through a question panel. Panelists can directly ask a question in the question panel. Some of the questions can be answered immediately by peers. Others may have to be forwarded to subject matter experts. Once answers are received, they will be incorporated into the document collections.

4   Case Study

In order to test our implementation of CIR and iteratively improve it, we conducted a case study to gather the feedback from the potential panelists.

4.1 Procedure

The community issue used in this study is *inflationary tax indexing*. The proposal is that *real estate tax should be increased by at least inflation every year just to keep pace with the cost of providing services to the Borough*. We recruited fourteen participants as the citizen panel. Most of them were recruited via mailings that were sent at random based on the addresses provided the borough office. Three of them from specific student organizations were recruited via targeted email. The three students rent in the borough. The rest are homeowners. There are also four subject matter experts involved. Two of them are proponents that support the inflationary tax indexing, and two are opponents against the issue.

Fig. 3. Face-to-face meeting on Day 1

The study lasted ten days. On the first day, a short introduction and a training session were conducted in the face-to-face meeting. In the first session, the moderator introduced the community issue review in terms of its process, expected outcome and various roles. Then the community issue of *inflationary tax indexing* was introduced, followed by a *question and answer* period that allows the panelists to ask questions.

After the meeting, the panelists went home and began to work in the online environment. They were expected to follow CIR phases and collaboratively produce candidate statements for the final-day meeting to discuss. During this period, a facilitator kept monitoring the online activities and moderate the process when necessary. To ensure steady progress, the facilitator sent emails every morning, along with a summary of the progress by far. In the final day meeting, the panelists discussed and finalized the 20 citizen's statements.

We wanted to gather input from the participants as much as possible since this is still a preliminary study, thus an exploratory approach was employed to collect their feedback. During each of the work sessions, researchers conducted observations and asked the panelists to describe what they were doing and thinking aloud, especially the intentions behind behaviors. We only provided guidance and assistance whenever the participants had confusion.

4.2   Evaluation and Feedback

Based on the participants' feedback and our observations, we compiled a series of points and summarized them in this section.

Knowledge Crystallization Scheme. Without knowing how to decide and choose the knowledge schema, we adopted a set of themes as the knowledge crystallization scheme in this study. Each theme represents one important aspect of the issue and is shown as a phrase with detailed explanations on demand. For example, "Affordability" was used in the study as a theme, which indicates how a tax increase affects the price of owning and renting properties.

All the participants reported that the themes were only useful for the first phase to organize extracted nuggets. It was difficult for them to continue to use the themes as the extracted nuggets were transformed into claims. Instead, some of the participants suggested that several guiding questions would be more helpful for all phases.

Phase Transition. We organized CIR as an explicitly phase-based process following the IBKC framework (Fig. 2). Phases switch only when all participants feel that they have completed the current phase and ready to move on to the next phase. By enforcing phase-based process, panelists were expected to work synchronously and thus their contributions could be evaluated and utilized collaboratively.

However, Some participants reported that it was difficult for them to divide phase clearly; it caused confusion to them as they had to understand exactly the design of each phase. To address this problem, we enhanced our system by allowing panelists to be able to do all the work in one integrated interface where phases are implicitly enforced. We presented the revised interface to two participants and received positive feedback.

Learnability and Accessibility. The most common issue pointed by the participants was the usability of the online system. The participants were unaware of many available features and sometimes used the system in an incorrect way. The targeted users are ordinary citizens, among which many have insufficient computer skills. Therefore, on the one hand, the system should be designed to be easier to learn and operate. On the other hand, a more sophisticated technical support and training session should be provided.

Collaboration, Coordination, and Communication. Our observations show that participants communicated a lot in face-to-face meetings while they worked almost individually in the online environment, though a variety of communication channels were provided. One participant believed it is due to time delays in asynchronous communication while people do expect immediate responses or in-time notification. This was explained by [4].

One improvement is to provide subscription/notification service: Once a participant makes a contribution to an entity, she is considered to subscribe to the related thread. Whenever there is an update, e.g., another participant leaves a comment, the participant will be notified. The idea of the private and public workspace was also mentioned by some participants, which allows the participants to work in their private workspace and share with others only when necessary.

Flexibility of Organizing and Retrieving Contents. Currently all the entities involved in CIR, such as documents, extracted nuggets, assembled claims, and candidate statements, are structured in a linear fashion. Although some filters are provided that allow panelists to select, for example, the information nuggets tagged by a particular theme, it is still limiting the way of organizing them. Some participants would like to see the system provide more means of structuring the entities, for example, to cluster documents based on contents in advance.

Another feature the participants hope to have is a search function. We intentionally removed the search function as a way to enforce people to go through all the documents thoroughly rather than doing a keyword search when doing sense-making. However, the participants do have a need to revisit what they have read, and search function can support that. Bookmarking is also a solution to that.

5 Discussion and Conclusion

In this paper, we identified the challenges caused by information overload and knowledge deficit that prevent ordinary citizens from participating public life effectively. Drawing from observations of how local government decision-making works and theories of information, we proposed CIR, an instance of knowledge crystallization, as a solution to the above problem. We implemented CIR with the help online technologies and presented it to a group of citizens strategically selected. Based on lessons learned from their feedback, we developed a better understanding of CIR process and the need for improving this process.

Community Issue Review should be considered as a general framework that can be implemented in a variety of the contexts and processes. The current implementation of CIR (as described in this paper) is far from being perfect. On the technical side, many system-support features are to be further refined and optimized. We are incorporating the lessons learned from experimental observations and the feedback collected from the case study to enhance the support for collaboration and communication among panelists. On the social side, our design of the CIR process should consider the vulnerability of the process and outcomes to *power influences*. In our observation of CIR practices in State College Borough, the Borough's council members are clearly the power holders since they make the final decision. The council can influence the CIR process by framing the policy issues from the government point of view, imposing pressure on which issue to be reviewed and limiting policy options to be considered. To balance such potentials of power influence, we have explicitly included a few mechanisms in CIR to empower citizens. *First*, the citizen panel of CIR is the only body to execute the creation of the citizens' statement, and other players (subject matter experts, municipal staff, researchers) are all playing a supporting role during the process. *Second*, we run a special session of "issue-framing" in Day-1 of CIR to allow the panel to generate its own way of framing the policy issue and propose alternative solutions. *Second*, we asked the panel to deliberate on their value propositions and challenge those from the experts and the government. For the above reasons, we argue that citizens' participation in the CIR redistributes more power from the council to the citizens, compared to the existing citizen consultation methods that do not garner much participation.

Acknowledgments. We acknowledge the support of this research by NSF under award IIS-1211059. The work of the first author is also partially supported by a grant from the Chinese Natural Science Foundation under award 71373108.

References

1. Card, S.K., Mackinlay, J.D., Shneiderman, B.: Readings in Information Visualization: Using Vision to Think. Morgan Kaufmann, San Francisco (1999)
2. Chambers, S.: Deliberative democratic theory. Ann. Rev. Polit. Sci. **6**, 307–326 (2003)
3. Council, N.R.: Understanding Risk: Informing Decisions in a Democratic Society. National Academy Press, Washington, D.C. (1996)
4. Curtis, D.D., Lawson, M.J.: Exploring collaborative online learning. J. Asynchr. Learn. Netw. **5**(1), 21–34 (2001)
5. Elliman, T., Macintosh, A., Irani, Z.: A model building tool to support group deliberation (eDelib). Int. J. Cases Electron. Comm. **3**(3), 33–44 (2007)
6. Friess, D., Eilders, C.: A systematic review of online deliberation research. Policy Internet **7**(3), 319–339 (2015)
7. Gastil, J., Levine, P.: The Deliberative Democracy Handbook: Strategies for Effective Civic Engagement in the 21st Century. Jossey-Bass, San Francisco (2005)
8. Gastil, J., Richards, R.: Making direct democracy deliberative through random assemblies. Politics Soc. **41**(2), 253–281 (2013)
9. Gudowsky, N., Bechtold, U.: The role of information in public participation. J. Publ. Deliber. **9**(1) (2013)
10. Hagen, L., Harrison, T.M., Uzuner, Ö., Fake, T., Lamanna, D., Kotfila, C.: Introducing textual analysis tools for policy informatics: a case study of e-petitions. In: Proceedings of the 16th Annual International Conference on Digital Government Research (dg.o 2015), pp. 10–19 (2015)

11. Kavanaugh, A., Ahuja, A., Pérez-Quiñones, M., Tedesco, J., Madondo, K.: Encouraging civic participation through local news aggregation. In: Proceedings of the 14th Annual International Conference on Digital Government Research, pp. 172–179 (2013)

12. Kropczynski, J.N., Cai, G., Carroll, J.M.: Understanding the roles of artifacts in democratic deliberation from the citizens initiative review. J. Soc. Med. Organ. **3**(2), 1–22 (2015)

13. Moore, C.W.: The Mediation Process: Practical Strategies for Resolving Conflict. Wiley, New York (2014)

14. North, C., Chang, R., Endert, A., Dou, W., May, R., Pike, B., Fink, G.: Analytic provenance: process+interaction+insight. In: CHI 2011 Extended Abstracts on Human Factors in Computing Systems (CHI EA 2011), NY, USA, pp. 33–36. ACM, New York (2011)

15. Panagiotopoulos, P., Gionis, G., Psarras, J., Askounis, D.: Supporting public decision making in policy deliberations: an ontological approach. Oper. Res. **11**(3), 281–298 (2011)

16. Price, V., Neijens, P.: Opinion quality in public opinion research. Int. J. Publ. Opinion Res. **9**(4), 336–360 (1997)

17. Resnikoff, H.L.: Concurrent computer and human information processing. In: Zunde, P., Agrawal, J.C. (eds.) Empirical Foundations of Information and Software Science IV, pp. 63–73. Springer, Boston (1987)

18. Richards, G., Belcher, K., Noble, B.: Informational barriers to effective policy-public communication: a case study of wind energy planning in Saskatchewan Canada. Canad. Publ. Policy **39**(3), 431–450 (2013)

19. Rowley, J.: The wisdom hierarchy: representations of the DIKW hierarchy. J. Inf. Sci. **33**(2), 163–180 (2007)

20. Yin, Z., Cao, L., Gu, Q., Han, J.: Latent community topic analysis: integration of community discovery with topic modeling. ACM Trans. Intell. Syst. Technol. (TIST) **3**(4), 1–21 (2012)

Revealing the Factors Influencing E-participation Development in Russia

Lyudmila Vidiasova[✉], Dmitrii Trutnev, and Evgenii Vidiasov

ITMO University, Saint Petersburg, Russia
bershadskaya.lyudmila@gmail.com, trutnev@ego-center.ru,
vidyasov@lawexp.com

Abstract. International rankings of e-participation development provide useful information for making strategic decisions for a more successful information society development. However, when we start the interpretation of the ranking details, it is important to consider the context, as well as national factors and existed barriers on the way. The paper presents some results and conclusions drawn from the expert survey and aiming to detect the factors which affect e-participation development in Russia. The authors conducted an expert poll with the participation of 41 experts from government, business, NGO, scientific and education structures, and city-activists. The survey results allowed to detect the target of e-participation tools development in Russia; to determine the factors that influence positively and negatively on its development. The major finding of the survey showed the following trend: e-participation tools in Russia served to optimize the authorities' work and fight such barriers as administrative, regulative and lack of citizens' trust in e-participation tools.

Keywords: E-participation · Expert survey · Factors of development · Assessment

1 Introduction

The global trends belonged to the term "e-participation" assume a technological mechanism for linking citizens' demands and needs and the politicians. According to the last world ranking on E-participation development prepared by UN in 2016 [8], the world leadership in this field belongs to the United Kingdom, Australia, Japan, South Korea, Netherlands, New Zealand, Spain, Singapore, Canada, Finland, Italy. Russia occupies the 32nd place losing two positions from the previous rating and receiving 91,2% (out of 100) for e-information, 63,2% for e-consultation and just 28,6% for e-decision-making directions.

With the purpose to determine the reasons for such un-proportional development we conducted an expert survey focusing on factors which influence positively and negatively on e-participation development in Russia.

© IFIP International Federation for Information Processing 2017
Published by Springer International Publishing AG 2017. All Rights Reserved
P. Parycek et al. (Eds.): ePart 2017, LNCS 10429, pp. 65–74, 2017.
DOI: 10.1007/978-3-319-64322-9_6

2   E-participation Development Factors

Russia, following global trends, attempts to activate the citizens' participation in solving various issues of state and public life through ICT [23]. Over the past few years several legal acts that form the basis of electronic interaction between the state bodies and the citizens have been adopted. For instance, the Concept for e-democracy mechanisms development in the Russian Federation till 2020, developed by the Ministry of Communications and Mass Communications, forms the institutional environment for this phenomenon.

The concept determines a direct relationship between the transition to e-democracy practice and the process of strengthening and further development of Russian civil society: "… the active introduction of ICT in the social and political relations can significantly enhance the ability of Russian citizens in terms of their social and political participation and creating conditions for the civil activity growth, which contributes to the formation of a qualitatively new level of citizen activity" [5]. In addition, the Concept identifies several barriers for e-democracy development in Russia. The following barriers from the list related to e-participation: the lack of efficiency, poor organization and technical support, inadequate attention to the issues of citizens' identification and authentication, digital divide in the Russian regions, inequality between the federal, regional and municipal levels.

When we looked at the world research practice, we found a variety of factors that determine the success of e-participation development. According to the South Korean survey, conducted in 2015 in 125 countries around the world, there is a statistically significant correlation between the degree of citizens' e-participation and groups of indicators characterizing ICT development, the level of democracy, political institutions and human capital (literacy, education, income, etc.) [25]. J. Fountain argues that the institutional and organizational contexts act as an intermediary in ICT implementation [9]. Without a conceptual scheme that incorporates e-participation in politics, government, institutional structure and behavior, researchers can only ascertain the destructive internecine fighting bureaucracy and individual cases of outstanding innovation, but they are not able to recognize the more general models of institutional behavior.

For effective political participation, A. Kurochkin highlights the presence of a stable institutional environment (legal and informal institutions), defining clear rules for all actors, as well as guaranteeing their freedom of activity in the network [14]. I. Kharechko also draws attention to the fact that e-democracy should be developed and implemented in society in parallel with the electronic board. The author points out the need for a unified national technical platform, adapted to the needs and IT skills of ordinary citizens, as well as the supervisory organizational structure for monitoring and analysis the situation in the regions development [13].

According to J.Parfenova's survey, a low level of trust in public authorities serves a critical factor of e-participation development, affecting the low use of e-participation tools [18]. Foreign researchers, among the reasons for citizens' low online activity, stressed the insufficient politicians' involvement in e-participation projects. This fact entails the reduction of citizens' confidence and disbelief that their opinions are taken into account in policy-making [4].

A. Golubeva and D. Ishmatova noted that the lack of institutional support and political involvement is a major obstacle to the successful implementation of e-participation [11]. Furthermore, it may be institutional and political resistance to the development of new participation forms, since they can undermine the authority of established political institutions, expanding access to decision-making processes and, as a result, changing the political balance of power [16]. According to the European studies, poor support for projects at the institutional and administrative levels, as well as resistance to e-participation development usually influence negatively on citizens' activity [4].

According to A. Golubeva and D. Ishmatova findings, the main reason for the low level of citizens' participation is the lack of confidence in the political process and lack of trust in influence on the state policy. These researchers underline the transparency of e-participation results and its impact on political decisions. Also, the initiation of e-participation projects is likely to face the problem of institutional and political resistance. From the opposite side, the citizens' indifference to political life is another factor impeding the development.

Thus, in the field of e-participation regulatory and institutional environment, a contradictory situation is observed in Russia. On the one hand, ICT is a powerful tool for civic and political participation, and on the other - an effective instrument for political control. This view is also supported by the Russian researchers A. Sokolov and E. Grushina, [21] who say that "the spread of the Internet, power delegitimizing, the protest increases, and social tension - all this results in Internet activities' growth. At the same time, the "anti-piracy" law, an attempt to introduce roll-call identification lead to restriction of Internet activity".

Based on literature review, we analyzed research results and revealed more than 30 factors detected by foreign and the Russian scientists. Then we organized an expert research group and systemized them into the following lists of factors that influence the e-participation development:

- human capital characteristics [19],
- scale of technological development [2],
- level of democracy, nature of participation [12],
- decision-making procedures and its legal acceptance [17];
- institutional and political resistance [16]/reform orientation [1];
- different stakeholders' involvement [24];
- digital divide and level of adequate skills [12] and regional differentiation [7];
- privacy concerns and autonomy, identification procedures [6, 10];
- trust to e-participation tools [20] and government institutions [4];
- level of income and social welfare [15];
- existence of the monitoring system [3].

The analysis of research publications leads to the conclusion that the variety of factors makes an impact on e-participation development in both directions, positive and negative. In this research, we used this data to create a questionnaire for experts to assess different factors influence on e-participation in Russia.

3   Research Methodology

In this survey, we understood e-participation as "the process of engaging citizens through ICTs in policy, decision-making, and service design and delivery in order to make it participatory, inclusive, and deliberative" [22].

With the aim to detect the factors that influence positively and negatively on e-participation in Russia, we conducted an expert poll survey. The poll has been organized in August–September 2016. The list of experts being invited to the survey included representatives of federal, regional and municipal authorities, scientific structures and IT-companies. The listed consisted of 121 respondents. We also checked the data on active e-participation portals, revealed its' activists and contacted them directly with the purpose to involve this part of the targeted audience in the survey. Ultimately, 41 experts took part in the survey: 39% - from government, 32% - from science and education, 12% - from business, 10% - from NGOs and 7% - active portals' users.

The majority of experts have been working in e-governance and e-participation sphere for 3–10 years. Moreover, 14.6% of them had more than ten years' experience in this field.

The research addressed the following issues:

– detecting the purpose of e-participation tools development;
– determine the factors influence positively on e-participation development in Russia;
– revealing the barriers of e-participation development in Russia.

An automated questionnaire was designed for the survey. The experts received the questionnaire containing questions of closed and open types. According to research methodology, we created lists of barriers and positively influence factors which experts could evaluate using a special scale. The correspondence between the list of factors revealed from the literature review and those appeared in the questionnaire is presented at Table 1.

In addition, experts were encouraged to supplement the questionnaire with their own suggestions and comments, as well as to provide solutions on the current barriers.

4   Research Findings

The experts were asked to detect the purpose of e-participation tools' development in Russia. This question supposed to show not the experts' knowledge in the regulations but their personal opinions and feelings about the current situation. It's interesting to note, that 1/5 part of experts underlined the optimization of the administrative process, focusing more on civil servants' side than on citizens (Fig. 1). It also should be noted that the 3rd most popular answer touched the ostentatious nature of this phenomenon in Russia: the experts supposed that some of the actions in the field of opening governments and involving citizens' in the political process just seemed to act like real e-participation tools. However, these tools don't work well in real life. Some of the experts also made an accent on the fact that institutions of direct democracy (treatment, civil initiatives)

Table 1. The correspondence of the factors used in the survey with the list of factors revealed from literature review

Literature review	Questionnaire	
	Factors for development	Barriers
Human capital characteristics	Citizens' computer literacy	Low computer literacy
	Citizens' benefits	
Scale of technological development	Easy use	Insufficient usability
	Quality of information	
	Quick confirmation, alerts	
Level of democracy, nature of participation	Leaders and activists' existence	Administrative barriers
		Lack of motivation
Decision-making procedures and its legal acceptance	Proper regulations	Administrative barriers
	Civil servants' responsibility for timely response	
Institutional and political resistance/reform orientation	Political activity	Political indifference
	Promotion	
Different stakeholders' involvement	Business involvement	Lack of motivation and benefits
	NGO's involvement	
	Civil servants' active involvement	
Digital divide and level of adequate skills	Citizens' motivation	Digital divide
Privacy concerns and autonomy, identification procedures	Easy registration procedure	Liability for Internet publications
Trust to e-participation tools	High trust	Low trust
Level of income and social welfare	Citizen's level of income	Citizen's low level of income
Existence of the monitoring system	Assessment of users' satisfaction	Lack of monitoring and evaluation

are still more popular in Russia. In this way, the developing tools repeat the political landscape of the state very much.

The experts from business companies were rather skeptical about the increasing citizens' activity in the socio-political life of the country. The respondents from science and education sphere often mentioned the desire to meet international standards.

While answering this question, the experts could also give their comments on e-participation tools development. Some experts noted the uneven development of regional e-participation tools, together with the established quite formal purposes. *"The goal of creating visibility of public participation and the possibility to make proposals is a dominant at the regional level, with exception of top-ranked regions"*, - said the expert - a representative of a scientific structure.

The respondents evaluated the importance of the possible factors e-participation tools development, using a 5-marks scale, where: 1 - not significant, and 5 - very

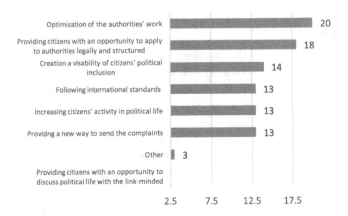

Fig. 1. Expert's answers to question "What is the purpose of e-participation tools development in Russia?", %

significant. Figure 2 represents average marks which experts gave to all the factors from the proposed list. The study found that the greatest significance belonged the following factors: easy use of tools (about 90% of respondents noted these factors as very significant), civil servants' responsibility for the timely reaction to citizens' requests, and quick feedback. Almost 78% of the respondents indicated a positive impact on e-participation tools development in the case when citizens got real benefits from their involvement in new services creation.

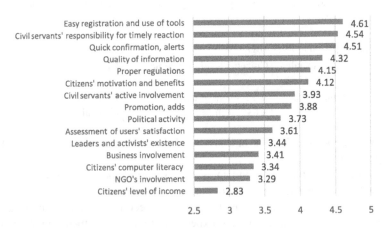

Fig. 2. Factors influencing positively on e-participation development in Russia, experts' evaluation

Among the other important factors listed by the experts, we should note the following:

- a significant number of e-participation successful cases resulted in decision-making;
- mandatory actions on supported decisions,

- 100% mandatory publication of the decisions taken by officials and their public evaluation.

Using the same scale, the experts rated the barriers of e-participation development in Russia. Figure 3 summarizes this assessment. The higher average rank in the graph means a higher importance of the existed barrier in Russia.

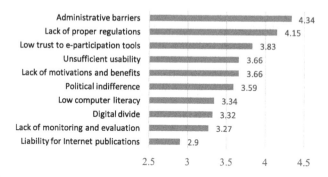

Fig. 3. Barriers to e-participation development in Russia, experts' evaluation

The most significant barriers to e-participation development, according to experts, linked with the administrative barriers, as well as the absence of a legal framework covering the authorities' working procedures with citizens' electronic applications (80.5% and 75.6% of experts respectively marked them as "very significant" or "rather significant").

The second group of important barriers addressed the human capital issues, such as low level of trust in e-participation tools, lack of motivation while communicating with authorities via the Internet, and insufficient usability level of existed services.

During the research, we have summarized experts' proposals to address the most critical issues. The respondents suggested the development of regulations with penalties for the late response to citizens' applications or incomplete feedback. Some experts, however, believed that such mechanisms had already existed and functioned, but due to the lack of responsible civil servants' qualification and/or their insufficient number, the authorities could not cope with the flow of requests effectively.

As a possible way to overcome the low trust, the experts proposed a stronger advertising and promotion of e-participation tools, including information about successful cases of real participation in decision-making processes. It's very important to show not just the cases from international practice, but national stories as well. The experts paid special attention to the transparency and openness of e-participation mechanisms in order to improve the level of citizens' confidence, as well as the feedback efficiency. One of the experts expressed the following opinion: *"if participation is anonymous, citizens are willing to participate. While publishing their data caused fears that this information could be used against themselves"*. As a possible way to improve the situation, the expert pointed out the necessity to save the anonymity of published petitions. Also, the expert highlighted the idea of block-chain technology and external audit introduction in the authorities.

5   Conclusions

The study found several administrative, regulatory, institutional and human-capital related barriers for e-participation development in Russia.

The experts confirmed that the declared purposes of e-participation tools development in Russia related to the improvement of authorities' administrative procedures and providing a way to apply the authorities online. However, the inner nature peculiarities of these initiatives in Russia lead to their low-performance and don't create any benefits for stakeholders. That all results in a low citizens' inclusion in the decision-making processes.

The study showed a correspondence between the key barriers of e-participation tools development and the factors which should be managed to improve the situation:

- administrative barriers and the need to actively involve civil servants' in e-participation tools' usage;
- lack of proper regulations and the need to establish civil servants' responsibility for timely reaction to citizens' requests,
- low citizens' trust and the proposal to increase personal benefits and motivation in e-participation tools,
- insufficient usability and the necessity to provide quick feedback and alerts system.

The research results lead to the assumption that institutional development could provide a positive impact on more comprehensive e-participation tools creation. Another important conclusion is about the opposite effect: if citizens see personal benefit in the proposed e-participation services and their possible ability to influence on state policy, they are ready to overcome the serious administrative and technical barriers on their own. Conversely, the absence of significant values makes administrative and technical barriers insurmountable due to the lack of citizens' interest.

The conducted research has some limitations due to the focus on experts' assessment. Taking into considerations the opinions of active e-participation tools' users (involved in the survey), we tried to reveal those respondents who already used such tools, because it isn't very much popular now. But the opinions of the citizens who don't use the tools, or even don't use the Internet stay unstudied now.

The experts also noted the importance of drawing up a comprehensive evaluation criteria for e-participation assessment including the following parameters: citizens' demand, the tools' credibility, transparency, social needs, qualitative changes as a result of e-participation tools, citizens' level of trust, level of motivation, the degree of influence on the actual decision-making.

The authors are going to continue the future research in the following directions:

- to expand the scope of the study to cover various target groups among the population;
- measuring political, social and economic impacts from e-participation tools' use by citizens to find the emerging benefits and opportunities for public values creation;
- detailed analysis of successful and not successful e-petitions for detection the public mood and forecasting the most critical issues and possible protests.

Acknowledgements. This work was conducted with support of the Grant of the President of the Russian Federation to young scientists №MK-5953.2016.6 "The research of e-participation tools development factors in Russian Federation".

References

1. Alreemy, Z., Chang, R.W., Wills, G.: Critical success factors (CSFs) for information technology governance (ITG). Gov. Inf. Q. **36**(6), 907–916 (2016)
2. Astrom, J., Karlsson, M., Linde, J., Pirannjad, A.: Understanding the rise of e-participation in non-democracies: domestic and international factors. Gov. Inf. Q. **29**, 142–150 (2012)
3. Bershadskaya, L., Chugunov, A., Dzhusupova, Z.: Understanding e-government development barriers in CIS countries and exploring mechanisms for regional cooperation. In: Kő, A., Leitner, C., Leitold, H., Prosser, A. (eds.) EGOVIS/EDEM 2013, LNCS, vol. 8061, pp. 87–101. Springer, Heidelberg (2013)
4. Charalabidis, Y., Tsitsanis, T., Koussouris, S., Matzakou, I.: Momentum deliverable 2.7: e-participation projects consolidated results. http://www.epomentum.eu/LinkClick.aspx?fileticket=3pkZY45Ect8%3d&tabid=57&mid=492. Accessed 14 June 2017
5. Concept for e-democracy mechanisms in Russia development till 2020. http://rario.ru/projects/Congress_conception.php. Accessed 14 June 2017
6. Delopoulos, H.N.: Barriers and opportunities for the adoption of e-governance services. Int. Scholar. Sci. Res. Innov. **4**(60), 883–886 (2010)
7. Domnina, A.: Development of mechanisms of e-democracy in modern Russia. Nizhny Novgorod Univ. Herald **3**(2), 72 (2014). (In Russian)
8. E-Government Survey: UN Report (2016) http://workspace.unpan.org/sites/Internet/Documents/UNPAN96407.pdf. Accessed 14 June 2017
9. Fountain, J.: Building the Virtual State. Brookings Institution Press, Washington, D.C. (2001)
10. Gil-Garcia, J.R., Pardo, T.: E-government success factors: mapping practical tools to theoretical foundations. Gov. Inf. Q. **22**(2), 187–216 (2005). doi:10.1016/j.giq.2005.02.001
11. Golubeva, A., Ishmatova, D.: E-Democracy in Russia: the formation of the tradition of political awareness and participation. Quest. State Municipal Manage. **4**, 54 (2012)
12. Karlsson, F., Holgersson, J., Soderstrom, E., Hedstrom, K.: Exploring web participation approaches in public e-services development. Gov. Inf. Q. **29**, 158–168 (2012)
13. Kharechko, I.: E-democracy as a model to improve political participation of citizens: foreign experience. Perm Univ. Herald Ser. Politics **3**, 120 (2013). (In Russian)
14. Kurochkin, A.: Public administration and innovation policy in a network society, pp. 126. Ph.D. thesis, Saint Petersburg (2014). (In Russian)
15. Lancee, B., Van der Werthorst, H.G.: Income inequality and participation: a comparison of 24 European countries. Soc. Sci. Res. **41**(5), 1166–1178 (2012)
16. Macintosh, A., Coleman, S., Schneeberger, A.: E-participation: the research gaps. In: Macintosh, A., Tambouris, E. (eds.) Electronic Participation. ePart 2009, LNCS, vol. 5694, pp. 1–11. Springer, Berlin, Heidelberg (2009)
17. Nour, M.A., AbdelRahman, A.A.: A context-based integrative framework for e-government initiatives. Gov. Inf. Q. **25**, 448–461 (2008)
18. Parfenova, J.: Formation of a stable institutional environment as a condition of communicative efficiency of the network of political participation. Soc. Policy Econ. Law **5**, 33 (2016). (In Russian)

19. Satish, K., Teo, T.S.H., Lim, V.K.G.: Contextual factors, e-participation, and e-government development: testing a multiple-mediation model. In: Proceedings of PACIS 2012, pp. 113 (2012). http://aisel.aisnet.org/pacis2012/113. Accessed 14 June 2017
20. Scherer, S., Wimmer, M.: Trust in e-participation: literature review and emerging needs. In: Proceedings of the 8th International Conference on Theory and Practice of Electronic Governance (ICEGOV 2014), pp. 61–70. ACM Press, Guimaraes (2014)
21. Sokolov, A., Grushina, E.: Terms of development of political activity on the Internet. Perm Univ. Herald 1, 29 (2015). (In Russian)
22. UNDESA: Developing capacity for participatory governance through e-participation: engaging citizens in policy and decision-making process using ICTs. http://workspace.unpan.org/sites/internet/Documents/CONCEPT%20PAPER%20e-Participation%2001.30.13.pdf. Accessed 14 June 2017
23. Vidiasova, L.: A framework for e-participation effectiveness assessment. Commun. Comput. Inf. Sci. 674, 145–154 (2016)
24. Weerakkody, V., El-Haddadeh, R., Sabol, T., Ghoneim, A., Dzupka, P.: E-government implementation strategies in developed and transition economies: a comparative study. Inf. J. Inf. Manage. 32(1), 66–74 (2012)
25. Whasun, J., Song, K.J.: Institutional and technological determinants of civil e-Participation: solo or duet? Gov. Inf. Q. 32, 488–495 (2015)

Technocracy to Democracy Knowledge Transfer Using Social Media and Reputation Management

Aggeliki Androutsopoulou ⓘD, Yannis Charalabidis, and Euripidis Loukis^(✉) ⓘD

Department of Information and Communication Systems Engineering,
University of the Aegean, Samos, Greece
{ag.andr,yannisx,eloukis}@aegean.gr

Abstract. Previous political sciences research has highlighted the importance of both 'democracy' (democratic processes and consultation with stakeholder groups) and 'technocracy' (specialized knowledge of experts) as main foundations for the development of effective public policies, and the need for balance as well as interaction between them. The use of information and communication technologies (ICT) for supporting this exchange can be highly beneficial. Our paper makes a contribution in this direction, by evaluating an ICT-based 'expert-sourcing' method that has been developed for supporting the transfer of knowledge from 'technocracy' (i.e. knowledgeable experts) to 'democracy' (i.e. participants of the democratic processes, such as citizens' representatives, elected officials and various public policies' stakeholder groups). This method exploits policy-related content that has already been published by experts in numerous social media, adopting a selective approach (filtering this content in order to extract the highest quality parts of it that have been authored by the most knowledgeable experts) based on reputation management techniques. From the evaluation of this ICT-based 'expert-sourcing' method useful conclusions have been drawn concerning its strengths and weaknesses, as well as directions for the improvement of it and the enhancement of its value.

Keywords: Social media · Reputation management · Expert-sourcing · Democracy · Technocracy

1 Introduction

Previous political sciences research has highlighted the importance of both 'democracy' (democratic processes and consultation with stakeholder groups) and 'technocracy' (specialized knowledge of experts) for the development of effective public policies, and the need for balance as well as interaction between them [11, 13, 27, 28]. This research has concluded first that the domination of one of them over the other can have negative impact on the quality and effectiveness of the resulting public policies; and second, that each of them needs inputs from the other, so extensive exchange of knowledge between them is required. The use of information and communication technologies (ICT) for supporting this exchange can be highly beneficial. Previous research in the information systems (IS) domain has revealed that ICT can significantly support and increase the

© IFIP International Federation for Information Processing 2017
Published by Springer International Publishing AG 2017. All Rights Reserved
P. Parycek et al. (Eds.): ePart 2017, LNCS 10429, pp. 75–86, 2017.
DOI: 10.1007/978-3-319-64322-9_7

effectiveness of knowledge transfer [17]. However, there has been a lack of research on ICT-based support of knowledge transfer in the above context, between 'technocracy' and 'democracy', despite its criticality for public policy development. So extensive research is required for the development of ICT-based methods that can effectively support the effective exchange of policy related knowledge between 'technocracy' and 'democracy', as well as for their evaluation, in order to identify their strengths and weaknesses, and also make improvements of them in order to enhance their value, so that finally high levels of maturity can be achieved in this novel area.

Our paper makes a contribution in this direction, by evaluating an ICT-based 'expert-sourcing' method that has been developed for supporting the transfer of knowledge from 'technocracy' (i.e. knowledgeable experts) to 'democracy' (i.e. participants of the democratic processes, such as citizens' representatives, elected officials and various stakeholder groups), in order to identify its strengths and weaknesses, as well as value enhancing improvements of it. This method has been developed within the European research project 'EU-Community' (project.eucommunity.eu/), which has been partially funded by the 'ICT for Governance and Policy Modelling' research initiative of the European Commission. It exploits policy-related content that has already been published by experts in numerous social media, adopting a selective approach: it filters this content, in order to extract the highest quality parts of it that have been authored by the most knowledgeable experts, based on reputation management techniques. A comprehensive description of this method is provided in [1], however for the sake of completeness of this paper an outline of it is presented in Sect. 3.

So, the research objectives of this paper are:

(i) to evaluate the above method in order to identify its strengths and weaknesses,
(ii) as well as to make improvements of it that can enhance its value.

The paper is structured in six sections. In the following Sect. 2 the background of our research is presented. The abovementioned ICT-based expert-sourcing method is outlined in Sect. 3, while the data and method of our study are described in Sect. 4. Then the results of the evaluation are presented in Sect. 5. Finally, in Sect. 6 the conclusions are summarized and future research directions are proposed.

2   Background

2.1   Democracy vs Technocracy

There has been considerable political sciences research, as well as political debate, concerning the relationships between public policies formulation, democracy (i.e. the role of democratic processes and consultations with stakeholder groups) and technocracy (i.e. the role of knowledgeable experts). On one hand the development of the 'participative democracy' ideas have resulted in a growing involvement of stakeholder groups in the formulation of public policies [2, 21, 24, 25, 30, 31]. In [31] public participation is defined as 'the practice of consulting and involving members of the public in the agenda-setting, decision-making and policy forming activities of organizations or institutions responsible for policy development'. Public participation constitutes a move away from an 'elitist model' of public policy development, in which managers and experts are the basic source of policies, towards a new more 'democratic model', in which the citizens have an active role and voice in policies' formulation. It should be noted that the development of the 'participatory democracy' does not aim at the replacement of the existing 'representative democracy' (and its institutions, such as the Parliaments and other representative institutions, and the elected officials), but on the contrary at the enhancement and revitalization of it. However, throughout the public participation literature it is emphasized that in order to be successful it is necessary the participating stakeholders to be sufficiently informed about the complex social problems under discussion, and the existing options for addressing them (various alternative interventions that government can undertake for this purpose, as well as advantages and disadvantages of them, short and long term impacts, etc.). The increasing complexity of the problems and the needs of modern societies have increased the importance of knowledge and expertise for the design and implementation of relevant public policies. This has led to the establishment and growing influence of various expert bodies (having various forms, ranging from committees to separate organizations, such as economic institutes), in both government agencies competent for the formulation of public policies, and also the other public policy stakeholders (e.g. associations of professions, labor unions and other interest groups). These expert bodies have become today highly important for and influential on the formulation of public policies, and this is termed 'technocracy' [6, 11, 14, 15, 27, 28]. So today it is widely recognized that the two fundamental and mutually complementary foundations of public policy making are democracy (representative institutions and elected officials) and technocracy.

Political sciences research in this area has highlighted the need of balance as well as relationship, interaction and exchange of knowledge between them, as each of them needs inputs from the other, while both make significant but different contributions to the design of public policies. In particular, participants in the democratic processes (citizens' representatives, elected officials, various stakeholder groups) need extensive knowledge and expertise on the social problems they are dealing with, while the lack of them can have quite negative impacts on the quality and effectiveness of the formulated public policies [11, 32]. At the same time experts dealing with important social problems often tend to 'de-politicize' them [11, 13, 14], or give low priority to important aspects of public policies, such as employment generation, poverty eradication, inclusive social protection, etc. [32]; in order to reduce these negative tendencies, experts need inputs from the democratic political process, concerning diverse values and concerns of different stakeholder groups, as well as their diverse perspectives, approaches and ideologies. So, Gilley [14] argues that 'democratic sovereignty and technocratic expertise must coexist', with each of them being necessary conditions for the other, and concludes that 'a healthy democracy requires a healthy technocracy and vice versa'.

The ICT can be very useful for supporting the above required interaction and exchange of knowledge between these two important foundations of modern public policy making, the 'democracy' and the 'technocracy'. However, as mentioned in the Introduction, limited research has been conducted in this direction. Our paper contributes to filling this research gap, by analyzing and evaluating an ICT-based method that supports the transfer of knowledge from the latter to the former, and identifying its strengths and weaknesses, and proposing improvements for increasing its value.

2.2 Government Citizen-Sourcing

The public sector, motivated by the multiple 'success stories' of crowdsourcing in the private sector [4, 5, 16], has started moving to this direction as well, using the ICT, and especially the social media, in order to exploit 'collective wisdom', giving rise to the gradual development of 'citizen-sourcing' [12, 18, 20, 22, 23, 26]. Most of these first citizen-sourcing initiatives follow the 'active citizen-sourcing' paradigm, in which government agencies' web-sites or social media accounts are used in order to pose a particular social problem or public policy (existing or under development), and solicit relevant information, knowledge, opinions and ideas from the general public [7, 12, 22]. Recently, there has been some research interest in the 'passive citizen-sourcing' paradigm, which aims to exploit policy-related content that has been generated by citizens freely, without any direct stimulation or direction by government, in various external (i.e. not belonging to government agencies) web-sites or social media, such as political fora, news web-sites, political blogs, Facebook, Twitter, etc. accounts; the analysis of this content can provide useful information, knowledge and ideas concerning important social problems and public policies [3, 8, 20]

However, a common characteristic of the first citizen-sourcing initiatives is that they aim to collect policy relevant knowledge and perceptions from the general public, and this has resulted in outcomes of varying quality levels. So, it would be useful, additionally to attempt collect relevant knowledge from experts as well, and this leads to the development of the new paradigm of 'expert-sourcing'; this paper contributes to the development of it, by analysing and evaluating an ICT-based passive expert-sourcing method (outlined in the following Sect. 3), and identifying its strengths, weaknesses, as well as valuable improvements of it.

3   An ICT-Based Passive Expert-Sourcing Method

As mentioned previously, an advanced passive ICT-based expert-sourcing method has been developed in the European research project 'EU-Community' (see project.eucommunity.eu/)'; a comprehensive description of it is provided in [1], however for the sake of completeness of this paper an outline of it is presented in this section. It is based on the automated retrieval from multiple online sources at regular time intervals of information about experts on various policy related topics, as well as relevant online texts and postings already published by such experts in multiple social media and web-sites; so it does not require from experts to create new content (which would be problematic as usually they are under pressure of time), conducting a selective 'passive' crowd-sourcing [3, 8, 20]. The retrieved content is filtered, in order to extract the highest quality parts of it that have been authored by the most knowledgeable experts, using reputation management techniques, in combination with text/opinion mining. This is a novel feature of this method in comparison with previous government citizen-sourcing methods, which target the general public, aiming to collect policy relevant knowledge and perceptions from it [e.g. 7, 8, 12, 19, 20].

In particular, one component of the ICT platform supporting the application of this method maintains a directory of profiles of individuals possessing high levels of knowledge, expertise and credibility in one or more predefined topics related with EU policies. Data about these individuals are collected and included in the corresponding database automatically by the crawlers sub-component (that crawls at regular time intervals numerous external sources, which can be pre-defined websites (e.g. Euractiv.com, EUR-Lex, Europa Whoiswho directory, RSS Feeds, blogs and news sites) and social media accounts (e.g. LinkedIn, Twitter)), or even can be entered manually by interested individuals (self-registration - in this case a validation by the system administrators follows). Furthermore, this component provides rankings of the expert profiles on one or more topics, based on their relevant expertise, through 'reputation scores' calculated by a reputation management sub-component. For this purpose is used a synthetic algorithm based on the following criteria (having different weights): self-evaluation; peer-assessment (based on endorsements from other experts); 'business card' reputation (based on the reputation ranking of the organization he works in, or committees he belongs to, and his/her position in it); documents assessments (results of his/her authored documents' assessments by their readers); network value (level of influence as the sum of his/her network connections); proximity trust (degree of connection in social media); past rankings (taking into account reputation rankings in previous months; offline reputation (manually added for persons with no online presence). This component provides multiple experts' search capabilities, e.g. by name, country or EU policy or topic, and returns experts found in its database in descending reputation score order (i.e. showing first the most reputable ones).

Another component of the ICT platform supporting the application of this method maintains a database of relevant documents concerning the above predefined policy related topics of interest. For this purpose it crawls at regular time intervals various external sources of content related to EU policies, such as relevant blogs, websites of EU institutions (e.g. European Commission), relevant media (such as EurActiv, European Voice, EU Observer) and various EU policy stakeholders' websites (such as various business and professional associations and NGOs' portals), and also social media accounts, where relevant positions and opinions are published, and updates with new content the corresponding documents' database. These documents (blog posts, social media content, online comments, word/pdf documents, web pages, etc.) are first correlated with the most relevant policy topic and subtopics (one document may match more than one subtopics), and possibly linked to one or more authors of the above individual experts' database. Next, for each document its quality is rated with respect to the above policy topic/subtopic(s), using an algorithm based on the following criteria: author (his/her credibility ranking for the specific topic/subtopic as provided by the reputation management module described above); ratings by other experts submitted in the platform, with respect to quality, accuracy, value, relevance and timeliness (which are weighted based on the reputation of the individuals who provide them). Also, these documents undergo sophisticated processing using text/opinion mining and sentiment classification techniques, in order to assess their sentiment (positive, negative or neutral).

These documents are structured around 'policy processes' (as policy process can be modelled any prospective, ongoing or completed E.U. legislative procedure, or any political debate in general), which can be created by system users. Furthermore, this component provides a timeline visualization (see Fig. 1), which shows the main documents (based on quality ratings, as assessed using the above algorithm) associated with a policy process selected by the user in a temporal order; different types of documents are represented by different shapes, while the sizes of the shapes reflecting their quality. A complete view of all documents associated with the process is provided through a tabular visualization provided by the component.

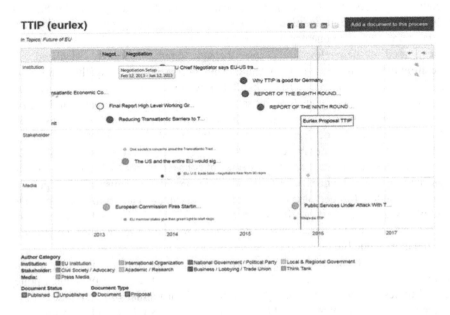

Fig. 1. Documents' timeline visualization

4   Data and Method

For the evaluation of the ICT-based passive expert-sourcing method outlined in previous Sect. 3 three pilot applications of it have been conducted, concerning three important EU policy related topics agreed among the 'EU-Community' project partners: Innovation and Entrepreneurship, Energy Union and Future of the European EU. In particular, for each of them numerous online sources were crawled, in order to retrieve and store expert profiles, and also various types of relevant documents (e.g. blog posts, social media content, online comments, word/pdf documents, web pages, etc.); then they were all processed as described in the previous section. Next, five interviews were conducted with Members of the Greek Parliament, with each of them having a duration of about 1.5 h. They included initially a presentation of this ICT-based passive expert-sourcing method, its supporting ICT platform, as well as the abovementioned three pilot applications; then the interviewees were asked to use the platform in order to perform searches of experts and documents concerning the above three topics, examine and understand the results' visualizations, and then see in more detail document-level information and content, with our assistance.

In order to collect evaluation data from the interviewees about this ICT-based passive expert-sourcing method we used mainly qualitative techniques, however complemented by quantitative ones. According to relevant literature [9, 29], the qualitative techniques allow a more in-depth examination of a social phenomenon, and enable the generation of deeper knowledge about it, its positive and negative aspects as well as a deeper explanation of them ('how' and 'why'). However, the quantitative techniques offer the advantage of enabling the summarization of positive and negative aspects into a few numbers, which make it easier to draw conclusions.

For these reasons, in order to combine the abovementioned advantages of the qualitative and the quantitative techniques, in each of these interviews initially we conducted a qualitative in depth discussion about the usefulness of this method from the technocracy to democracy knowledge transfer perspective [10]:

 (i) for the acquisition/collection of high quality expert knowledge concerning a specific public policy (existing, under development or proposed) we are interested in;
 (ii) for the transfer of policy related knowledge from experts to the participants of the democratic processes (such as members of parliaments and their assistants, representatives of various policy stakeholder groups, etc.);
(iii) and for assisting the above participants of the democratic processes for having a better, more substantial and constructive participation in public policy debates;

The above qualitative discussions were recorded, and then transcribed and coded manually using an open coding approach [9].

Then we asked the interviewees to fill a short evaluation questionnaire, which included three questions corresponding to the above three discussion topics; they were converted to positive statements, and the interviewees were asked to provide the degree of their agreement/disagreement with each of them in a five-levels scale (1 = strongly disagree, 2 = disagree, 3 = neutral, 4 = agree, 5 = strongly agree), as a summary/aggregation of all the positives and negatives they mentioned in our discussion.

5   Results

In Table 1 we can see the results of the processing of the quantitative evaluation data collected through the questionnaire; for each question are shown the frequencies/numbers of the responses 'strongly disagree' (SD), 'disagree'(D), 'neutral'(N), 'agree' (A) and 'strongly agree' (SA) respectively.

From the above Table we can see that there is a medium to high level of agreement concerning the usefulness of this ICT-based method for the acquisition of high quality expert knowledge concerning a particular public policy, as 2 out of the 5 interviewees agree on this, 1 strongly agrees, and the remaining two are neutral. However, most of the interviewees agree (4), and one strongly agrees, that this ICT-based method is useful for its main objective: the transfer of policy related knowledge from experts to the participants of the democratic processes. Furthermore, most of the interviewees agree (4), and one is neutral, that this method can assist the above participants of the democratic public policy formulation processes for having a better, more substantial and constructive participation and contribution in public policy debates.

Table 1. Results of processing the quantitative evaluation data collected through the questionnaire (frequencies of interviewees' responses)

To what extent this ICT-based method is useful:					
- for the acquisition/collection of high quality expert knowledge concerning a specific public policy (existing, under development or proposed) we are interested in	0	0	2	2	1
- for the transfer of policy related knowledge from experts to the participants of the democratic public policy formulation processes (such as members of parliaments and their assistants, representatives of various policy stakeholder groups, etc.)	0	0	0	4	1
- for assisting the above participants of the democratic public policy formulation processes for having a better, more substantial and constructive participation in public policy debates	0	0	1	4	0

In the qualitative in depth discussions it has been mentioned by the interviewees that the policy related documents provided by the platform seem to be of high quality, authored by knowledgeable experts, and contain useful expert knowledge on these specific important policy related topics, so this is an important strength. They consider this method as a useful tool that could complement other mechanisms they already use for finding relevant information and knowledge on public policies under discussion; however they would like, beyond the automated identification of experts and documents, as well as their rating and ranking, which are performed automatically by the system, some human presence, in order to double check and curate this content. As characteristically expressed by one of the interviewees *"My biggest concern is to what extent the information and knowledge I get from the system is checked and reliable, so it can save me from the effort of checking it myself again and again. My experience shows that there is much fake information, so we have every day to ensure that information is coming from real experts"*. Others suggested that the proposed platform could be used as an entry point of reference, from where they could go to the original sources to cross-check the reliability of the content.

The first weakness mentioned by the interviewees in the qualitative in depth discussions is that the knowledge contained in the documents provided per topic by the system is not directly accessible, as the user has to read these documents (most of them being rather lengthy) in order to extract this knowledge; it has been mentioned by one of the interviewees that *"a policy analysis has to be read in detail in order for someone to gain the picture"*. So it was suggested that it would be highly beneficial to make further 'deeper' processing of these documents, in order to automatically extract the relevant knowledge they contain, instead of the user having to do this manually. A first step in this direction might be to extract the main terms mentioned in each document, as well as in groups of related documents, using advanced methods of text/opinion miming, and then presenting a visualization of the results possibly in the form of 'word cloud' (with the most frequently used words shown bigger). Some interviewees mentioned another issue of the algorithms used for assessing the reputation of experts and the quality and relevance of the documents: they take into account factors concerning authors' social media presence and connections, 'business card' reputation (i.e. being part of highly reputable organizations or committees), and also documents' ratings by users (such as quality, accuracy, value and relevance ratings). Taking into account the existing 'populism' in the political debates in general, many actors (mainly politicians, but also sometimes scientists as well) tend to support popular and 'pleasant' positions, instead of less pleasant but more beneficial ones in the long run; so 'popular' does not necessary mean scientifically sound. This means that a popular politician would probably be assigned high rating and ranking for a topic by our algorithms, although he/she may not be really knowledgeable about it, by being highly popular (having numerous social media connections, and receiving high assessments for the documents he/she authors), and/or by being a member in important institutional committees. One of our interviewees mentioned *"I can see institutional experts in the tool, who claim expertise because they are associated with a particular committee or a position, but to me these do not imply that they are experts in the topic"*. In order to address this issue two main improvements of our method have been proposed: (i) the weights for the popularity and the 'business card' related factors should not be very high, so that they do not influence too much the ratings of experts and documents; (ii) a more radical intervention might be to distinguish between two classes of experts: the politicians-experts and the scientists/academics – experts, with each of them having different rankings, criteria and weights; the same applies for the documents: there should be a differentiation between politicians-experts' documents and scientists/academics – experts' documents, having different criteria and weights for assessing the quality of these two types of documents.

It was also emphasized that the trustworthiness of the results depends on the size and the diversity of the community that will be built around this ICT platform. This community will result in a large number of diverse multi-perspective policy related documents; furthermore it will provide large numbers of diverse assessments of the documents identified in the crawled sources, resulting in higher quality of ratings and rankings of the documents, and through them higher quality ratings and rankings of their authors. It has been mentioned by one of the interviewees that *"If sufficient number of experts exists in the database, I would trust more the results concerning credible experts and documents; it is important a 'critical mass' to be achieved on a policy topic, with respect to experts and documents, so that it is covered to a sufficient extent"*. Therefore it is important to build and maintain an extensive high quality and diverse community around this ICT platform.

Finally, another remark concerned an important type of useful policy related content not captured by our method: speeches in Parliaments (or other bodies of citizens' representatives, such as regional or municipal councils), by politicians and invited experts, which are not recorded in minutes. It has been argued that such speeches contain useful high quality information and knowledge on the debated social problems and public policies; however, some of this content is not recorded in the minutes, but it is recorded as audio or video. So a very useful extension of our method would be to add capabilities of processing and analyzing such multimedia content.

6   Conclusions

In the previous sections of this paper has been presented an evaluation of an ICT-based 'expert-sourcing' method, aiming to support the transfer of knowledge from 'technocracy' (i.e. knowledgeable experts) to 'democracy' (i.e. participants of the democratic processes, such as citizens' representatives, elected officials and various public policies' stakeholder groups). This evaluation has been based mainly on qualitative data, complemented by quantitative ones, collected though five interviews with Members of the Greek Parliament.

Our results are in general encouraging. The interviewees perceive a medium to high level of usefulness of this method for the acquisition of high quality experts' knowledge concerning social problems and public policies we are interested in. At the same time they identified some weaknesses of the method, which have led to proposals for improvements of it that can significantly enhance its usefulness and value:

- The most important of them is to proceed to a 'deeper' processing of the text of the policy related experts' documents provided by this method, in order to extract the knowledge they contain (so that the users do not have to do this manually, by reading lengthy documents).
- Another important improvement might be the discrimination between two classes of experts: the politicians-experts and the scientists/academics – experts, with each of them having different rankings, criteria and weights; and also the differentiation between politicians-experts' documents and scientists/academics – experts' documents.
- Also, in the experts' and documents' rating algorithms of this method are required appropriate settings of the weights for the social media presence, connections, popularity and 'business card' related factors, so that they do not influence too much the ratings of experts and documents.
- Human intervention will be useful for double-checking and curating the automatically collected content (through crawlers), in order to improve the reliability of the results.
- Finally technical capabilities should be enriched, enabling the processing and analysing of not only textual content, but also multimedia as well.

In general, taking into account both the strengths and the weaknesses of this method, it is perceived as a highly useful mechanism for the transfer of policy related knowledge from experts to the participants of the democratic public policy formulation processes (such as members of parliaments and their assistants, representatives of various policy stakeholder groups, etc.); and also for providing assistance to the latter in order to have a better, more substantial and constructive participation in public policy debates.

Further research is required for more extensive evaluation of the specific ICT-based technocracy to democracy knowledge transfer method by different groups of participants in the democratic processes (not only by Members of Parliaments, but also by citizens' representatives at lower administrative levels, such as regional, municipal, etc., as well as other policy stakeholders, such as associations of professions, labor unions and other interest groups). Also evaluation of it should be conducted from more perspectives of the political and management sciences, in order to develop a wider base of knowledge about different dimensions of advantages/strengths and disadvantages/weaknesses of this method. Furthermore, research is required towards the abovementioned improvements proposed by the interviewees. Additional research should also be conducted concerning the exploitation of ICT for the transfer of knowledge in the opposite direction (which is equally important – see [14, 15, 28]): from the democratic processes towards the experts/technocracy (concerning diverse needs, values and concerns of different stakeholder groups on the particular social problem or public policy the experts are dealing with).

References

1. Androutsopoulou, A., Mureddu, F., Loukis, E., Charalabidis, Y.: Passive expert-sourcing for policy making in the European Union. In: Proceedings of IFIP EGOV-EPART 2016 Conference, Guimarães, Portugal (2016)
2. Barber, B.: Strong Democracy. University of California Press, Berkeley (1984)
3. Bekkers, V., Edwards, A., de Kool, D.: Social media monitoring: responsive governance in the shadow of surveillance? Gov. Inf. Q. 30(4), 335–342 (2013)
4. Brabham, D.: Crowdsourcing as a model for problem solving: an introduction and cases. Convergence Int. J. Res. New Media Technol. 14(1), 75–90 (2008)
5. Brabham, D.: Crowdsourcing. The MIT Press, Cambridge (2013)
6. Brown, M.: Science in Democracy: Expertise, Institutions, and Representation. MIT Press, Cambridge (2009)
7. Charalabidis, Y., Loukis, E.: Participative public policy making through multiple social media platforms utilization. Int. J. Electron. Gov. Res. 8(3), 78–97 (2012)
8. Charalabidis, Y., Loukis, E., Androutsopoulou, A., Karkaletsis, V., Triantafillou, A.: Passive crowdsourcing in government using social media. Transforming Gov. People Process Policy 8(2), 283–308 (2014)
9. Cooper, D., Schindler, P.: Business Research Methods, 12th edn. McGraw-Hill, New York (2013)
10. Davis, F.: Perceived usefulness, perceived ease of use, and user acceptance of information technology. MIS Q. 13(3), 319–339 (1989)
11. Esmark, A.: Maybe it is time to rediscover technocracy? - An old framework for a new analysis of administrative reforms in the governance era. J. Public Admin. Res. Theory (2016, in-press)
12. Ferro, E., Loukis, E., Charalabidis, Y., Osella, M.: Policy making 2.0: from theory to practice. Gov. Inf. Q. 30(4), 359–368 (2013)
13. Fischer, F.: Technocracy and the Politics of Expertise. Sage, London (1990)
14. Gilley, B.: Technocracy and democracy as spheres of justice in public policy. Policy Sci. (2016, in press)

15. Harcourt, A., Radaelli, C.: Limits to EU technocratic regulation? Euro. J. Polit. Res. **35**, 107–122 (1999)
16. Hossain, M., Kauranen, I.: Crowdsourcing: a comprehensive literature review. Strateg. Outsourcing Int. J. **8**(1), 2–22 (2015)
17. Iyengar, K., Sweeney, R., Montealegre, R.: Information technology use as a learning mechanism: the impact of IT use on knowledge transfer effectiveness, absorptive capacity, and franchisee performance. MIS Q. **39**(3), 615–641 (2015)
18. Linders, D.: From e-government to we-government: defining a typology for citizen coproduction in the age of social media. Gov. Inf. Q. **29**, 446–454 (2012)
19. Loukis, E., Charalabidis, Y., Androutsopoulou, A.: An analysis of multiple social media consultations in the european parliament from a public policy perspective. In: European Conference on Information Systems (ECIS) 2014, Tel Aviv, Israel (2014)
20. Loukis, E., Charalabidis, Y., Androutsopoulou, A.: Promoting open innovation in the public sector through social media monitoring. Gov. Inf. Q. **34**(1), 99–109 (2016)
21. Macpherson, C.B.: The Life and Times of Liberal Democracy. Oxford University Press, London and New York (1977)
22. Mergel, I., Desouza, K.C.: Implementing open innovation in the public sector: the case of challenge.gov. Public Adm. Rev. **73**(6), 882–890 (2013)
23. Nam, T.: Suggesting frameworks of citizen-sourcing via government 2.0. Gov. Inf. Q. **29**, 12–20 (2012)
24. Organization for Economic Co-operation & Development (OECD). Evaluating Public Participation in Policy Making. OECD, Paris (2005)
25. Organization for Economic Co-operation & Development (OECD). Focus on Citizens: Public Engagement for Better Policy and Services - Policy Brief. OECD,s Paris (2009)
26. Prpić, J., Taeihagh, A., Melton, J.: The fundamentals of policy crowdsourcing. Policy Internet **7**(3), 340–361 (2015)
27. Radaelli, C.M.: The role of knowledge in the policy process. J. Eur. Public Policy **2**(2), 159–183 (1995)
28. Radaelli, C.M.: The public policy of the European Union: whither politics of expertise? J. Eur. Public Policy **6**(5), 757–774 (1999)
29. Ragin, C., Amoroso, L.: Constructing Social Research: The Unity and Diversity of Method, 2nd edn. Pine Forge Press – Sage Publications, California (2011)
30. Rowe, G., Frewer, J.: Public participation methods: a framework for evaluation. Sci. Technol. Hum. Values **25**(1), 3–29 (2000)
31. Rowe, G., Frewer, J.: Evaluating public-participation exercises: a research agenda. Sci. Technol. Hum. Values **29**(4), 512–557 (2004)
32. United Nations Research Institute for Social Development. Technocratic Policy Making and Democratic Accountability, UNRISD Research and Policy Brief no. 3, United Nations Research Institute for Social Development (UNRISD), Switzerland (2004)

Policy Modeling and Policy Informatics

Predicting the Outcome of Appeal Decisions in Germany's Tax Law

Bernhard Waltl[(⊠)], Georg Bonczek, Elena Scepankova, Jörg Landthaler, and Florian Matthes

Software Engineering for Business Information Systems,
Technical University of Munich, 85748 Garching bei München, Germany
b.waltl@tum.de

Abstract. Predicting the outcome or the probability of winning a legal case has always been highly attractive in legal sciences and practice. Hardly any attempt has been made to predict the outcome of German cases, although prior court decisions become more and more important in various legal domains of Germany's jurisdiction, e.g., tax law.

This paper summarizes our research on training a machine learning classifier to determine likelihood ratios and thus predict the outcome of a restricted set of cases from Germany's jurisdiction. Based on a data set of German tax law cases (44 285 documents from 1945 to 2016) we selected those cases which belong to an appeal decision (5 990 documents). We used the provided meta-data and natural language processing to extract 11 relevant features and trained a Naive Bayes classifier to predict whether an appeal is going to be successful or not.

The evaluation (10-fold cross validation) on the data set has shown a performance regarding F_1-score between 0.53 and 0.58. This score indicates that there is room for improvement. We expect that the high relevancy for legal practice, the availability of data, and advance machine learning techniques will foster more research in this area.

1 Introduction

The formal procedure of modern societies allows to take legal actions in order to claim someone's right. Thereby, courts and judges decide the case based on a given set of facts (evidence) and the applicable law. From an economical point of view, those cases can be resource intensive, as to time, money, and data. This does not only count for legislation, and consequently the society, but also for the claiming individual, i.e. the plaintiff. Therefore, predicting the result of a case or a probability approximation of whether a case is successful or not, is highly desirable. Within this paper we describe our approach and results of predicting the outcome of cases for a narrow but relevant set of cases within the German tax law, namely the success rate of appeal decisions of German Fiscal Courts.

The Federal Fiscal Court being one of the five highest courts in Germany, is a court of last resort responsible for the interpretation and application of German

© IFIP International Federation for Information Processing 2017
Published by Springer International Publishing AG 2017. All Rights Reserved
P. Parycek et al. (Eds.): ePart 2017, LNCS 10429, pp. 89–99, 2017.
DOI: 10.1007/978-3-319-64322-9_8

tax law (exempt criminal tax law). In most cases, people refrain from going into appeal, as for non-legals it is extremely difficult to assess their success odds correctly and thus the financial risk if losing the case. As a result, many people do not even try to challenge the first instance court decisions, remaining ignorant and losing on their chances of getting their legitimate right. Only about 4–5% of about 70 000 currently pending cases at financial courts go into appeal [1]. This seems particularly problematic from the view of the rule of law principle in Germany. The decision if to appeal or not, depends on a couple of factors from an individual's perspective. By helping to predict the outcome of an appeal, we aim to find a fair deal between seeking justice and the economic risks of legal proceedings.

2   German Judicial Procedures: Fiscal Courts and Appeal Decisions

The judicial procedures in the German fiscal domain follow a clear structure. The process is initiated by a plaintiff, who brings his case to one out of 18 different fiscal courts (Finanzgericht FG) in Germany. The FG collects and structures the evidence and decides on the case. In case the plaintiff does not agree with the outcome, he can initiate an appeal procedure, which directly goes to the Federal Fiscal Court (Bundesfinanzhof BFH), which is located in Munich, Bavaria. In contrast to different jurisdictions, the tax law system only consists of two instances, with the BFH being the second and last instance for tax law related cases. Now the BFH investigates the case and decides whether the decision of the FG was compliant with applicable laws. If European legislation is decisive for the case outcome, the BFH is obliged to consult the European Court of Justice (EuGH), and await its binding ruling. Finally, the BFH renders a judgment which either confirms or overrules the decision of the fiscal court as court of first instance. Under certain circumstances, the BFH has to refer the case back to the fiscal court which decides the case anew. Finally, the case is decided and the plaintiff is informed.

We analyzed and modeled fiscal court decisions (Step 1a) and trained machine learning algorithms to predict the outcome of future appeal decision. Thereby, we collected cases from FG and BFH (responses of Step 1a and 2a) (see Sect. 5), processed them, proposed a model and extracted eleven different features (see Sect. 6). Those features served as the base line for a multinomial Naive Bayes classifier (see Sect. 7). Finally, we evaluated the performance of the classifier and discussed steps for improvements (see Sect. 8).

3   Related Work

One of the earliest approaches regarding predictions applied a nearest neighbor approach, where the cases closest to a problem are determined in terms of similarity measures and an outcome is assigned with regard to the majority of those cases [4]. Popple, in 1996, using a nearest neighbor algorithm, added more complexity to the similarity measures by assigning weights to different fact descriptors [6]. In our view, a nearest neighbor approach is limited by its definition to the circle of identifiable neighbors and does not allow for precise predictions outside this scope.

The IBP (Issue-Based Prediction Model) integrates case-based reasoning with a model of abstract legal issues associated with a legal claim of trade secret misappropriation [2]. The model's restriction to cases concerning trade secret misappropriation reflects the difficulty of a transfer to other fields of law. When the legal issues and relationships in the IBP Domain Model are "a distillation and interpretation of two authoritative sources on the law of trade secret misappropriation (a statute and a Restatement provision)" [2], this shows this model's strong connection to the legal content of cases. The identification of relevant issues in this model is thus time- and knowledge-intensive and has to be done anew for any other field of law, hindering the development of a universal prediction model.

Katz's prediction model leverages the random forest method together with feature engineering for the prediction of Supreme Court decisions [3]. Based on the extensive Supreme Court's database, where each case is assigned with around 240 variables, many of which are categorical, a number of formal features is derived. Except for the lack of a comparably extensive database and the information about judges "behavior" who don't play a dominant role in civil law jurisdictions as Germany, the use of formal features sets the possibility of creating a universal prediction model in a way we are aiming at.

4   Approach

This section briefly describes the steps performed within our approach, which follow a classical machine learning approach by beginning with a data preparation and pre-processing step. Subsequently, we came up with a model (features and priorities) which serves as the base line for the prediction algorithm. Based on that, we extracted the required features and trained a classifier, which we tested afterwards.

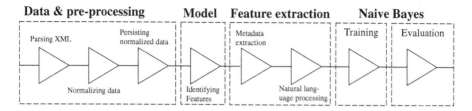

Fig. 1. Stepwise and subsequent pre-processing, feature extraction, and training with evaluation of a Naive Bayes classifier to predict the outcome of fiscal court appeal decisions.

Data and Pre-processing. The available data (see Sect. 5) needs to be processed. Therefore, it was necessary to develop specified importing routines and normalized the data such that it fits to one common data scheme, which is persisted in a database to easily enable data-intensive machine learning procedures.

Modeling. During the model we have defined parameters that potentially indicate the outcome of an appeal case and that are available in the data at hand. Thereby, we have identified different variables, so-called features, and summarized them within a table (see Sect. 6). In addition, we assigned a priority to each feature indicating its suspected importance.

Feature selection. Based on the collection of features, we have developed several routines extracting those from the data set. Thereby, we analyzed the metadata, such as author, publishing date, etc. and created the desired set of features for each of the document (see Sect. 6). We mainly used regular expressions for this step.

Naive Bayes classifier. Using an existing machine learning framework, we trained and tested a common and simple probabilistic classifier, namely Naive Bayes. We have compared different classifiers and found that Naive Bayes is performing best. We split up the available data into a training and a test data set. Thereby, we used a common strategy, namely 10-fold cross validation (see Sect. 7).

Figure 1 shows the subsequent steps but it does not reflect the workload that was spent on each individual task. Especially data & pre-processing, modeling and the feature selection parts require lots of time and different implementations. Compared to that, training and testing the classifier can be done straight-forward. Existing machine learning libraries and frameworks can easily be integrated and used once the data is pre-processed, the modeling part done, and the required features extracted.

5   Data

The data we base our research on is a corpus, maintained by professional editors, consisting of 44 285 judgments of German fiscal courts, which date back to 1945, whereas the most recent documents were issued in 2016. Out of these 44 285 documents, 27 055 depict first instance cases (FG), the remaining 17 230 are judgments ruled by the BFH. Ultimately, after cleaning documents which lack important data for feature extraction, our dataset contained 5 990 complete proceedings.

Each data point consists of a tuple: A first instance case, and a corresponding appeal decision, i.e. revision. The effectively used dataset consists of judgments from 1990 until 2015. Our data is relatively up-to-date, but there is a significant drop of cases from 2012, since those cases have not been decided yet. This might cause a so-called cold start issue during the training phase of machine learning algorithms. An analysis of the temporal distribution of the data set implies that the dataset does not cover many major changes in German fiscal legislation. One can expect however the dataset to be representative for the German fiscal legislation of the last years. As stated above, although the German tax law is part of a civil law jurisdiction and the main acts, e.g., EStG, have statutory character, the case law is particularly important for legal practice, e.g., tax consultants, auditors, etc.

The data is structured in XML documents collection, whereas each XML file represents one judgment. Each XML file contains a variety of different metadata such as referenced legal norms, decision date, filing numbers, years of dispute, the ruling court and a general markup for structuring the judgment text itself into different sections, e.g. statement of facts, reasoning, etc. Advanced information of the decision results such as the information whether the court ruled in favor of the plaintiff, what kind of juristic person the plaintiff constitutes etc. are not explicitly given. After its extraction, this data, in combination with the meta-data, is used as features (see Sect. 6.2).

In addition, we have access to a manually created and editorially maintained thesaurus containing numerous terms of the German tax law. The thesaurus is available in JSON format, can easily be accessed, and provides information about synonyms, hyponyms, abbreviations and similar terms to a given term. This thesaurus in its entirety includes 16 019 of such groups (synsets) and overall 42 598 tokens, i.e. terms.

6 Processing and Feature Extraction

6.1 Pre-processing

The pre-processing consists of two main parts. The first one constitutes the simple extraction of meta data of the concerning documents, whereas the second one contains several text mining tasks in order to extract features that are not already given.

We extracted four features: The references within the factual findings, since not all existing references are also stated in meta-data, the factual findings themselves and reasons given in the judgment as well as the type of juristic person that represents the plaintiff (if applicable). In the process of determining those features we acted on the assumption that legal texts often follow certain patterns of formulation. This approach allows us to extract the desired features with standard natural language processing techniques.

Dataset Generation. In order to ascertain the result of the appeal, we needed to label our testing and training data. Thereby, we used the circumstance that the information, if the appeal got rejected or sustained, could be at the very beginning of the reasons part within the ruling. Also, the wording is carefully chosen, so the dismissal of a case is formulated with just a few adjectives. By means of several selected terms, it is possible to classify this first sentence and therefore determine the outcome of the judgment. Despite the small feature space of 8 different terms indicating the outcome, this method works reasonably good for all documents.

6.2   Modeling and Feature Selection

All information for our model was derived and is knowable prior to the date of the estimated decision (out-of-sample applicability). Consequently, the model allows to generate ex ante predictions, i.e. predicting in the real sense. Another characteristic of our model is generality and consistency. This means that our model generates predictions irrespective of changes in the composition of the courts (e.g., retirement, recusal, etc.) and not limited to specific time periods.

We considered a number of features, e.g. the year of dispute, the specific courts, the nature of the petitioner, the duration of a case, the decisive legal norms, the overall cited norms, the guiding principles and the heading. The different grade of impact each one of those features might have on the decision result, we are expressing in different weights manually attributed to them.

Considering the year of dispute the assumption is that different time periods correspond to different legal amendments with specific grades of legal complexity which influences the probability of reversals. Compared to other fields of law, tax law is immensely important for the state budget and thus highly influenced by political considerations, which result in more legal changes and amendments than in any other legal area. The more those amendments intervene with the overall tax law system, the more careful they have to be drafted in order to guarantee the application consistency within the tax law system itself (Table 1).

We distinguished geographically between different courts and the specific Chambers deciding the case (German: Gerichtskammer). Courts having jurisdiction ratione loci and ratione materiae decide autonomously within their circuit, which leads to inconsistency between the different court circuits. In a comparable way, Chambers as parts of the same court are autonomous in deciding cases, often dominated by the concrete personal composition. The observed autonomous deciding is grounded in the principle of the judge being bound only by law and his own consciousness. We assume that there is some correlation between the outcomes of the case and case durations on the one hand, and court locations, including Chamber specifications, on the other hand.

Selecting legal norms is motivated by the fact that legal norms are the decisive factor when adjudicating a case. Moreover, our feature selection considered norms not just as a whole, but - following its specific citation in the case - splits it into paragraphs, articles, sentences, numbers, letters etc. Certain norms, or rather elements of a norm are more controversial in their application than others, i.e., creating more scope for different interpretations. This is why the splitting is necessary for more precise predictions. We distinguished between decisive legal norms, which are explicitly cited at the beginning of a case, and the overall cited norms in the judgment text.

Considering the petitioner as a selective feature we looked into the function he is acting in - as an individual or as a legal person. The assumption is that courts might be more willing to attribute rights to individuals than to legal entities,

Table 1. An overview of the selected features, description and corresponding priority we attributed to them.

Feature	Description & rational	Priority ↓
Courts	Courts having jurisdiction ratione loci and ratione materiae, decide autonomously in their geographically assigned circuit, leading to inconsistency within the circuits	High
Court chambers	Chambers of the same court may and do decide autonomously, leading to inconsistency within the same court	High
Decisive legal norms	Those have the function of legally justifying the outcome of the case	High
Guiding principals	Those summarize the legal statement of the decided case in a few sentences	High
Petitioner	The different groups of petitioners (individuals and corporate entities) incorporate different values with regard to the public law domain of tax law	High
Cited legal norms	Those are necessary for legal reasoning, albeit not of decisive nature for the outcome of the case	Middle
Duration of the case	This reflects either the complexity of a case or the workload in a specific court	Middle
Keywords of statement of facts	The 'statement of facts' section contains by law only the legally essential, resp. for the legal reasoning relevant facts of a case	Middle
Keywords of the 'legal reasoning' part	The legal reasoning part is dominated by legal language - extracted keywords thus support semantically the outcome of a case	Middle
Year of dispute	This time period reflects the applicable law at the time of the dispute	Middle
Heading	This serves as a quick classification of judgments without the aim to reflect the legal reasoning	Low

as the former are usually in an (economically) weaker position than the latter ones. Exerting influence on this imbalance of powers might be a factor on the subconscious level of judges as decision makers. We further grouped legal entities into two categories, the private entities (German: "Personengesellschaften") and the corporate entities (German: "Kapitalgesellschaften").

Another feature is the duration of cases as the time period from the year of the case filling to the actual decision date. The case duration may reflect both the complexity of a case or the workload at a particular court. By extracting the workload cases by way of comparisons, we filtered the factual or legally complex cases. Complexity itself increases the probability of different interpretations and thus the risk of reversal.

Feature Extraction. A part of the references used by the court are already contained in the meta-data of the document. The remaining norms were extracted by parsing the textual content of the case. Since we only considered a relatively small subset of German legal texts, we used regular expressions to detect those references. After finding such a reference we normalized it, such that it corresponds the format that is used throughout the corpus.

For the extraction of the information whether the plaintiff represents a certain type of juristic person, we again relied on certain structures in legal formulations. We analyzed the first few sentences of the facts which cover the basic traits of the plaintiff. Those also cover whether it is a juristic or natural person raising the claim. Afterwards, we searched for the terms referring to the plaintiff. We extracted common terms and phrases that occur in combination with the most relevant forms of juristic persons. In order to avoid false positives arising through formulations such as "the plaintiff works at X-GmbH", we did not consider sentences that contain verbs indicating some form of employment. Despite this method obviously not being the most effective one, we consider it to be more efficient in comparison to more advanced techniques with respect to implementation efforts.

Processing of Textual Data. After extracting the textual features, we normalized them with respect to the thesaurus mentioned earlier. For each concept in this thesaurus, we chose one representative with which we replaced all occurrences that pose an abbreviation, synonym or similar term to this representative. Furthermore, for the facts and reasons we only kept a bag of words that contain the keywords (also their multiplicity) appearing in the thesaurus. This allowed us to preserve the legal terms, while removing terms and nouns that induce noise due to their irrelevance for the legal case. By replacing the synonyms etc., we expect an edge in efficiency when classifying, since the semantic relation between words is not taken into account. When unifying terms that are similar to each other, we might lose some nuance that differentiates them, but we consider the advantage in the classification step worth this hypothetical loss, since there is no other trivial way of creating a relation between them. After these steps, we also apply stop-word removal and stemming.

7   Predictive Analytics and Performance

For the training and classification we used the scikit-learn [5] machine learning framework. We passed different features through a pipeline, calculating TF-IDF vectors for textual features and count-based vectors for the remaining features. After trying different common estimators, the multinomial Naive Bayes classifier has performed best producing the most promising results. Using a 10-fold cross-validation, we achieved a F_1-score of 0.57 (see Table 2).

We see that both types of judgments, the ones in favor of the plaintiff and the ones in favor of the defendant, have been classified by our approach (precision). Also, 60% of the judgments with positive outcome have correctly been identified

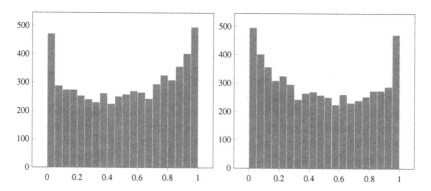

Fig. 2. Histogram of predicted probabilities for positive (left chart) and negative outcomes (right chart).

Table 2. Confusion matrix summarizing the performance of the prediction using a multinomial naive Bayes estimator (evaluation using a 10-fold cross-validation).

	Precision	Recall	F_1-score	Support	Support (rel)
Pos. outcome	0.57	0.60	0.58	3 012	50.28%
Neg. outcome	0.57	0.53	0.55	2 978	49.72%
Avg/total	0.57	0.57	0.57	5 990	100.00%

having no negative outcome. Since the overall precision and recall are both 57%, so is the F_1-score. In Sect. 8 we will interpret these values in this specific application, thereby we differentiate between three different aspects: Quality of features and feature extraction, accuracy of predictions, and potential for improvements.

We also used feature weighting, but initial parameter studies have been of little success. We also observed loss in both precision and recall when lowering auxiliary feature weights such as court, plaintiff type or references. Based on this fact, we conclude that there is in fact potential for hyperparameter tuning since the likelihood of ideal parameters being the default ones is quite low.

A detailed inspection of the classifiers outcome is shown in Fig. 2. The figure shows two histograms for the classifiers performance on predicting positive (left chart), and negative outcomes (right chart). The histograms show the confidence with which the classifier predicts a certain outcome. Maybe one would expect the classifier to decide very confident on a subset of cases but this only holds for a small set of cases in which his prediction is above 80 or 90%. Instead the distribution shows that the classifier's confidence is, with a few minor exceptions, equally distributed and covers the whole range from high confidence ($\geq 90\%$) to very low confidence ($\leq 10\%$).

8   Discussion

8.1   Quality of Features and Feature Selection

The features we are currently using largely represent data about the legal process. When it comes to the content of the document, its title, the head-note, the types of plaintiffs as well as keywords of judicial relevance contained in the facts or the reasoning of the court are considered. These chosen features mainly constitute the factual basis of a judgment and are thus in our opinion essential for its efficient classification. However, the actual benefit of supporting features is to be put into question. The impacts of features such as the duration of the process are nominal and could turn out to be the source of overfitting. In addition, the extraction of metadata and especially of features using natural language processing (NLP) is — up to a certain degree — always vulnerable to errors. Hardly any technique from NLP can be performed without any error.

However, the formal nature of the features we selected for our model allows to build a prediction model across different legal areas. In contrast to successful, however predominantly issue-based prediction models (e.g. IBP [2]) our model bears the chance to create a universal prediction model, applicable across different legal areas.

8.2   Accuracy of Predictions

Regarding the overall complexity, it is hard to define a "minimal" threshold for a F_1-score to be considered meaningful or valuable for legal practice. Due to the low precision and recall scores, it is currently not feasible to make any final statements about the ability to classify judgments of the fiscal courts. However, our results support the hypothesis that a classification of such judgments is principally possible. It also should be kept in mind that we use a rather small feature set, so adding more high quality features we expect a further increase both in precision and recall.

9   Conclusion

This paper summarizes the results of an interdisciplinary research topic on using machine learning to predict the outcome of court decisions based on a huge set of prior cases. We restricted ourselves to predict the outcome of appeal decisions within the German tax law. Thereby, a plaintiff can appeal if he does not agree with the result of the fiscal court (first instance). The appeal goes directly to the German Federal Fiscal Court (BFH). This consumes a lot of time and monetary resources both of the plaintiff and the German State financing jurisdiction. Using the meta-data and natural language processing, we analyzed 5 990 documents and extracted 11 different features for each case. This served as the input for a multinomial Naive Bayes classifier. The evaluation has shown that the classifier's performance is limited (F_1-score between 0.53 and 0.58).

Although the overall performance of the classifier is not satisfying at the current stage, there is strong evidence that the performance could be improved by taking more features and additional data into account. Since more and more data is going to be publicly available, a synthesis of those combined with powerful machine learning algorithms could lead to better performing algorithms that could potentially be used by legal practitioners, e.g. judges and lawyers, or legislators to evaluate and improve the current legal situation.

References

1. The Federal Supreme Finance Court. https://www.bundesfinanzhof.de/sites/default/files/Booklet.pdf
2. Ashley, K.D., Brüninghaus, S.: Automatically classifying case texts and predicting outcomes. Artif. Intell. Law **17**(2), 125–165 (2009). http://dx.doi.org/10.1007/s10506-009-9077-9
3. Katz, D.M., Bommarito, I., Michael, J., Blackman, J.: A general approach for predicting the behavior of the supreme court of the united states. arXiv preprint arXiv:1612.03473 (2016)
4. Mackaay, E., Robillard, P.: Predicting judicial decisions: the nearest neighbour rule and visual representation of case patterns. Datenverarbeitung im Recht (1974)
5. Pedregosa, F., Varoquaux, G., Gramfort, A., Michel, V., Thirion, B., Grisel, O., Blondel, M., Prettenhofer, P., Weiss, R., Dubourg, V., Vanderplas, J., Passos, A., Cournapeau, D., Brucher, M., Perrot, M., Duchesnay, E.: Scikit-learn: machine learning in Python. J. Mach. Learn. Res. **12**, 2825–2830 (2011)
6. Popple, J.: A pragmatic legal expert system. In: Applied Legal Philosophy Series (1996)

Data-Driven Policy Making: The Policy Lab Approach

Anne Fleur van Veenstra[(✉)] and Bas Kotterink

TNO Strategy & Policy, Anna van Buerenplein 1, 2595 DA The Hague, The Netherlands
{annefleur.vanveenstra,bas.kotterink}@tno.nl

Abstract. Societal challenges such as migration, poverty, and climate change can be considered 'wicked problems' for which no optimal solution exists. To address such problems, public administrations increasingly aim for *data-driven policy making*. Data-driven policy making aims to make optimal use of sensor data, and collaborate with citizens to co-create policy. However, few public administrations have realized this so far. Therefore, in this paper an approach for data-driven policy making is developed that can be used in the setting of a Policy Lab. A Policy Lab is an experimental environment in which stakeholders collaborate to develop and test policy. Based on literature, we first identify innovations in data-driven policy making. Subsequently, we map these innovations to the stages of the policy cycle. We found that most innovations are concerned with using new data sources in traditional statistics and that methodologies capturing the benefits of data-driven policy making are still under development. Further research should focus on policy experimentation while developing new methodologies for data-driven policy making at the same time.

Keywords: Data-driven policy making · Data for policy · Co-creation · Policy Lab

1 Introduction

Today's society faces complex 'wicked problems', such as migration, poverty, and climate change, for which not one optimal solution exists [1, 2]. In order to address such problems, governments aim to realize *public sector innovation* that gears them towards becoming platforms of open governance, making optimal use of information and communication technologies (ICTs) to create public value [1]. Increasingly, ICTs are not only used for improving the daily operations of government, but also for enhancing the process of policy making [2]. Policies address societal problems by formulating and implementing laws, rules and guidelines, and policy making is the process of creating and monitoring these policies. Hence, it is often conceptualized as a policy cycle, consisting of several different phases, such as agenda setting, policy formulation, decision-making, implementation and evaluation [3]. ICTs may be used to support and enhance different phases of the policy cycle and enable experimentation [1, 2].

Data-driven policy making uses ICTs to capture the benefits of new data sources [4, 5], and to support collaboration with relevant stakeholders and citizens [2, 6, 7]. It builds on the notion of evidence-based policy making [see, for instance, 8, 9]. In

P. Parycek et al. (Eds.): ePart 2017, LNCS 10429, pp. 100–111, 2017.
DOI: 10.1007/978-3-319-64322-9_9

the literature on evidence-based policy making three types of evidence are considered relevant: "systematic ('scientific') research, program management experience ('practice'), and political judgement" [9, p. 1]. Data-driven policy making acknowledges the importance of these types of evidence, but can be distinguished from evidence-based policy making, since it is mainly concerned with the inclusion of big and open data sources into policy making as well as with co-creation of policy by involving citizens. Data-driven policy making is not only expected to result in better policies, but also aims to create legitimacy [10]. Involvement of citizens in a data-driven policy making process is especially important since public data and statistics are increasingly met by citizens' distrust [11].

To allow for better collaboration and involve citizens, public administrations around the world have set up Policy Labs to allow for experimentation and facilitate the involvement of relevant stakeholders [12, 13]. They, thus, address the need for experimentation and design-thinking to deal with wicked policy issues [1, 2]. Therefore, in this paper we develop a Policy Lab approach for data-driven policy making. First, based on literature of public sector innovation, we identify innovations in the use of data for policy making and co-creation of policy. Secondly, we map these innovations to different phases of the policy cycle. And thirdly, we develop an approach that can be used to guide data-driven policy making in a Policy Lab setting. The next section presents the theoretical background of public sector innovation. Section 3 discusses data-driven policy making and identifies innovations. Subsequently, Sect. 4 presents the development of the Policy Lab approach, followed by a discussion and recommendations for further research in Sect. 5. Finally, Sect. 6 presents the conclusion.

2   Public Sector Innovation

Public sector innovation holds that "[p]ublic policy and services need to become more open and innovative as well as being efficient and effective" [1, p. 2], making optimal use of ICTs [1]. As such, it encompasses a myriad of aspects. Gil-Garcia, Zhang and Puron-Cid [14] refer to as much as fourteen aspects of smartness in government, including evidence-based, technology savviness, openness, citizen engagement, and innovation. According to Millard [1], public sector innovation means that public administrations operate as a platform [15, 16] and use ICT to collaborate across organizational borders [17] and to involve citizens and other relevant stakeholders [6, 7, 18, 19] with the purpose of creating public value [20–22]. Over the past decades, ICTs have had a great impact on services delivery [23], opened up public datasets [24] and increased citizens' participation [25]. The use of ICTs for policy making can, thus, be seen as a next step in public sector innovation [2].

The use of ICTs benefits policy making in two ways. The first is the use of new data sources, such as (real-time) sensor data, either physical (e.g. traffic monitoring [2, 4]), or virtual (e.g. social media data [2, 6]). "Data-driven decisions and intensive use of data, through ubiquitous sensing, advanced metering and integrated applications enable governments to make more informed decisions and improve the effectiveness of public policies and programs" [14, p. 527]. Secondly, it requires from governments to collaborate across organizational borders and with citizens and businesses to enable co-creation of policies [1, 6, 7, 16]. "Co-creation is understood as the active flow and exchange of ideas, information, components and products across society (academia, government, business, civil society and citizens) which allows for a better understanding of participation, engagement and empowerment in policy development" [1, p. 5].

Besides the deployment of ICTs to use new data sources and enable co-creation of policies, public sector innovation is concerned with the ability of public administrations to experiment, using innovative approaches such as gaming, simulation, and installing of sensors for do-it-yourself measurements, and deploy 'design-thinking' [1, 2, 14]. In order to do so, many public administrations have set up Policy Labs [12, 13]. "Policy Labs are emerging structures that construct public policies in an innovative, design-oriented fashion, in particular by engaging citizens and companies working within the public sector" [13, p. 2]. Policy Labs exist in all shapes and sizes and on different levels of government (national, regional and municipal) [13]. The majority of Policy Labs do not focus on a specific type of policy or on a specific phase of the policy cycle, but they employ a design and experimentation based approach to policy making [13]. As such, Policy Labs can be considered as a specific instance of Living Labs, which aim to "support public open innovation processes" [26, p. 90]. While Living Labs are concerned with the involvement of private sector organizations as well as citizens in public open innovation processes in general [26], Policy Labs focus on the involvement of citizens (and also other stakeholders) into the policy making process specifically.

3 Innovations in Data-Driven Policy Making

Data-driven policy making thus aims to use new data sources such as (real-time) sensor data and new techniques for processing these data and to realize co-creation of policies, involving citizens and other relevant stakeholders. However, realizing data-driven policy making is complex: many challenges related to the capturing, integration and re-use of data exist [4, 5], as well as to the involvement of citizens and other stakeholders in policy making [2, 6, 7]. This section identifies innovations of data-driven policy making based on literature.

3.1 Use of New Data Sources in Policy Making

The use of new data sources holds big promises: it is expected to offer organizations greater operational efficiency and effectiveness, and lead to the development of new products, services and business models [27–29]. In the context of governments, "we are faced with a deluge of data that, when combined with new technologies and analysis techniques, has the potential to inform decision and policy making in unprecedented ways" [4, p. 10]. Big data is often defined as "vast datasets that cannot be analyzed using conventional software and analytic tools" [4, p. 2]. Since many 'big data' sources can be stored on a USB-stick nowadays, in the context of public administration, important characteristics of big data are not so much that they require large processing power, but more the variety and the interoperability because of its different data sources and formats

[4]. The use of (sensor) data in policy making encompasses three steps: capturing data, integrating data from different sources, and applying these data [30]. Table 1 summarizes the main opportunities, challenges and innovations per step.

Table 1. Opportunities, challenges and innovations of new data sources for policy making.

Steps of data use	Opportunities	Challenges	Innovations
Capturing data	Availability of (real-time) sensor data [2, 14, 31], open data [5, 31] and social media data [2, 14, 31]	Variety in data [1], data quality [4, 5, 18], reliability of data [4, 5, 18], and security of data [17, 18]	Crowdsourcing [2, 6, 14]; nowcasting [32]
Integrating data	Cross-organizational collaboration [4, 14, 17]; linking new data sources to traditional statistics [4, 31, 33]	Interoperability [5]; lack of standardization, architectures, and portals [4, 5, 17]; legacy systems [4, 5]	Sentiment analysis [31], location mapping [4, 14, 31], advanced social network analysis [14, 31]
Application of data	Real-time monitoring of policy [31]; transparency and accountability [14]	Sense-making and interpretation [31]	Visualization techniques [19, 31]; computer simulation [14, 19]

Table 1 shows that public administrations increasingly see opportunities for the use of new data sources, mainly (real-time) sensor data [2, 14]. These data can be physical, such as roadside monitoring, but also virtual, such as social media data. A study from 2015 finds that governments mainly make use of two types of data for data-driven policy making: "public datasets (administrative (open) data and statistics about populations, economic indicators, education, etc.) that typically contain descriptive statistics, which are now used on a larger scale, used more intensively, and linked [... and ...] social media, sensors and mobile phones that are [...] analyzed with novel methods such as sentiment analysis, location mapping or advanced social network analysis" [31, p. 3]. Main issues are whether the data are of sufficient quality [4, 5, 18], and whether they are reliable and secure [4, 5, 17, 18]. Otherwise, they may undermine the policy making process [4]. Innovations in capturing data are crowdsourcing [6], and nowcasting, which is the capturing of search engine data [32].

Regarding integration of data, to make successful use of big and open data in organizational processes, cross-boundary information integration (in between government agencies and between not-for-profit organizations and private firms and the public sector) is necessary [14, 17]. The integration of data is becoming more important: linking these data sources with data sources that are traditionally used for policy making such as statistics, surveys and organizational databases is becoming the norm [31, 33]. However, many challenges exist: interoperability of data and lack of standardization, architectures and portals [4, 5, 17]. Another issue are legacy systems that may negatively influence this linking [4, 5]. Poel et al. [31] conclude that currently privately held data is of less relevance, as they are still hardly shared.

Opportunities for data integration include sentiment analysis, location mapping, and social network analysis [4, 14, 31].

The third step in the use of new data sources is application and sense-making. While social media analysis and network analysis can be seen as forms of data integration that can be used to support the policy making, we consider the use of visualization tools and computer simulations to be applications of data to the actual process of policy making [19]. However, "[a]mong the initiatives examined, there is little use of advanced analytics or visualization techniques" [31, p. 4]. Another opportunity is to realize greater accountability [14]. Likely, the most innovative use of new datasets take place in the hidden spheres of fighting crime and terrorism [31].

3.2 Co-creation of Policy

Another essential element of smartness in government is *co-creation of policy*, as ICT not only allows for collaborating with other organizations (public or private), but also with citizens [1, 2, 6, 14]. Co-creation is the exchange of ideas and information between relevant actors, such as governments, businesses, civil society and citizens that lead to the develop of policies [1, 6]. Involvement of citizens in policy making is especially important since public data and statistics are increasingly met by citizens' distrust [11]. This can take on different forms, depending on the level of involvement [2]: it may range from merely informing public administrations, for example by tapping discussion fora, opinion polls and using social media [2, 6, 19], to participating in decision making and in policy implementation. Table 2, which is based on Janssen and Helbig [2], summarizes the main innovations and challenges to co-creation of policies.

Table 2. Opportunities, challenges and innovations in co-creation of policies.

Levels of involvement	Opportunities	Challenges	Innovations
Informing and signaling	Citizens identify problems and set the agenda [2]	Social inclusion and overcoming exclusion [6, 19, 31]; lack of stability of social media [6]	Crowdsourcing [2, 6]; online petitions [2]; participatory sensing [19]
Decision making	Citizens being involved in selecting options [2, 6]	Citizens' skills and motivation [2, 16]; skills and culture of the government agency [6]	Computer simulation and serious games [2, 19]; cross-platform social media analysis [6]
Implementation	Co-creation between governments, citizen and businesses [2]; policy evaluation [19]; transparency and accountability [6]	Privacy and security [2, 6]; accuracy [6]	Camera surveillance, smart phone data, use of sensors [2]; agile implementation [19]

The most basic form of citizen involvement is informing and signaling, meaning that citizens' information is used for identifying problems and setting the agenda [2]. Main challenges for this level are to make sure that different groups of citizens are represented, without excluding relevant groups [6]. Examples of this happening can be found in literature on using social media data during disasters and disease outbreak. While nowcasting using search engine data for predicting flu outbreaks can be an accurate predictive methodology; for predicting Ebola, this method proved to be much less accurate since in the areas where the main outbreak was, internet access is still scarce [31]. Furthermore, the stability of social media is a challenge for its use in signaling problems [6]. Innovations in using citizens' ideas include crowdsourcing [2, 6], online petitions [2], and participatory sensing [19].

The inclusion of citizens' opinions in decision making refers to a higher level of involvement. This means that citizens are involved in the evaluation of policy options [2, 6]. The most elaborate form of this is the organization of a referendum, but using social media or other online tools, this could be done more efficiently and effectively [1, 2]. Important challenges are to ensure that both citizens' and skills and motivation [2, 16] and that civil servants' skills and culture [6] are sufficient. Innovations in involving citizens in the choice for different policy options and decision making are computer simulations and serious games [2, 19], and cross-platform social media analysis [6].

The third level of involvement is implementation of policies, which can be seen as the most immersive level of co-creation. Opportunities for co-creation include collaboration between public administrations, private companies and citizens in policy implementation [2], policy evaluation [19], and transparency and accountability [6]. Challenges include privacy and security [2, 6] and accuracy [6]. Innovations in this level of involvement include camera surveillance, the use of smart phone data and sensors [2], and allowing for agile implementation, delivering faster and better innovations because of regular and short-cycle interactions [19].

4   The Policy Lab Approach

In the previous section we identified opportunities, challenges, and innovations based on literature of new technologies and co-creation in policy making. This section aims to present a coherent Policy Lab approach to data-driven policy making based on the innovations in these fields. Since the framework is to be used for policy making, we mapped these innovations to phases of the policy cycle [3]. Inspired by Janssen and Helbig [2], we distinguish three phases: *predictive and problem definition*, *design and experimentation*, and *evaluation and implementation*. Table 3 elaborates innovations and impact per phase of the Policy Lab approach, and identifies challenges.

Table 3. Innovations, impact and challenges of data-driven policy making.

Policy cycle phase	Innovations	Impact	Challenges
Predictive & problem definition	Use of (real-time) sensor data from citizens (e.g. social media data, crowd-sourcing), business and government for problem definition and prediction	Problem definition based on (real-time) data from different actors, rather than merely expert based	Capturing different data sources and ensuring data quality, reliability and security as well as representativeness of the data
Design & experimentation	Using advanced analyses, such as sentiment analysis, location mapping, social network analysis, visualization, computer simulation and serious games for decision making	Cross-organizational collaboration and involvement of citizens require more advanced analyses to be able to select policy options	Creating an infrastructure ensuring interoperability and allowing for integration of data, in the form of standards, architectures, and portals
Evaluation & implementation	Collaborative data-driven policy implementation by governments, citizens and businesses, allowing for agility of processes	Public value creation, improved transparency and accountability, but it may also lead to more surveillance	Accuracy of data and data models, ensuring privacy and security. Citizens' skills and motivation and skills and culture of the government agency need to be sufficient

The first phase of policy making – predictive and problem definition, (real-time) sensor data is used, comprising physical sensor data such as roadside traffic data, and virtual data such as social media data. Furthermore, innovative approaches such as crowdsourcing and nowcasting are also used to predict and identify problems. This leads to the availability of (real-time) information that allows more precise predictions than those that are merely expert based. However, experts are still important to provide context information to the trends spotted by the data. Main challenges are the availability, quality, reliability and security of the data as well as representativeness of the data that should include viewpoints of different groups of citizens without excluding relevant groups. In a study on the use of data for policy making from 2015, over half of the cases identified were used for this first phase of policy making [31].

The second phase of policy making – design and experimentation, should ensure collaboration between government, private organizations, and citizens in the decision making process and choice for policy options. This requires the use of more advanced analytical approaches such as sentiment analysis, location mapping, social network analysis, visualization techniques, computer simulation and serious games to allow for the involvement of other stakeholders in the decision making. A major challenge for the integration of different data sources, the performance of more advanced analyses, and ensuring involvement of citizens is setting up an infrastructure that allows for interoperability and integration of data [17]. Standards, architectures and portals can be instruments for this. Traditionally, governments more often involve citizens after this phase, in the implementation, rather than in the process of decision making. This is reflected in the lower number of best practices in this phase [31].

Evaluation and implementation – the third phase of policy making, allows for joint policy implementation and co-creation of services by government, businesses and citizens. An advantage of the use of new data sets and technologies is the use of an agile approach [15] that allows for short cycles of decision making and implementation. The involvement of relevant stakeholders in the implementation and ongoing monitoring of policy creates public value [20–22]. More insight and collaboration may result in greater transparency and accountability, but also to more surveillance. Accuracy of data and data models and ensuring privacy and security are major challenges. Furthermore, co-creation of policy requires specific skills and motivation of citizens as well as specific skills and culture of the government agency [2, 16]. While in traditional e-participation, citizens are involved in policy implementation, actual co-creation involving citizens in the production of services is less often found in practice [7].

These innovations are challenging and in practice most governments do use new technologies and data sets for policy making, but they use this to enrich traditional statistical data rather than achieving co-creation [31]. Therefore, besides allowing for experimentation with policy making, new methodologies need to be developed that are able to make use of these new data sources and technologies. Using a design science approach [34], we developed the Policy Lab approach that can be used to guide innovations in data-driven policy making, allowing for experimentation with new policies and developing new data-driven methodologies at the same time. To validate this approach we held five internal workshops with experts that took place over the course of 2016. Furthermore, throughout this process we consulted academic and governmental stakeholders: four representatives of three academic institutions and six representatives of the national and local levels of government were involved. The Policy Lab approach is graphically presented in Fig. 1.

The conceptualization of the Policy Lab approach presented in Fig. 1 consist of two circles. The inner circle is represents the policy making process, consisting of several phases, such as agenda setting, policy formulation, decision-making, implementation and evaluation. The outer circle of the Policy Lab approach focuses on the development of data-driven methodologies and co-creation. This approach allows the two circles to mutually influence each other: policy experiments can be used to develop and test new methodologies, that, in turn can be used for developing and evaluation policies.

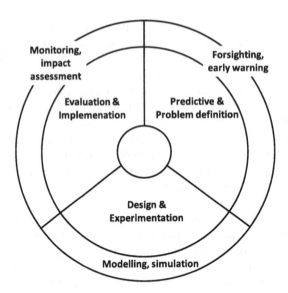

Fig. 1. The policy lab approach for data-driven policy making.

5   Discussion

Based on the literature review, we found that most applications of new data sources, such as (real-time) sensor data are to link them to traditional statistics and few innovative methodologies are used for policy making [31]. However, "utilizing such [social] channels for policy making purposes does not constitute an established approach yet" [19]. This means that first of all instruments and methodologies for the use of these new data sets in traditional statistical and econometric methodologies should be developed [35]. Furthermore, in order for governments to become used to these methodology, they could very well use the use the 'design-thinking approach' of a Policy Lab that allows for experimentation. This means that the Policy Lab approach, effectively, has three pillars: using new technologies and data sources for policy making, enabling co-creation and allowing for experimentation.

The use of new datasets in traditional statistical or econometric studies is widely regarded to have a large potential for policy making. Traditional data sources are often text based or have a strong qualitative character rather than a numerical or machine generated form. Newer data sources are often human generated (social media) data, or machine generated sensor data. This can also be seen as the main distinction between data-driven and evidence-based policy. Using these newer data sources means that not only new methodologies need to deal with the size of these new data sets, but also with the variety of data, that may range from traditional statistics, to (real-time) sensor data to human generated text based social media data to images, video streams or geo-data. Statisticians and econometrists aiming to deal with these new (big) data sets, need to learn ways to incorporate them into their traditional methodologies [35].

Fundamentally, there are no contradictions between big data and traditional econometric approaches, but the two have developed independently. For example, the use of big data sets enhances statistics in prediction methods (out-of-sample), which is often not possible in traditional econometrics because data sets are not large enough [35]. Furthermore, when using big data sets it makes more sense to focus on model uncertainty than on sampling uncertainty, which is often examined in traditional econometrics. Finally, machine learning techniques such as decision tree learning may give a better picture than logistic regression [35]. Traditional statistics, in turn, provide useful methods to help variable selection in big data models such as stepwise regression penalized regressions and Bayesian techniques (including time series analysis) [35].

However, while these new methodologies could benefit from the incorporation of big data and linking them with traditional methodologies, traditional policy models are far from obsolete. Big data mainly concerns the discovery of correlations, while policy models present causations that have been developed based on practical experience [36]. Causation hypotheses can ultimately be confirmed using controlled or natural experiments, and, thus, cannot be replaced with big data analyses alone. The degree to which the outcomes of such combinations of big data and statistical models can be explained, thus, represents a major issue. Therefore, the involvement of citizens and experimentation become paramount. This is even more the case in this 'post-factual' era, in which citizens are critical of official statistics and data [11]. A Policy Lab setting can be used for controlled experimentation allowing people to 'buy into' data, statistical methods and data-driven policies.

Similar to the challenges that Living Labs face, the Policy Lab approach, as a specific instance of a Living Lab, presents the risk of becoming primarily focused the implementation of an open innovation approach, rather than with achieving specific results [26]. While involvement of new data sources and citizens in the policy making process are important objectives, the primary aim should be to improve policy making. If this is not achieved, this may result in a limited application of data-driven policies outside of the Policy Lab environment. This also means, as is the case for Living Labs, that scaling and sustainability are major challenges [26].

Further research should thus focus on the development of these new methodologies that allow for combination of new data sources with traditional statistical data and the combination of big data methodologies with econometrics. Furthermore, experiments with policy development that address wicked problems should be carried out both to involve citizens and increase legitimacy of these policies and to capture the benefits of these new approaches for policy makers. This means that the Policy Lab approach should be validated and expanded based on these experiments. Finally, the issue of scalability and sustainability should be further explored to capture the benefits of data-driven policy making outside of the Policy Lab setting.

6   Conclusion

New data sources and ICTs have great potential for improving policy making. However, data-driven policy initiatives are scarce and the existing initiatives are, often, cases linking (real-time) sensor data to traditional statistical analyses. Therefore, using a design science approach, this paper develops a Policy Lab approach. Based on literature, we identified innovations in the use of new data sources and in co-creation of policies. The involvement of citizens will likely become more important for the legitimacy of statistics and data and policies. Subsequently, we mapped these innovations to the different phases of the policy cycle. Based on this overview, the Policy Lab approach draws on three aspects: using new data sources, co-creation and experimentation with policy making focusing on real-life wicked problems. The experiments can be used to develop data-driven policies as well as to develop new data-driven methodologies. Further research should focus on the development of methodologies for incorporating big data analyses into traditional statistical analysis and on experimentation with policy issues, thereby validating the Policy Lab approach.

References

1. Millard, J.: Open governance systems: doing more with more. Gov. Inf. Q. (2015, in press)
2. Janssen, M., Helbig, N.: Innovating and changing the policy-cycle: policy-makers be prepared! Gov. Inf. Q. (2015, in press)
3. Lasswell, H.: The policy orientation. In: Lerner, D., Lasswell, H. (eds.) The Policy Sciences: Recent Developments in Scope and Method, pp. 3–15. University Press, Stanford (1951)
4. Bertot, J.C., Choi, H.: Big data and E-government: issues, policies, and recommendations. In: Proceedings of the 14th Annual International Conference on Digital Government Research. dg.o. 2013, 17–20 June, Quebec City, pp. 1–10 (2013)
5. Janssen, M., Charalabidis, Y., Zuiderwijk, A.: Benefits, adoption barriers and myths of open data and open government. Inf. Syst. Manag. 29(4), 258–268 (2012)
6. Ferro, E., Loukis, E.N., Charalabidis, Y., Osella, M.: Policy making 2.0: from theory to practice. Gov. Inf. Q. 30(4), 359–368 (2013)
7. Linders, D.: From E-government to we-government: defining a typology for citizen coproduction in the age of social media. Gov. Inf. Q. 29(4), 446–454 (2012)
8. Solesbury, W.: Evidence Based Policy: Where it Came and Where it's Going. ESRC UK Centre for Evidence Based Policy and Practice, Queen Mary, University of London (2001). https://www.kcl.ac.uk/sspp/departments/politicaleconomy/research/cep/pubs/papers/assets/wp1.pdf
9. Head, B.W.: Three lenses of evidence-based policy. Aust. J. Public Adm. 67(1), 1–11 (2008)
10. Bijlsma, R.M., Bots, P.W.G., Wolters, H.A., Hoekstra, A.Y.: An empirical analysis of stakeholders' influence on policy development. Ecol. Soc. 16(1), 51–66 (2011)
11. Davies, W.: How statistics lost their power – and why we should fear what comes next. The Guardian, 19 January 2017. https://www.theguardian.com/politics/2017/jan/19/crisis-of-statistics-big-data-democracy
12. Williamson, B.: Governing methods: policy innovation labs, design and data science in the digital governance of education. J. Educ. Adm. Hist. 47(3), 251–271 (2015)
13. Fuller, M., Lochard, A.: Public policy labs in European Union Member States. EUR 28044 EN June (2016). http://publications.jrc.ec.europa.eu/repository/bitstream/JRC102665/final%20report%20w%20identifiers.pdf
14. Gil-Garcia, J.R., Zhang, J., Puron-Cid, G.: Conceptualizing smartness in government: an integrative and multi-dimensional view. Gov. Inf. Q. 33(3), 524–534 (2016)
15. Janssen, M., Estevez, E.: Lean government and platform-based governance – doing more with less. Gov. Inf. Q. 30(S1), S1–S8 (2013)
16. Meijer, A.: E-governance innovation: barriers and strategies. Gov. Inf. Q. 32(2), 198–206 (2015)

17. Gil-Garcia, J.R., Sayogo, D.S.: Government inter-organizational information sharing initiatives: understanding the main determinants of success. Gov. Inf. Q. **33**(3), 572–582 (2016)
18. Hui, G., Hayllar, M.R.: Creating public value in E-government: a public-private-citizen collaboration framework in web 2.0. Aust. J. Public Adm. **69**(S1), S120–S131 (2010)
19. Koussouris, S., Lampathaki, F., Kokkinakos, P., Askounis, D., Misuraca, G.: Accelerating policy making 2.0: innovation directions and research perspectives as distilled from four standout cases. Gov. Inf. Q. **32**(2), 142–153 (2015)
20. Moore, M.H.: Creating Public Value Strategic Management in Government. Harvard University Press, Cambridge (1995)
21. Stoker, G.: Public value management a new narrative for governance? Am. Rev. Public Adm. **36**(1), 41–57 (2006)
22. Bannister, F., Connolly, R.: ICT, public values and transformative government: a framework and programme for research. Gov. Inf. Q. **31**(1), 119–128 (2014)
23. Dawes, S.S.: The evolution and continuing challenges of E-governance. Public Adm. Rev. **68**(4), S86–102 (2008)
24. McDermott, P.: Building open government. Gov. Inf. Q. **27**(4), 401–413 (2010)
25. Chadwick, A.: Bringing e-democracy back in why it matters for future research on E-governance. Soc. Sci. Comput. Rev. **21**(4), 443–455 (2003)
26. Gasco, M.: Living labs: implementing open innovation in the public sector. Gov. Inf. Q. **34**(1), 90–98 (2017)
27. Manyika, J., Chui, M., Brown, B., Bughin, J., Dobbs, R., Roxburgh, C., Hung Byers, A.: Big data: the next frontier for innovation, competition, and productivity. McKinsey Global Institute (2011). http://www.mckinsey.com/insights/business_technology/big_data_the_next_frontier_for_innovation
28. Cukier, K., Mayer-Schönberger, V.: Big Data: A Revolution That Will Transform How We Live, Work, and Think. Houghton Mifflin Harcourt Publishing Company, Boston (2013)
29. Chen, L., Chiang, R.H.L., Storey, V.C.: Business intelligence and analytics: from big data to big impact. MIS Q. **36**(4), 1165–1188 (2012)
30. Harrison, C., Eckman, B., Hamilton, R., Hartswick, P., Kalagnanam, J., Paraszczak, J., Williams, P.: Foundations for smarter cities. IBM J. Res. Dev. **54**(4), 1–16 (2010)
31. Poel, M., Schroeder, R., Treperman, J., Rubinstein, M., Meyer, E., Mahieu, B., Scholten, C., Svetachova, M.: Data for policy: a study of big data and other innovative data-driven approaches for evidence-informed policymaking. Report about the State-of-the-Art (2015). http://media.wix.com/ugd/c04ef4_20afdcc09aa14df38fb646a33e624b75.pdf
32. Taylor, L., Schroeder, R., Meyer, E.: Emerging practices and perspectives on big data analysis in economics: Bigger and better or more of the same? Big Data Soc. **1**(2), 1–10 (2014)
33. van den Brakel, J., Söhler, E., Daas, P., Buelens, B.: Social media as a data source for official statistics; the Dutch consumer confidence index. Discussion Paper 2016-01, Statistics Netherlands (2016). https://www.cbs.nl/nlnl/achtergrond/2016/07/social-media-as-a-data-source-for-official-statistics-thedutch-consumer-confidence-index
34. Hevner, A.R., March, T.S., Park, J., Ram, S.: Design science in information systems research. MIS Q. **28**(1), 75–105 (2004)
35. Varian, H.R.: Big data: new tricks for econometrics. J. Econ. Perspect. **28**(2), 3–28 (2014)
36. Cowls, J., Schroeder, R.: Causation, correlation, and big data in social science. Policy Internet **7**(4), 447–472 (2015)

A Systematic Literature Review of the Relationships Between Policy Analysis and Information Technologies: Understanding and Integrating Multiple Conceptualizations

Cesar Renteria[(✉)] and J. Ramon Gil-Garcia

University at Albany, State University of New York, Albany, NY, USA
crenteria@albany.edu, jgil-garcia@ctg.albany.edu

Abstract. Researchers and practitioners are increasingly aware of changes in the environment, broadly defined, that affect the policy process and the current capabilities for policy analysis. Examples of these changes are emergent information technologies, big and interconnected data, and the availability of computational power to perform analysis at a very disaggregate level. These and other forces have the potential to significantly change multiple stages of the policy process, from design to implementation and evaluation. The emergence of this phenomenon has led to the use of a variety of labels to define it. Potentially, a variety of labels might contribute to some conceptual confusion, but most importantly to concept stretching. This article aims to provide a conceptual space by identifying the attributes that compose the phenomenon. Based on a systematic literature review, this paper identifies the terms that have been used to refer to this phenomenon and analyzes their associated attributes. Based on Gerring & Barrosi's Min-Max strategy of concept formation, we propose two sets of attributes to define the phenomenon.

Keywords: Policy informatics · Policy analytics · IT-enabled policy analysis · E-policy-making · Systematic literature review · Policy analysis · Policy process

1 Introduction

Recent technological and analytical developments have grabbed the attention of researchers and practitioners as potential innovations that could improve the quality and timeliness of the policy process, compared with more traditional methods and approaches to collecting and analyzing information for policymaking. In this paper, we broadly refer to this as the relationship between policy analysis and information technologies. This relationship involves, among other things, new data sources and structures, improved computational capacity, and new methods of analysis that could contribute to better address the increasing complexity, interconnectedness, and uncertainty of public problems [1–4].

P. Parycek et al. (Eds.): ePart 2017, LNCS 10429, pp. 112–124, 2017.
DOI: 10.1007/978-3-319-64322-9_10

Recent academic interest has been brought on the matter from diverse fields, such as health [5], policy analysis [6–8], statistics [9], electronic government [10], population studies [11], complexity science [2], computational science [12], and informatics [2, 3, 13]. There is a variety of terms of concepts that have emerged from these backgrounds to refer to that phenomenon. For example, Janssen [2] identified the following terms: e-policy-making, computational intelligence, digital policy sciences, and policy informatics. Other authors have associated the terms IT-enabled policy analysis, policy modeling, and data-driven decision-making as well as other forms to label the same phenomenon [2, 14].

The high number of different terms to refer, arguably, to approximately the same phenomenon is a problem of conceptual clarity [15, 16]. Because every term has associated certain attributes, a number of terms imply a loose constellation of attributes associated with the same phenomenon. This conceptual ambiguity (in the constitutive attributes) might limit the possibility to build knowledge on top of previous works. Conceptual clarity is not to prefer a label rather than others, but to provide insights to facilitate future research on the matter. For example, as a basis for case selection or comparative analysis, for the operationalization of measurements, or to undergo a revision of the conceptual definition of current terms. Conceptual clarity also contributes to mitigate conceptual stretching, which is defined by Goertz [17] as "concepts [that] are loosened up so that they apply to additive cases. Thus, we seek to contribute in the study of the relationship of policy analysis and information technologies by defining a conceptual space[1] for the phenomenon of interest, as well as to provide two sets of attributes that best suit the definition of the phenomenon and have clear conceptual boundaries. Based on this, our research question is: what are the common and distinct attributes of the terms defining the relationship between policy analysis and information technologies?

The article is structured in five sections, including the present introduction. Section two explains the methodological approach used to develop the proposed conceptual space. This is followed by a brief description of the terms' backgrounds and an assessment of their conceptual clarity (or ambiguity). Section four provides a description of the minimal and ideal-type definitions, as well as the set of the constitutive attributes of the proposed conceptual space. In the final section, we provide some conclusions and discuss future research directions.

2   Methodological Approach

2.1   Min-Max Strategy of Concept Formation

The Min-Max strategy of concept formation was proposed by Gerring and Barresi [15] as a mechanism to provide conceptual clarity, by uncovering the defining attributes of a concept. The strategy is particularly useful when uncovering these attributes across contesting defining terms. This is because the strategy focus on identifying the *non-idiosyncratic definitions* (those that are less dependent on particularities of certain field or period). Gerring & Barresi's strategy is based on Sartori's

---

[1] A conceptual space is defined here as the range of attributes extracted from the concepts or terms aforementioned.

propositions of the "ladder of abstraction." This is in reference to the generality or specificity of a concept due to the augment or decrease of the concept's *intension*. The intension of a concept is the set of properties or attributes that determine the constitutive elements belonging to a concept [16]. The concepts are found to be more general by simply reducing the set of attributes, whereas the concept is more specific by adding or unfolding attributes [16]. These changes have a direct effect on the *extension*, which is the group of observations that have the attributes specified in the concept. Thus, the *extension* increases as *intension* decreases, and vice versa.

To define what attributes should be kept in a prototypical definition, Gerring & Barresi propose two strategies. The first strategy is a *minimal definition*. This refers to a set of necessary attributes that must be present in all terms or concepts. Identifying such attributes is an empirical endeavor, rather than theoretical. The goal is to identify the attributes that are present across all the concepts reviewed. This strategy aims to find a *non-idiosyncratic definition* (i.e. a set of attributes that will not vary across the terms used). The second strategy is an *ideal-type definition*. This strategy seeks to identify a definition that is "maximal" in that it includes all the attributes that could possibly compose the definition [15].

The empirical strategy proposed by Gerring & Barresi is unfolded in three steps. The first step is to gather a representative sample of the terms or concepts of interests. In this regard, our work departs from the lists presented in the introduction. Next, we did a systematic literature review to find the relevant manuscripts that use the terms or concepts of interest. The protocol of the systematic literature review is presented in the next section. The second step is to typologize the attributes from analyzing the manuscripts found in the systematic literature review. We built a typology of attributes by obtaining explicit referenced attributes (characterized here as "strong" attributes) and by interpreting implicit attributes (characterized as "weak" attributes). The third step corresponds to the organization of the attributes in two sets. The first set corresponds to a *minimal definition* and an *ideal-type definition*.

2.2 Systematic Literature Review

We conducted a systematic literature review of the relationship between policy analysis and information technologies in academic publications, following the widely used Preferred Reporting Items for Systematic Reviews and Meta-Analyses (PRISMA) statement. The PRISMA protocol confers to the research process limited bias, transparency, and replicability [18]. We collected publications from three digital libraries to cover the publications in social sciences: Scopus, Web of Science, and JSTOR. These libraries combined offer the best coverage of publications in social sciences [19, 20]. In addition, we selected the digital library DBLP that accounts for the most extended coverage in computer science [21].

Our inclusion criteria were as follows. In terms of publications, we considered peer-reviewed articles, books or book chapters, and conference proceedings. All types of study designs were considered. We considered publications that: (1) provided or was related with a descriptive or conceptual discussion about policy analysis and information technologies; and/or (2) provided an application of an innovative approach, method or technology in the policy process. Our exclusion criteria were to limit the search to the following research fields: computer science, complexity science, health, informatics, and social sciences, which are the fields from which we had previous knowledge of being using related terms. We also discarded the publications that did not made a substantial reference to policy analysis, policy process or policy cycle.

Based on our previous knowledge of the topic, we considered the following search terms: (1) "policy informatics", (2) "e-policy-making", (3) "IT-enabled policy analysis", (4) "policy modeling", (5) "computational intelligence", (6) "digital policy science", (7) "policy analytics", (8) "data science", (9) "computational social sciences", (10) "digital science", (11) "data-driven decision-making". For the database searching, we followed two rounds of search queries with clearly defined query rules.[2] The first round was based on a search of the exact terms, after the application of the inclusion criteria. In the first round, we noticed that our search strategy needed further specificity for some terms, since the publications retrieved were populous. For example, we retrieved 2,087 for "computational social sciences" (see Table 1). In the second searching round, all exact concepts were combined with common concepts in public administration literature ("governance", "public administration", "policy analysis", "policy-making", and "policy process"). The reason of this intersection was to automatically reduce the possibility of including articles that did not match the inclusion criteria, without scanning the titles or abstracts. This was a practical solution to address massive matches in broader concepts such as "computational intelligence", "data science" or "policy modeling".

Table 1. Publications retrieved by first and second rounds of refinement

Concept	First round	Second round
Policy informatics	121	31
E-Policy-Making	15	6
IT-Enabled policy analysis	10	9
Policy modeling	18,979	1,301
Computational intelligence	175,418	34,760
Digital policy science	52	12
Data science	11,504	2,083
Computational social sciences	893	76
Digital science	1,156	104
Data-Driven Decision-Making	920	303

---

[2] Illustratively, the search query string for policy informatics in the first round is shown below. All the terms followed the same string. ALL ("policy informatics"). In the second round was: ALL ("policy informatics") AND (ALL("governance") OR ALL ("public administration") OR ALL ("policy analysis") OR ALL ("policy-making") OR ("policy process")).

The search period of our review spans from 2000 to December 27th, 2016. By testing the search queries, we observed that most of the publications are not older than 8 years; however, we decided to extend the search period to 16 years to make sure we have a thorough coverage of research publications (thus, the lower bound is 2000).

Based on the results of the second round of search queries, we discarded some concepts from the study. The terms "computational social sciences", "data science", "digital science", "data-driven decision-making", "policy modeling", and "computational intelligence" were discarded as being considered too broad for the purposes of this research. We acknowledge that there is a chance that a subset of the articles retrieved with these terms might be related with the policy cycle and are not captured in the present study. In these cases, future research is needed in understanding whether these concepts could be associated with the policy analysis and how.[3] Finally, the concept "digital policy science", although we found publications in the search queries, this concept did not pass the fourth step in our PRISMA flowchart. Thus, we also discarded this term. The final list of terms was the following: (1) policy informatics, (2) e-policy-making, (3) IT-enabled policy analysis, and (4) policy analytics.

The search strategy consisted of five steps (see Fig. 1). In the first step, we performed database searching following the inclusion and exclusion criteria defined above. The number of records identified in the first step was 367. In the second step, we extracted the reference metadata from the digital libraries and placed them into the reference manager software Mendeley, grouping the references by term. We then search for duplicates with the managing tools provided by Mendeley. As some records mentioned more than one term, we discarded duplicates within groups of references. We also grouped all records in a single file and searched for duplicates across groups, but keeping a research memo on the records that included many terms. The number of records after all duplicates were removed was 342. In the third step, we screened the titles and abstracts of the records to exclude the records that did not meet our inclusion. The number of records after screening titles and abstracts was 62. In the fourth step, we screened the full-text in the remaining records and removed those that did not meet the inclusion criteria. The third and fourth steps discarded mostly records that did not make any substantial reference to policy analysis, policy process or policy cycle. Finally, we included records identified while reading the selected records and were not identified through the search queries. This snowball sampling contributed to the identification of 6 relevant records that were included in the final sample. Based on that, the final number of records included in the systematic review was 43.

---

[3] Furthermore, at the end of the literature review, we found three other related terms: "social data science", "data-centered policy-making", "data science for government and policy-making", and policymaking 2.0.

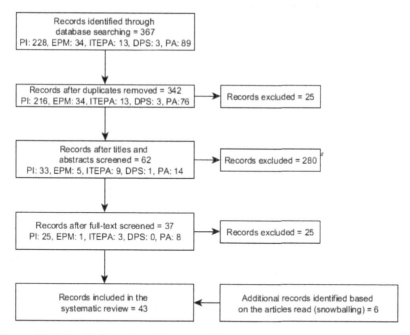

Notes: PI: Policy Informatics; EPM: E-Policy-Making; ITEPA: IT-Enabled Policy
Analysis; DPS: Digital Policy Science; PA: Policy Analytics.

Fig. 1. Flow diagram of the search strategy and results

3   Understanding the Multiple Conceptualizations

3.1   "Insufficiently" Developed Terms

Aside from the terms that we considered not pertaining exclusively to policy analysis, policy
process or policy cycle (computational social sciences, quantitative social sciences, data
science, digital science, data-driven decision-making, policy modeling, and computational
intelligence), we concluded that two of the terms reviewed lack of constituent attributes or
they are vaguely defined. The first term that lies within this vagueness is Digital Policy
Science, from which although we found little evidence of its use in academic literature, there
is neither an explicit definition, nor an implicit description of its constitutive attributes. The
second term is e-policy or e-policy-making, which, although we found some attributes, we
perceive them as weakly defined. In fact, the defining attributes found in the literature make
direct reference to the defining attributes of other terms. As Hochtl [22] states, e-policy-
making conceptually "shares many features of 'policy informatics,' such as analysis, administration, and governance [3], and 'policymaking 2.0,' [...]" [22]. Sticking with the rule of
discriminatory power in the intentionality of the attributes, we concluded that this term fails
to set clearly some definitional boundaries as the definitional attributes are not described
beyond these types of superficial descriptions.

3.2   Brief Presentation of Studied Terms

So far, the set of developments that have been perceived as useful for improving the policy process have been conceptualized in different terms. Janssen and Wimmer [2] include e-policy-making, computational intelligence, digital policy sciences, and policy informatics. Additionally, other authors have associated IT-enabled policy analysis, policy modeling, and data-driven decision-making as emergent concepts that also affect the policy process. Among these concepts, some have evolved recently as more complex conceptualizations than others, perhaps setting a framework for understanding the processes through which emergent developments could affect public policy.

For instance, IT-enabled policy analysis (ITEPA) is a framework that seeks to advance the study of policy analysis by integrating the views of Bardach's policy cycle with Sterman's system dynamics approach. This framework also expands the conceptualization of policy analysis as a task with a necessary combination of institutions, actors, data, and information technologies. ITEPA is a perspective primarily concerned with the relationship between government and citizens. Its background spans through the study of e-government and governance. In this perspective, the substantial change in policymaking is caused by the development of open government and open data initiatives [10, 14, 23]. In this sense, the deployment of open government policies, and the release of open data in particular can strengthen new mechanisms of government-citizen relationships such as co-production, collaboration, and participation of the citizens in public processes as they are provided with new sources of information on public issues. Because data is regularly an input for decision-making, the increased availability of public data in the public domain may shift the approach to policymaking from a top-down decision-making approach towards a networked participatory approach. Furthermore, potential changes in policymaking are not only driven by data and technology possibilities, but also by a set of governing principles on the rise: transparency, participation, collaboration, and empowerment.

E-Policy-Making (EPM) is a term less used and developed in its contents. This terms refers to the use of "e-governance processes" in policymaking. Hochtl [22] points out that the concept formation intersects the attributes of policy informatics and Policymaking 2.0. Furthermore, the authors imply that the study of e-policy-making encompass both the improvements of already existing structures in policymaking by the incorporation of technology, as well the transformation of the policymaking structure itself [22].

Policy analytics is a concept formed to encompass different methods able to cope with the growing challenges that the rise of Big Data poses on data analysis [24, 25]. Its conceptualization is an adaptation of the idea of "business analytics" in the private sector, but applied to public policies. The focus of this conceptualization is to understand which methods or approaches could contribute to leverage the emergence of massive, complex and unstructured data production for the decision-making in the policy process. Thus, policy analytics is a field of study about how to adapt the set of skills, applications, methods, and technologies that lie within the field of data science to assist the construction of evidence for decision-making. Policy analytics is a perspective primarily concerned with the exploit of data quality, quantity and availability commonly known as the data revolution [24–26]. Overall, analytics are perceived as a way to solve the challenges associated with analyzing massive and unstructured data [25]. The term comes primarily from the field of operations research, as an attempt to understand the implications of adopting quantitative decision support methods in the private sector known as business analytics. Business analytics is a collection of innovative computational techniques to leverage and, at the same time, cope with the challenges of managing big data to inform decision-making.

Decision-making under this perspective pursues the ideal of evidence-based decision-making, where big data features and data science techniques are perceived as more accurate, rich, and timely, as well as less costly than traditional methods of collecting data [24, 25]. Furthermore, these are perceived as less biased in the collection and interpretation processes [24, 26]. As for the policy process, this perspective directly implies the incorporation of new sources of information for decision-making; remarkably, Daniell [25] has attempted to organize the blending of data sources and data science techniques and associate them as tools for policy analysis at different stages in the policy cycle. In addition, policy analytics indirectly implies the incorporation of predictive analysis to the toolkit of policy analysts (Table 2).

Table 2. Summary of definitions

Concept	Definition
E-policy-making	"The act of policymaking in e-government using e-governance processes, with the distinctive feature that evaluation happens as an integral part of all along the policy cycle rather than a s a separate step at the end of policymaking process" [22]
IT-enabled policy analysis	"The use of IT tools, mathematical modeling and analytical methods to take advantage of the available data to aid individuals and groups make policy options or solve policy problems" [14]
Policy informatics	"The study of how computation and communication technology is leveraged to understand and address complex public policy and administration problems and realize innovations in governance processes and institutions" [3]
Policy analytics	"The development and application of [...] skills, methodologies, methods, and technologies, which aim to support relevant stakeholders engaged at any stage of a policy cycle, with the aim of facilitating meaningful and informative hindsight, insight and foresight" [27]

4   Integrating the Attributes from Multiple Terms: A Min-Max Approach

Even though the Min-Max strategy is generally used to set the conceptual space of a given concept (i.e. democracy or culture), here we used this method to ensemble the attributes of a constellation of concepts that we hypothesized belong to the same latent concept. The argument is that this latent concept has been characterized through different lenses, where each lens has its own background and thus would likely assign different attributes to the same phenomenon.

Each concept formation offers, explicitly or implicitly, a variety of definitional attributes, where some of them will intersect each other, whereas others are context-specific reminiscent or idiosyncratic attributes [15, 28]. Thus, the *minimal definition* comprises the attributes that are common to all perspectives, providing a more general and agnostic perspective on the phenomenon.

The relationship between policy analysis and information technologies, minimally defined, is a phenomenon composed by the development of methods, technology, and data. Adding the idiosyncratic attributes allows to broaden the definition to a more overarching idea without blurring the definitional boundaries. This *ideal-type definition* includes all the attributes that comprise the conceptual space of the phenomenon, regardless of the perspective. The *ideal-type definition* is equivalent to the conceptual space in that both comprise the full range of attributes. Thus, as will be described below, the conceptual space is composed by five attributes: human resources, governance, methods, technology, and data (see Table 3).

Table 3. Table of attributes, by term

	Human resources	Governance	Methods	Technology	Data
E-policy-making		Weak	Weak	Weak	Weak
IT-enabled policy analysis	Strong	Strong	Strong	Strong	Strong
Policy informatics		Strong	Strong	Strong	Strong
Policy analytics			Strong	Weak	Strong
Typology of attribute	Ideal-Type	Ideal-Type	Minimal	Minimal	Minimal

Note: "Strong" stands for strongly defined attribute, whereas "Weak" means weakly defined attribute.

We also found that some terms had a stronger identification of attributes than others. For example, e-policy-making had a weak definition of attributes (i.e. subject to textual exegesis). Policy analytics has a strong emphasis on data as the fundamental attribute constitutive of the concept, whereas there is a weak connection with technologies. As for IT-enabled policy analysis and policy informatics, there is an evenly strong identification of attributes across the definitional works reviewed. Interestingly, although the IT-enabled policy analysis framework has more constitutive attributes than policy informatics, the authors consider this as a possible variation of policy informatics [10].

The results show that the attributes observed across the concepts are convergent towards a unified core of attributes (the minimal definition). All these perspectives are relatively aligned, with some idiosyncratic attributes that are likely to be explained by their intellectual background.

4.1 Minimal Attributes

Methods

In this context, methods refer to the analytical tools that people, primarily in the public sector, use to obtain useful information insights or knowledge from data for decision-making. These methods are generally suited for the analysis of quantitative data, although Puron-Cid, Gil-Garcia and Luna-Reyes [14] also recognize analytical methods for qualitative data. The perceived constitutive methods of policy analysis span from a wide variety of fields, such as mathematics, statistics, economics, operations research, psychology, sociology, management, finance, and political science [14, 24, 25, 27, 29], although the focus is stressed in emergent methods or techniques from computer science. For example, text mining, exploratory data analysis, support vector machines, spreadsheet models, and machine learning [25]. Other methods considered that are not yet part of the traditional policy analyst's toolkit are group model building, multi-criteria analyses, simulation and optimization modelling, participatory planning, resource allocation modelling, real-time operations optimization, remote sensing, smart metering, and participatory GIS/evaluation [25]; simulation modelling, and cognitive mapping [2, 3, 14, 25]. There is no clarity however, on whether the list of methods considered as part of this phenomenon is pertaining to a single technological innovation (i.e. data revolution) or the concept should be extended to all methods that eventually would fit technological innovations in the future.

Data

Data is an input for decision making in the policy process [10, 30–32]. This is regarded as sets of measurements of social activity that require analytical skills or methods to be transformed into useful information or knowledge for decision making. Data is also perceived as an element that could be easily spread into the public domain, contributing to re-shape the relationships between government and citizens. Under certain circumstances, data is also perceived as a potential driver towards networked governance, transparency, and other activities beyond policy decision-making [14]. Although this attribute also refers to traditional data (e.g. survey data), the primary focus is on big data, which is perceived as massive, usually costless, and unstructured. There are several types of such data, primarily organized by its source; for example, commercial data, administrative data, open data, electronic data, on-line data, cellphone data, geospatial data, daily census data, as well as data from sensor readings and crowd computing sources.

Technology

Technology or IT tools refers to the computational infrastructure that contributes to increase government's capacity [14, 30, 33–35]. This increased capacity comes in a variety of activities linked with both decision-making and governing. These activities are the likes of visualization technologies for the communication of policy analysis or decisions, technologies to process and manage information overload and ambiguity, technologies to generate and collect data, technologies for understanding patterns and detect trends in data, to increase the reach of the policy discussion, to enable collaborative networks, or to crowdsource public policy analysis, policy monitoring, evaluation or implementation.

4.2 Idiosyncratic Attributes

Human Resources

This attribute refers to the stock of capacities and skills for policymaking in the human resources available in an organization [14]. Any given development in computation and communication in the organization requires a body of expertise and knowledge in the human resources to effectively accomplish any task. More specifically, human resources refer to the personnel in charge of tasks such as producing insights for or advising decision-making, as well as being responsible for decisions in any given stage of the policy cycle.

Governance

Governance refers to the technological infrastructure through which governance processes could occur [14, 36–42]. The governance platforms are perceived to have the capacity to improve the flexibility and responsiveness of bureaucracies [39]. In addition, improved computation and communication capabilities in government activities could improve the interaction between citizens and government, as well as among government agencies. As a constitutive element for decisions in policymaking, governance represents the institutional and social arrangements in which a decision-making process takes place. As such, governance is highly intertwined with the rest of the constitutive elements of policy analysis and information technologies, since it might be shaped by data or technologies or it might determine the use of types of data and technologies in the policy process.

5 Conclusion

Rising literature on this topic suggests that information technologies and the availability of new types of data are already affecting the policy process and the way people think about policy analysis. The increasing computational power and alternative analytical methods also add to this situation and make it complex and not easy to conceptualize. In this paper, we have shown that there are many labels to refer to this phenomenon, including policy informatics, IT-enabled policy analysis, and E-Policy, among others. Despite the very diverse labels there are some important commonalities that should be part of our understanding of this phenomenon and a more comprehensive, but concise definition. There are aspects related to methods, data, technology, human resources, and governance and all of them contribute to a rich conceptualization of the relationships between information technologies and policy analysis.

In addition, this analysis identifies some terms with insufficient conceptual development, and other that are not clearly related to the policy process. In contrast, there are a core set of conceptualizations that help to identify the common attributes and specific attributes of the phenomenon in our approach. There are also references to the policy cycle, but almost no strong links to theories of the policy process. This is still a limitation of the existing terms and their respective conceptual definitions. Finally, there is also the challenge of identifying and integrating new technologies or analytical methods when they emerge. The usefulness of a concept related to these important and frequently rapid changes is also related to its capacity to leverage past research and being useful for future research. This paper aimed to contribute to conceptual clarity by uncovering some underlying attributes and structure them into two sets of definitions. Since ideas are not set in stone, it may well make sense to use these insights as material to reassess the conceptual definition of current terms.

References

1. Desai, A., Kim, Y.: Symposium on policy informatics. J. Policy Anal. Manag. **34**, 354–357 (2015)
2. Janssen, M., Wimmer, M.A.: Introduction to policy-making in the digital age (2015)
3. Johnston, E.W., Desouza, K.C.: Governance in the Information Era: Theory and Practice of Policy Informatics. Routledge, New York (2015)
4. Lazer, D., Pentland, A.S., Adamic, L., Aral, S., Barabasi, A.L., Brewer, D., Christakis, N., Contractor, N., Fowler, J., Gutmann, M.: Life in the network: the coming age of computational social science. Science **323**, 721 (2009)
5. Martin, E.G., MacDonald, R.H., Smith, L.C., Gordon, D.E., Tesoriero, J.M., Laufer, F.N., Leung, S.J., O'Connell, D.A.: Policy modeling to support administrative decisionmaking on the New York State HIV testing law. J. Policy Anal. Manag. **34**, 403–423 (2015)
6. Blume, G., Scott, T., Pirog, M.: Empirical innovations in policy analysis. Policy Stud. J. **42**, 33–50 (2014)
7. Cook, T.D.: "Big data" in research on social policy. J. Policy Anal. Manag. **33**, 544–547 (2014)
8. Pirog, M.A.: Data will drive innovation in public policy and management research in the next decade. J. Policy Anal. Manag. **33**, 537–543 (2014)
9. Crosas, M., King, G., Honaker, J., Sweeney, L.: Automating open science for big data. Ann. Am. Acad. Polit. Soc. Sci. **659**, 260–273 (2015)
10. Puron Cid, G., Gil-Garcia, J.R., Luna-Reyes, L.F., Puron-Cid, G., Gil-Garcia, J.R., Luna-Reyes, L.F.: IT-enabled policy analysis: new technologies, sophisticated analysis and open data for better government decisions. In: DG.O, pp. 97–106. ACM (2012)
11. Kum, H.-C., Krishnamurthy, A., Machanavajjhala, A., Ahalt, S.C.: Social genome: putting big data to work for population informatics. Computer **47**, 56–63 (2014)
12. Zeng, D.: Policy informatics for smart policy-making. IEEE Intell. Syst. **30**, 2–3 (2015)
13. Longo, J., Wald, D.M., Hondula, D.M.: The future of policy informatics. In: Johnston, E.W. (ed.) Governance in the Information Era: Theory and Practice of Policy Informatics, pp. 335–352. Routledge, New York (2015)
14. Puron-Cid, G., Ramon Gil-Garcia, J., Luna-Reyes, L.F.: Opportunities and challenges of policy informatics: tackling complex problems through the combination of open data, technology and analytics. Int. J. Public Adm. Digit. Age **3**, 66–85 (2016)
15. Gerring, J., Barresi, P.A.: Putting ordinary language to work: a min-max strategy of concept formation in the social sciences. J. Theor. Polit. **15**, 201–232 (2003)
16. Sartori, G.: Concept misformation in comparative politics. Am. Polit. Sci. Rev. **64**, 1033–1053 (1970)
17. Goertz, G.: Social Science Concepts: A User's Guide. Princeton University Press, Princeton (2006)
18. Petticrew, M., Roberts, H.: How to appraise the studies: an introduction to assessing study quality. Syst. Rev. Soc. Sci. Pract. Guide 125–163 (2006)
19. Albarillo, F.: Language in social science databases: English versus non-English articles in JSTOR and scopus. Behav. Soc. Sci. Libr. **33**, 77–90 (2014)

20. Norris, M., Oppenheim, C.: Comparing alternatives to the web of science for coverage of the social sciences' literature. J. Informetr. **1**, 161–169 (2007)
21. Cavacini, A.: What is the best database for computer science journal articles? Scientometrics **102**, 2059–2071 (2015)
22. Höchtl, J., Parycek, P., Schöllhammer, R.: Big data in the policy cycle: policy decision making in the digital era. J. Organ. Comput. Electron. Commer. **26**, 147–169 (2016)
23. Sandoval-Almazán, R.: Open government and transparency: building a conceptual framework (2015)
24. De Marchi, G., Lucertini, G., Tsoukiàs, A., Marchi, G.De, Lucertini, G., Tsoukiàs, A.: From evidence-based policy making to policy analytics. Ann. Oper. Res. **236**, 15–38 (2016)
25. Daniell, K.A., Morton, A., Insua, D.R.: Policy analysis and policy analytics (2016)
26. Larsson, A., Taylor, S., Wandhöfer, T., Koulolias, V.: Exploiting online data in the policy making process (2015)
27. Tsoukias, A., Montibeller, G., Lucertini, G., Belton, V.: Policy analytics: an agenda for research and practice. EURO J. Decis. Process. **1**, 115–134 (2013)
28. Dreyer, D.R.: Unifying conceptualizations of interstate rivalry: a min–max approach. Coop. Confl. **49**, 501–518 (2014)
29. Scharaschkin, A., McBride, T.: Policy analytics and accountability mechanisms: judging the "value for money" of policy implementation (2016)
30. Barrett, C.L., Eubank, S., Marathe, A., Marathe, M.V., Pan, Z., Swarup, S.: Information integration to support model-based policy informatics. Innov. J. **16** (2011)
31. Henman, P.: e-Government, public policy and the growth of conditionality (2005)
32. Kokkinakos, P., Koussouris, S., Markaki, O.I., Koutras, K., Psarras, J.E., Glickman, Y., Loehe, M., Lee, H.: Open Data Driven Policy Analysis and Impact Evaluation. In: EEPM@eGOV (2015)
33. Tait, E.: Web 2.0 for eParticipation: transformational tweeting or devaluation of democracy? (2013)
34. Charalabidis, Y., Loukis, E.: Participative public policy making through multiple social media platforms utilization. Int. J. Electron. Gov. Res. **8**, 78–97 (2012)
35. Lampe, C., Zube, P., Lee, J., Park, C.H., Johnston, E.: Crowdsourcing civility: a natural experiment examining the effects of distributed moderation in online forums. Gov. Inf. Q. **31**, 317–326 (2014)
36. Johnston, E.: Governance infrastructures in 2020. Public Adm. Rev. **70**, S122–S128 (2010)
37. Kim, Y., McGraw, C.: Use of agent-based modeling for e-governance research. In: ACM International Conference Proceeding Series (2012)
38. Krishnamurthy, R., Desouza, K.C., Johnston, E.W., Bhagwatwar, A.: A glimpse into policy informatics: the case of participatory platforms that generate synthetic empathy. Commun. Assoc. Inf. Syst. **33**, 21 (2013)
39. Wachhaus, T.A.: Governance as a framework to support informatics. Innov. J. **16** (2011)
40. Prpić, J., Taeihagh, A., Melton, J.: The fundamentals of policy crowdsourcing. Policy Internet **7**, 340–361 (2015)
41. Lampe, C., LaRose, R., Steinfield, C., DeMaagd, K.: Inherent barriers to the use of social media for public policy informatics. Innov. J. **16**, 1–17 (2011)
42. Kelley, T.M., Johnston, E.: Discovering the appropriate role of serious games in the design of open governance platforms. Public Adm. Q. **36**, 504–554 (2012)

Critical Reflections

Towards Participatory E-Government?: Learning from E-Government Project Evaluations

Wouter Bronsgeest[1(✉)], Rex Arendsen[2], and Jan van Dijk[1]

[1] Centre for E-Government Studies, University of Twente, Drienerlolaan 5,
7522 NB Enschede, The Netherlands
wl.bronsgeest@belastingdienst.nl, j.a.g.m.vandijk@utwente.nl
[2] Leiden University, Steenschuur 25, 2311 ES Leiden, The Netherlands
r.arendsen@law.leidenuniv.nl

Abstract. The question is whether citizens are sufficiently involved in the development of the facilities used to support e-Government, so they can safeguard the quality of these facilities. It is a relevant issue, as the projects in which these facilities are created often provide insufficient functionality. Based on a sample test, we selected evaluation reports of such projects and studied them based on a perceptual framework. It turns out that e-Government projects have been poorly evaluated and thereby governed. The evaluation governance instruments did not include any participative role of stakeholders. Principles of modern public administration theories are not sufficiently visible within the government in this regard. The quality can be improved substantially by involving representatives of industry and professional organizations, and by introducing co-creation before, during and after completion of projects, as well as during the corresponding evaluations and reflections.

Keywords: E-Governance · Evaluation · New public government

1 Introduction

The government utilizes ICT for several purposes. Naturally, ICT helps in improving the efficiency and effectiveness of executing the internal primary processes within a government organization. For that purpose, government organizations develop their own ICT facilities for their primary and supporting processes, or they purchase those facilities externally. In addition, ICT is essential for a government organization's contact with other government organizations, businesses and citizens. Finally, ICT often connects the interaction of the outside world with the digitalized processes within the government organization. Therefore, ICT is the enabler of e-Government in all three of these previously mentioned domains [7, 30].

E-Government is referred to as the technology-enabled transformation of government, and therefore governments' best hope to reduce costs, whilst promoting economic development, increasing transparency in government, improving service delivery and public administration, and facilitating the advancement of an information society [35].

© IFIP International Federation for Information Processing 2017
Published by Springer International Publishing AG 2017. All Rights Reserved
P. Parycek et al. (Eds.): ePart 2017, LNCS 10429, pp. 127–139, 2017.
DOI: 10.1007/978-3-319-64322-9_11

The purpose of e-Government is thus to work towards a more effective and more efficient government organization by utilizing new technologies and by involving citizens and businesses and, in doing so, listening to their needs [8, 20].

Citizens are therefore 'agents', so to speak, who, together with government representatives, and even together with business representatives, shape the services and processes of the government. This is in line with the principles of New Public Governance (NPG), in which the government is seen as part of a large and synchronized network of parties within society as a whole. It is essential that the interface between society and the total government system works properly, both for the political and the administrative system [20].

When it comes to e-Government, people often refer to e-Participation and, in particular, the various possibilities that this new technology offers [24, 30]. Macintosh [12] argues that e-Participation has several overarching objectives next to these technologies, including engaging a wider audience, and providing relevant information in a format that is both more accessible and more understandable. However, transparency and accountability do not receive as much attention [13]. This article specifically focuses on these issues. In addition to the involvement of citizens in making demands and creating IT facilities for the government, citizens also take on the additional role of monitoring the development process and therefore the quality of the facilities.

The question answered in this article is whether citizens are being sufficiently involved in monitoring the quality of the production processes and the implementation of facilities for e-Government. This would mean that citizens are involved during quality tests and especially during evaluations.

The involvement of citizens is relevant because society is setting increasingly high standards for the government regarding transparency, effectiveness, efficiency, possible influence and services provided [27]. For example, citizens want to know what information about them has been recorded by the government, and they want to know where 'their' tax money went [21]. People want this information to be easily accessible, preferably on a variety of mobile devices [9]. In addition, citizens also want to cooperate and offer their input for the solutions they are getting, an ambition that is in line with the public administrative theory of New Public Governance (NPG).

Safeguarding quality is relevant, because projects used to create IT facilities and the corresponding processes fail on a regular basis. Audits, quality checks and evaluations are subsequently used to see what can be learned from the projects, as well as what went wrong. As a result, a great deal of research has been done into success and fail factors of such ICT projects for both the public and private sectors [28]. These studies indicate that only a third of projects result in the desired end products within the specified time frame and within the budget. A third of the projects is terminated prematurely, and half of all projects end up costing nearly twice as much as was initially projected.

As a result of the disappointing performance of ICT projects within the government, governments focus more on monitoring by third parties. This corresponds to the attention for additional evaluations and audits, which Power and Clarke call the 'audit explosion' within the public domain [3, 22].

However, evaluations of ICT projects and the methods used for those evaluations are often lacking in quality. Nijland [15] states that evaluation methods are lacking in terms of management of costs and benefits of ICT. In the study into aspects of ICT projects within the Dutch government, it turns out that the most important learning experiences are not found in ICT but in related disciplines, in the processes of the organization itself, and in the effect of the organization on its environment – in other words: the business processes and citizens [36].

2   Theoretical Background

In order to better indicate the role of the citizens, the public administrative approach of New Public Governance (NPG) will prove useful. New Public Governance (NPG) is connected to the pluralistic and fragmented complexity of the twenty-first century [16]. While its predecessor, New Public Service (NPS), focuses more on the civilian's role and the optimal performance of the government organization, NPG focuses more on managing the government organization's environment. Through NPG, government managers are asked to manage while directing their attention outside of the organization, and to act in inter-organizational environments.

In addition to collaborating with citizens and offering services to citizens, the focus of NPG is also on negotiation about the added value and the management of networks and mutual relationships. This is in line with the observation that government organizations are starting to turn into network organizations within government organization chains [7], away from the vision that governments should treat citizens more like their customers, and focus on efficiency, effectiveness and economy as the New Public Management used to focus on [10].

The governmental chains exist in order to provide added value to citizens and businesses through products and services [25, 32]. E-Government can facilitate the process by providing full participation by citizens and businesses regarding both the creation and evaluation of the required facilities.

In this study, evaluation reports of IT-projects have been studied, in order to find evidence of citizen involvement in these evaluation. For the definition of evaluation, we chose the definition used by Stufflebeam and Shinkfield [29]: "Evaluation is the systematic assessment of an object's merit, worth, probity, feasibility, safety, significance and/ or equity." The core of this definition in its operationalization is the process-oriented, systematic research approach to evaluation. The definition used by Stufflebeam and Shinkfield [29] mentions a 'systematic assessment', exactly in the same way that Scriven [26] talks about evaluation as "...the process of determining the merit, worth and value of things, and evaluations are the products of that process."

The definitions describe a logical phasing of a number of steps in performing evaluations. In other words, an evaluation with a systematic research approach will follow steps like defining an objective, a problem and a research question, the construction of the theoretical framework, and subsequently defining a type of study, e.g. a descriptive, exploratory or evaluative study. Based on that, a choice will be made as to what population will be studied, and what method of information gathering and data analysis will be used. The final steps of such a study are the report and a phase of evaluation, recommendation and formulating follow-up steps [6].

Because evaluation research is a form of practical research, and because it usually involves a complex problem, an evaluation study will be conducted using an intervention cycle [34]. Such a cycle for evaluation consists of the following steps:

- A *motivation* that leads to performing an evaluation, and from which several concerns for the evaluation arise.
- The *decision* to perform an evaluation. The starting point for the evaluation is the moment the originator decides to have an evaluation performed.
- The *formulation* and *scope* of the evaluation. In doing so, the evaluator lays the foundation for their evaluation study. In the formulation phase, the criteria and substantive requirements to be used as preconditions for the evaluation are formulated as well [23].
- Choosing the *evaluation approach, evaluation type and evaluation techniques*. These are the choices the evaluator makes regarding the research method and approach from a scientific framework.
- *Performing* the evaluation, using the research and evaluation framework.
- *Finalizing* the evaluation. This step focuses on the importance of the end result, the way in which for example the report is handed to the originator of the evaluation, as well as the characteristics of the report [23].
- *Monitoring* the evaluation process as a whole, an activity that is performed during all steps of the evaluation. There is a particular focus on choosing the moment of evaluation and the (role of the) evaluator. This monitoring activity also initiates iterations in the process and the learning circles for the evaluator.

In an overview:

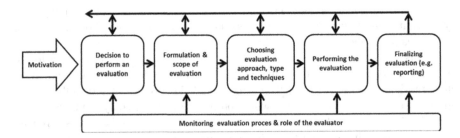

Fig. 1. Evaluation as an iterative process

Every process step comes with iterations during its execution, and iteration may take place after every step leading back to the previous step. The iterations may relate to continuous insight into the evaluation itself ('single loop'), or to the norms, criteria and preconditions within which the evaluation takes place ('double loop'), or to the conditions from the context that affect the evaluation ('triple loop'). With every iteration of this process, the evaluator will consider whether a subsequent step is essential and what changes need to take place.

The process of evaluation has nothing to do with the moment of evaluation: evaluations can take place both ex ante and ex post. The evaluation process can be used at any given time and has its own duration and dynamics. This process is independent from the ICT project being evaluated.

3 Research Method

A meta-evaluation

Citizen involvement is one of the aspects in evaluations of projects with an ICT component within the government. In order to study the overall quality of these evaluations, the evaluation reports of these projects have been studied. Obviously, not everything of value is put in evaluation reports. However, these reports give an indication of the evaluation as carried out. These reports are available upon request and can be studied based on a perceptual framework.

This approach can be more easily repeated as well, making additional and follow-up studies easier to carry out. By studying the evaluation reports, they are effectively subjected to a meta-evaluation. The meta-evaluation features two underlying levels for assessing evaluations:

1. Assessment of the process of the performed evaluation. Examples include the nature of the decision-making process surrounding an evaluation, the assignment description for the evaluation, the design of the evaluation study and the report.
2. Assessing whether the project evaluations meet content quality standards, e.g.:
    (a) Aspects in the process itself, the product resulting from a process, and the way in which people within the ICT project act and collaborate.
    (b) Assessing whether enough attention was paid to the relationship between the project and its environment during the evaluation.

In the study presented here, evaluation reports were requested from government organizations that apply ICT in their organizational processes and services: departments, government organizations that act at the federal level, and large municipalities. The criteria for the selection of the reports for this study are (a) that the reports are publicly available and (b) that the selected reports are about projects with an impact on computerized processes that took place between 2002 and 2010.

The population was determined based on two basic pieces of information. Firstly, the progress reports of large government projects sent to Parliament were studied. These include quality tests and evaluations per department and per project, listed by name. Secondly, an estimation of the possible number of projects was made for non-departmental government organizations and contracting organizations and municipalities, since a population for those could not be determined.

The requesting of these reports was based on a stratified random sample, after which the selected projects were requested. In case only the organizations were known, and not the reports or the projects, we approached the organizations. In these requests, we specifically stated that all reports will be treated confidentially, and that research results cannot be traced back to the report, the project or the organization. In total, this approach resulted in 88 evaluation reports for research purposes.

Assessment framework

In order to study the evaluation reports, specific criteria have been defined for every phase of the defined process (Fig. 1), derived from (a) literature about evaluation, and (b) literature of four related disciplines: (1) administrative and organizational science, (2) behavioural science, (3) accountancy and (IT) auditing, and (4) quality management.

Taken together, these criteria form the foundation of an extensive perceptual framework, consisting of 21 aspects with a variety of focus points. A detailed description of the framework can be found in: Bronsgeest [5]. Some of these focus points are about the extent to which citizens are involved when it comes to safeguarding the quality of the ICT-facilities during their creation.

Content analysis

In order to analyse the selected reports, we carried out a document analysis, using content analysis techniques. Document analysis is "...the techniques used to categorise, investigate, interpret and identify the limitations of physical sources, most commonly written documents whether in the private or public domain" [19]. Document analysis is often seen as a valuable addition to information obtained from interviews, for example, especially when talking about social studies: "In policy research, almost all likely sources of information, data, and ideas fall into two general types: documents and people" [1]. Document analysis can be carried out in multiple ways, namely through analytical reading, content analysis and quantitative analysis [4]. All three of these techniques were used within this study.

Document analysis as applied within this study employs content analysis techniques. With content analysis, the source or text is viewed as a piece of information for drawing conclusions about the meaning of these sources or text within a certain context. Berg [2] uses the following definition of content analysis, derived from Holsti: "Content analysis is any technique for making inferences by systematically and objectively identifying special characteristics of messages." According to Berg, this qualitative definition is broadly applicable on all kinds of written material, spoken material and visual material. Neuendorf [14] uses the term 'content analysis' and adds that the systematic and objective analysis is also quantitative. An objective analysis then becomes possible by determining explicit rules or criteria for the selection of these messages or research subjects before analysing the data [11]. When it comes to these definitions, it is essential for an analysis to be carried out using fixed procedures and methods, and for the approach to be repeatable.

In document analysis and content analysis, there is a methodological difference between manifest and latent content. Manifest content means the elements physically present, that can be observed and counted. Latent content means the interpretation of texts, e.g. its symbolic function or the underlying meaning of texts [2]. In this study's analysis, the manifest content of the evaluation reports was used.

Research approach

For the approach of document analysis, we used the basic model of the scientific method applied for a content analysis approach, as presented by Neuendorf [14]:

1. Determine what content will be analysed. In this study, the 88 evaluation reports.
2. Define and operationalize the variables to be studied. These have been included as focus areas within an operationalized and indexed perceptual framework of 21 focus areas. E-Government features in operationalization in parts, as follows:
   (a) The decision to have an evaluation carried out. The question is whether there is motivation from a political issue, questions from Parliament, or societal attention or unrest.
   (b) Which theoretical framework was used for this evaluation? In other words, are there any indications in the reports for, e.g., elements and instruments of New Public Governance?
   (c) Choosing evaluation techniques: Were approaches such as co-creation, participation taken into account, and were specific tools used to conduct research and to obtain, analyse and structure information?
   (d) The execution of a project, and the extent to which the content was analysed regarding what citizens think considering their participatory role and, if possible, how they affected the (project-oriented) creation, implementation, and monitoring of the projects. Topics such as usability, accessibility and various working methods like panels, sounding boards and design sessions are also part of the process.
3. Sampling of the content. Sampling is the selection of evaluation reports.
4. Train the coder(s). After initial training of the researcher, this was performed by carrying out a pilot of six cases, using a 'convenience selection'. In this pilot, evaluation reports were assessed by the researcher using the perceptual framework. The results were subsequently provided to eight informants for the purpose of assessment and improving reliability.
5. Coding. The researcher then coded the other evaluation reports.
6. Calculating reliability. We started with determining face validity and content validity. This was done by testing the perceptual framework in a workshop with external experts. The experts are people with at least 10 years of experience in both public and private organizations. Additionally, the reliability of the perceptual framework was tested using the intercoder reliability [14]. A person other than the researcher went through two of the cases. The achieved intercoder reliability as a representation of the percentage of similarities (percent agreement, PA_o) was calculated. In the analysis carried out, $PA_o = .76$. The formula for this calculation is as follows:

$$PA_0 = A/n$$

where A is the number of similarities between the coders and n is the total number of components coded by the coders.

7. Tabulation and reports. This was done in the form of the doctoral thesis and various articles.

4 Results

The results of the 88 meta-evaluations provide insight into the extent to which citizens are involved in the evaluation of e-Government projects, and to what extent the approach chosen facilitated this.

Decision-making process
Regarding the decision-making surrounding an evaluation, it is clear that many reports are not compiled with a political motive or a motive from within the organization itself. Many reports have a content-oriented motivation, and the decision to have an evaluation carried out was made in only 35 out of 88 reports. The role of the citizen in this decision-making process, e.g. as the person requesting an evaluation through representatives, social institution or lobby, could not be demonstrated. The relationship between the project and the outside world is limited, as the results show:

- In 83 out of 88 reports, there is no political issue, and no relationship with a political or social development was described.
- In 19 out of 88 reports, the evaluation was carried out because an audit plan was drafted within the organization, or because agreements were made for carrying out an evaluation prior to the project.
- For 12 out of 88 reports, we can see that the project featured an independent decision to have an evaluation carried out. This happened in the final stages of the project in all cases, in order to demonstrate the project results. Of the 12 times that a project was evaluated independently, there were indications on four occasions that the goal of doing so was to learn from the project.

Theoretical basis
Regarding the theoretical framework used, concepts of recent public administrative theories are virtually absent in evaluation reports. Elements such as (parts of) a network approach and attention for the projects' environments are featured in a very limited fashion. Stakeholder management is present in a very limited fashion and, if it is present, it mainly focuses on the stakeholders within a government organization. Broad attention to the organization's objectives in relation to the (social) environment could not be demonstrated in the evaluation reports reviewed. This means that, as expected, we did not find any evidence for the application of elements of New Public Governance (NPG), even though the reports were compiled in a period in which such elements could be reasonably assumed to have been fairly well known within the government.

Method of evaluation
In addition to the research approach, another point to consider in addition to the research approach is which of the techniques used for data collection and data analysis to use in

the research design. E-Participation was not used, but other techniques were. The most important techniques used were:

- In 48 out of 88 reports, interviews with individuals of (and surrounding) the project were conducted.
- In 33 out of 88 reports, a document study was carried out. In 32 situations, this happened prior to the interviews.
- In 19 out of 88 reports, group sessions were held in the form of focus groups (5), workshops (6) or group discussions (8).
- In 10 out of 88 evaluations, questionnaires were used.

Demands of citizens

In the meta-evaluation, we looked into whether evaluation reports paid attention to the extent to which the project itself looked at what citizens thought of it from their participatory role. No evidence was found: regarding the collection of demands of citizens and businesses, no framework was included in the reviewed evaluation reports. In the project evaluations, attention to topics like usability or accessibility, or the desires and demands of citizens regarding the internal processes and facilities of the government was seldom paid.

Degree of influence of citizens

Very little evidence was found regarding the opportunities citizens have to affect both the (project-oriented) creation, implementation and monitoring of the projects in the evaluation reports. Focus on various working methods, such as citizen panels, sounding board and design sessions in evaluations was not found. References to e-Government and supporting means to realize it are not mentioned in the evaluations either.

Service provision to citizens

Improved service to citizens was featured as a result to be evaluated in only five of the evaluation reports. In 13 evaluation reports, it was mentioned that the organization within which the project is positioned has a core task in the area of improved service provision to citizens. A core task from the organization gives projects some direction. The presence of a clear core task should therefore be studied in the evaluation. However, our study shows that evaluations of projects pay very little attention to it. As a result, this focus area is difficult to measure and demonstrate in the evaluations.

5 Conclusions

The focus of many evaluations follows the lines of Administrative Theory [17]. The central focus is on the idea of the government as an efficient organization, with hierarchical management and strong administrative management of responsibilities and authorizations. The corresponding evaluations are traditional in their approach and execution. The 88 evaluations we studied have a signature 'inside-in' or 'inside-out' approach. No evidence for an explicit 'outside-in' view for decision-making was found. Political issues or a clear connection to a social development were hardly found at all.

Our conclusion, therefore, is that the majority of the reports have more of an inward focus regarding the decision-making process surrounding evaluations, and consequently do not focus on the involvement of citizens, or their explicit desires and needs.

Additionally, we found little to no evidence in the studied evaluation reports of (elements of) a network approach and attention for the projects' environments. These are all important aspects of New Public Governance (NPG). Stakeholder management is present in a very limited fashion as an evaluation topic and, if it is present, it mainly focuses on the stakeholders within a government organization. Through NPG, government managers are asked to manage while directing their attention outside of the organization, and to act in inter-organizational environments. In addition to collaborating with citizens and offering services to citizens, the focus is also on negotiation about the added value and the management of networks and the mutual relationships.

As a result, and as expected, we found no evidence for the application of elements from New Public Governance (NPG). Elements of New Public Service (NPS) could not be found either, despite the fact that this public administrative movement has existed for a long time. The role of the citizen as a 'civilian', and issues like co-creation with the outside world, are not a topic of discussion in evaluations.

E-Participation also requires a different working method from government organizations. It was barely observed at all in the study. For example, citizens can offer their input and cooperate during the process of determining demands regarding IT facilities, or they may be involved during the creation process.

In addition, it is conceivable that citizens also play a bigger role in monitoring or even evaluating such projects. There are various intervention moments and techniques that can be used during such a process. Some working methods include requirements engineering, user tests and other types of input like expert opinions. Additionally, there are instruments for e-Participation, including methods to maintain contact with citizens, industry associations, professional organizations and knowledge institutes via the internet and other social media.

The general conclusion is therefore twofold. Firstly, the role citizens play in creating ICT facilities, though the means available to them via e-Participation, is limited. Citizens are not involved in the beginning, during, or after the completion of projects. Citizens are only involved in a limited number of usability tests, or in a campaign for the introduction of a new process or product.

Secondly, the question as to whether citizens are sufficiently involved in monitoring and evaluating the quality of the creation processes and the implementation of facilities for e-Government remains unanswered. This topic was not discussed in the evaluations reviewed. Monitoring projects, from the perspective of retrospective monitoring (i.e. not working with learning and looking forward in mind), is most common in the evaluations.

6   Recommendations and Discussion

Our most important recommendation to quickly improve evaluations from an e-Participation perspective is to start with the so-called low hanging fruit. That is to say, issues that can be targeted quickly and easily, and that can be solved to create short-term improvements. Within the government, for instance, an idea would be to direct attention outward in addition to directing it inward, e.g. by hiring professionals from government networks, industry and consumer organizations and professional organizations to obtain different viewpoints and better and broader input in projects and evaluations.

We also recommend using modern and creative working methods to involve project staff and citizens in evaluations. A lot of experience was gained regarding co-creation, and there are ample opportunities to use ICT applications and social media, both inside and outside of government organizations, to involve the various stakeholders and users. These are the forms of e-Participation that are clearly visible within the European and international context [18]. This is about involving people who work with the government's new ICT systems, as well as the citizens and businesses that experience the effects of government actions.

The application of evaluation in which citizens play a role (e-Evaluation) offers additional benefits. Since evaluations can be carried out more easily with modern electronic participatory means, is will become more easy to execute evaluations during different project stages. In addition, by using the resources of e-Government, boundaries of social status, position and area of expertise disappear. Everybody can be involved and can participate in evaluations, adding new insights and feedback. Even when disregarding the discussion of whether everyone has sufficient access to the digital channels provided by the government, participatory evaluation would be an improvement over the current method of evaluation.

Finally, the use of e-Evaluation could also result in a shift in the way in which the government executes projects. From the perspective of NPS and NPG, these projects use involved citizens before and during the project, as well as during the evaluation of said projects. Firstly, this results in different products for the purpose of interacting with citizens and businesses. And secondly, it results in a different way of implementing ICT products and related processes in the government organization and people using the ICT products [31]. This is also in line with the changes in project management and the way these projects create solutions for a variety of facilities: they are becoming increasingly multidisciplinary and agile [33]. This is exactly the type of approach where more intense involvement of citizens in drafting demands and monitoring quality is appropriate.

The study into the evaluation of projects with an ICT component within the government indicates, that the execution of projects *and* project evaluations in collaboration with citizens occurred infrequently, and that there is still much room for improvement in many aspects.

References

1. Bardach, E.: A Practical Guide for Policy Analysis, the Eightfold Path to More Effective Problem Solving, 3rd edn. CQ Press, Washington (2009)
2. Berg, B.L.: Quantative Research Methods for the Social Sciences. Allyn and Bacon, An Pearson Education Company, Boston (2001)
3. Bovaird, T., Löffler, E.: Public Management and Governance, 2nd edn. Routledge, Oxon (2009)

4. Bowen, G.A.: Document analysis as a qualitative research method. Qual. Res. J. **9**(2), 27–40 (2009)
5. Bronsgeest, W.L.: Meer vorm dan inhoud, Onderzoek naar evaluaties van ICT-projecten bij de overheid. Universiteit Twente, Enschede (2016)
6. Creswell, J.W.: Research design. In: Qualitative, Quantitative, and Mixed Methods Approaches, 3rd edition, Sage Publications Inc., London (2009)
7. Eggers, W.D.: Government 2.0. Rowman & Littlefield publishers Inc., Lanham (2007)
8. European Union (EU): Policy Department for Citizens', Potential and Challenges of e-Participation in the European Union (2016)
9. Hinssen, P.: The Network Always Wins, How to Survive in the Age of Uncertainty. Mach Media, Belgium (2014)
10. Hood, C.: The 'New Public Management' in the 1980s: variations on a theme. Acc. Organ. Soc. **20**(2/3), 93–109 (1995)
11. Krippendorff, K.: Content Analysis, an Introduction to Its Methodology, 3rd edn. Sage, Los Angeles (2013)
12. Macintosch, A.: Characterizing e-participation in policy-making. In: Proceedings of the 37th Hawaii International Conference on System Sciences (2004)
13. Mahmood, Z. (ed.): Developing E-Government Projects: Frameworks and Methodologies. Information Science Reference/IGI Global, Hershey (2013)
14. Neuendorf, K.A.: The Content Analysis Guidebook. Sage Publications, Thousand Oaks, California (2002)
15. Nijland, M.H.J.: Understanding the use of IT evaluation methods in organisations. London School of Economics (2004)
16. Osborne, S.D. (ed.): The New Public Governance? Emerging Perspectives on the Theory and Practice of Public Governance. Routledge, New York (2010)
17. Osland, J.S., Kolb, D.A., Rubin, I.M., Turner, M.E.: Organizational Behaviour, an Experimental Apporoach, 8th edn. Person International Edition, Upper Saddle River (2007)
18. Panopoulou, E., Tambouris, E., Tarabanis, K.: eParticipation initiatives: how is Europe progressing? Eur. J. ePractice, March 2009
19. Payne, G., Payne, J.: Key Concepts in Social Research. Sage Publications, London (2004)
20. Peristeras, V., Mentzas, G., Tarabanis, K.A., Abecker, A.: Transforming E-government and E-participation through IT. IEEE Intell. Syst. IEEE Comput. Soc. **24**, 1541–1672 (2009)
21. Pieterson, W.: Chanel Choice, Citizen' Behaviour and Public Service Channel Strategy. Universiteit Twente, Enschede (2009)
22. Power, M.: The Audit Explosion. Demos, UK (1999)
23. Russ-Eft, D., Preskill, H.: Evaluation in Organizations, a Systematic Approach to Enhancing Learning, Performance, and Change, 2nd edn. Basic Books, New York (2009)
24. Scholl, H.J., Janssen, M., Wimmer, M.A., Moe, C.E., Flak, L.S. (eds.): EGOV 2012. LNCS, vol. 7443. Springer, Heidelberg (2012). doi:10.1007/978-3-642-33489-4
25. Scott, W.R., Davis, G.F.: Organizations and Organizing, Rational, Natural, and Open System Perspectives. Pearson International Edition, Upper Saddle River (2007)
26. Scriven, M.: Evaluation Thesaurus, 4th edn. Sage Publications, Newbury Park (1991)
27. Smith, S., Dalakiouridou, E.: Contextualising public (e)Participation in the governance of the European Union. Eur. J. ePractice **7**, 47–50 (2009)
28. Standish Group International: The Winning Hand. Standish Group Int. Inc., Boston (2016)
29. Stufflebeam, D.L., Shinkfield, A.J.: Evaluation, Theory. Models & Applications, Jossey-Bass, San Francisco (2007)
30. Tambouris, E., Macintosh, A., Sæbø, Ø. (eds.): ePart 2012. LNCS, vol. 7444. Springer, Heidelberg (2012). doi:10.1007/978-3-642-33250-0

31. Tapscott, D., Williams, A.D.: Wikinomics, How Mass Collaboration Changes Everything. Penguin Group, Portfolio Series, New York (2007)
32. Tosi, H.L.: Theories of Organization. Sage Publications, Thousand Oaks (2008)
33. Unhelkar, B.: The art of Agile Practice, a composite approach for projects and organizations. CRC Press, Taylor & Francis Group, Auerbach Book, Boca Raton (2013)
34. Verschuren, P., Doorewaard, H.: Designing a Research Project, 2nd edn. Eleven International Publishing, The Hague (2010)
35. Worldbank: http://www.worldbank.org/en/topic/ict/brief/e-gov-resources#egov. Accessed 28 Apr 2017
36. WRR (Wetenschappelijke Raad voor het Regeringsbeleid): iOverheid. Amsterdam University Press, Den Haag/Amsterdam (2011)

Open Innovation and Co-creation in the Public Sector: Understanding the Role of Intermediaries

Mila Gasco-Hernandez[1](✉) [iD], Rodrigo Sandoval-Almazan[2] [iD],
and J. Ramon Gil-Garcia[1] [iD]

[1] Center for Technology in Government, University at Albany, Albany, USA
{mgasco,jgil-garcia}@ctg.albany.edu
[2] Universidad Autonoma Del Estado de Mexico, Toluca, Mexico
rsandovala@uaemex.mx

Abstract. Innovation is a recurring theme in public administration. Governments around the world are always exploring innovation alternatives. However, the way public organizations innovate has evolved in the last few years from "in-house" innovation to open innovation. Although the literature is rich in references to innovation in the private sector, how open innovation processes can become a true and effective tool for governments is still an underexplored topic. The few studies that have tackled it have mainly addressed one main question: how can a successful private sector practice be introduced in public sector organizations? In contrast, this paper aims at making a contribution to the existing literature on open innovation in the public sector by addressing one issue that is key in open innovation processes: the role of intermediaries. Intermediaries are important actors in the open innovation ecosystem as they facilitate activities in all stages of the innovation process and help government agencies to achieve their goals.

Keywords: Open innovation · Co-creation · Intermediaries · I-labs · Living labs

1 Introduction

Innovation is a recurring theme in public administration. It has been used to frame the transformation of public sector organizations in order to enhance the effectiveness, efficiency, and legitimacy of their public value creation processes [9]. As needs of citizens are changing, and technology is advancing, there is an immense need for innovation in the public sector. On one hand, citizens have higher expectations about public services and government interventions. On the other, public managers and elected politicians have growing ambitions concerning improved public governance mechanisms and tighter control. Finally, public tasks have become more and more complex and have developed into "tangled problems" or even "wicked problems" – problems that are often too difficult to be solved by a single entity and include many different layers of complexity [40].

Although innovation is not a new concept in the public sector [7, 17], the way public administrations have innovated throughout time has evolved, coinciding with different

P. Parycek et al. (Eds.): ePart 2017, LNCS 10429, pp. 140–148, 2017.
DOI: 10.1007/978-3-319-64322-9_12

waves of administrative reforms [37]. According to [32], public sector innovations can be the result of internal innovation processes (which are policy-induced and use employees' suggestions), externalized innovation processes (which depend on contractors and adapt to industry standards), and open innovation processes (which are based on crowdsourcing and involve external professional and amateur problem solvers).

Although the literature is rich in references to innovation in the private sector, how open innovation processes can become a true and effective tool for governments is still an underexplored topic [6, 20, 33]. Only recently such approach has been seen in research into public sector innovation [18].

Most of the studies that have addressed open innovation in the public sector have focused on drivers of adoption, success factors, and innovation outcomes (among other, [6, 10, 19, 20, 22, 23, 29, 33–35]). However, there is not enough research that specifically refers to public sector open innovation intermediaries and explores their role in innovation processes in the public sector [6].

Based on a review of recent literature, this paper proposes a government open innovation framework, which explicitly acknowledge the role of intermediaries. It analyzes theories and concepts of open innovation in the public sector and contributes to the public sector innovation literature by analyzing the role of intermediaries in open innovation processes that take place in the public sector.

The paper is organized in four sections, including the foregoing introduction. Section two presents the concept of open innovation and analyzes how it has been implemented in the public sector. The type and role of intermediaries in (public) open innovation processes is explained in section three. Finally, section four provides some conclusions and suggests ideas for further research on open innovation processes in the public sector.

2   Open Innovation

Open innovation is a term that was coined in the private sector. [12] defines open innovation as "the use of purposive inflows and outflows of knowledge to accelerate internal innovation, and expand the markets for external use of innovation, respectively" (p. 1). He actually sets open innovation in opposition to closed innovation [12, 13]. Regarding the latter, he states that "successful innovation requires control. In other words, companies must generate their own ideas that they would then develop, manufacture, market, distribute and service themselves (…). This approach calls for self-reliance: If you want something done right, you've got to do it yourself" ([13]: 36). At the same time, the author defines open innovation as a strategy by which firms commercialize external (as well as internal) ideas by deploying outside (as well as in-house) pathways to the market: "specifically, companies can commercialize internal ideas through channels outside of their current businesses in order to generate value for the organization (…) In addition, ideas can also originate outside the firm's own labs and be brought inside for commercialization. In other words, the boundary a firm and its surrounding environment is more porous, enabling innovation to move easily between the two" ([13]: 37).

[14] confirm the growth of academic research in the domain of open innovation. The authors present the fields in which open innovation has attracted most attention:

management, business, industrial engineering, operations research and management science, and planning and development. However, out of 1,965 articles, [14] only find 14 related to public administration, what leads the authors to insist on the opportunities of open innovation in the public sector as well as on the need to formulate public policies that support open innovation in a given society.

[34] shows that implementing open innovation methodologies in the public sector can indeed have myriad positive benefits, including improved awareness of social problems, more effective practices based on broad citizen experience, and increased trust between government and citizens. However, open innovation approaches in the private sector are context dependent: they cannot readily be transferred to the public sector [31, 34]. Consequently, the implementation of open innovation in the public sector needs to take the unique characteristics of the sector into consideration.

In the public sector, open innovation has inspired the concept of collaborative innovation: collaborative processes and interactions between internal and external stakeholders can spur innovation in the public sector and help find innovative solutions to complex problems. Therefore, collaborative innovation could have similar benefits as open innovation. However, although it is thought as happening across organizational boundaries, it is also inside government.

From a more practical point of view, most research on open innovation in the public sector has focused on open government and open data initiatives (among other, [11, 14, 27, 28, 33, 35, 45]). In these studies, open innovation has been conceptualized as a paradigm to move from closed organizations to open, transparent, and collaborative ones. Authors have therefore seen the potential of open data/open government projects, often based on prizes and contests that use online open innovation platforms, to boost open innovation in the public sector.

However, to realize the practical benefits of this transformative practice and to develop theory, still, more research needs to focus on understanding how innovation occurs through open data activities [45] but, also, on exploring additional topics that can make a contribution to the literature on open innovation in the public sector. It is necessary to go beyond open government and open data and focus on open innovation as the main topic and consider all the different examples or types of open innovation in the public sector. It also seems important to understand the role of different actors in the open innovation ecosystem.

3   Open Innovation Intermediaries in the Public Sector

In their review, [14] list some of the main themes that have emerged in the literature on open innovation. The innovation process is by far the most researched topic, followed by strategy, product development, and toolkit/users: "based on our analysis, we find that a large amount of research investigates the outside-in (inbound) side of open innovation. This research deals with how firms can leverage external knowledge and technology to accelerate internal innovation" (p. 8). Interestingly enough, the authors find several references to collaboration with intermediaries.

Innovation intermediaries can be defined as external organizations and individuals that support companies in their innovative activities by gathering, developing, controlling and disseminating external knowledge by providing various resources and regulating the innovation networks [6, 25].

[12] mentions that intermediaries can operate in different ways: some function as agents (representing one side of a transaction) and others as brokers (representing both sides of a transaction). More precise is [24] who considers the following roles of intermediaries in the private sector: (1) to help to facilitate internal and external technology commercialization, (2) to connect innovation seekers to innovation providers, (3) to help companies to screen external markets, (4) to understand the technology market better, (5) to make searching tasks easier for companies, (6) to reduce search cost of the companies, and (7) to in-license, co-develop and acquire external intellectual properties or technologies. Along the same lines, [30] indicates that innovation intermediaries have, indeed, a variety of profiles and functions that might be grouped under three general headings: connection, collaboration and support, and provision of technological services.

However, [24] also argues that the role of intermediaries is not just to link different parties, a commonly held belief, but also to search and transform ideas and provide personalized solutions that fit to individual clients. He also adds that intermediaries such as Yet2.com, Ninesigma, Innocentive, and IdeaConnection have changed the innovation spectrum dramatically giving rise to new industries.

The literature reveals a wide variety of innovation intermediaries [25] that range from public and private incubators to technological top institutes and, more recently, to living labs [1, 2, 6]. Most of these intermediaries have collaborated with private rather than public organizations [6].

Although in the context of private open innovation management, the role of intermediaries has been investigated thoroughly (among other, [3, 21, 25, 44]), there is not enough research that specifically refers to public sector open innovation intermediaries and explores their role in innovation processes in the public sector [6].

According to [6], public open innovation intermediaries can be understood as "public or private organizations that intermediate between city halls and other organizations" (p. 312). Building on this meaning and on the works of [5, 42], in this paper, we contribute a more elaborated definition that understands open innovation intermediaries as public and private organizations that intermediate between local/regional/national governments and other organizations and individuals with the purpose of enhancing public sector innovation capacity by means of applying open innovation methodologies: knowledge exchange, co-creation techniques and participatory methods.

Thus, intermediaries are important in at least two ways. First, they help to enhance government capabilities for open innovation. Second, they link governments with their context, including people and organizations that can contribute to their innovation efforts. Additionally, the concept also helps to focus the study of open government innovation on the actors involved and the role each of them plays in the innovation process. In sum, understanding the role of intermediaries contributes to the theory and practice of open innovation in the public sector.

The literature reveals two main types of public open innovation intermediary organizations: innovation labs and living labs.

Innovation labs, or i-labs, are seen as experimental forms of government acting as innovation catalysts [15]. [41] refer to them as experimental organizations, that is, spaces within the public sector to experiment and take risks. They are usually peripheral, agile, and smaller and operate under different rules than typical civil service organizations. Mindlab in Denmark and Nesta in the UK are examples of i-labs: "these are small organizations with low funding levels and diverse sources of funding, and they are typically engaged in short term projects and relatively removed from political leadership" [26].

There is very little research on public sector innovation labs beyond descriptive, and at times normative, overviews. In an attempt to bridge this gap, [41] analyzed 35 such organizations all over the world and concluded that:

- "I-labs were created to enable cross-disciplinary and citizen-driven approaches, while at the same time they produce most of their work for or with the ministerial departments and other government agencies" (p. 13).
- "I-labs are rather unique organizations and diverse in their mission, expected to act as change agents within public sector and enjoy large autonomy in setting their targets and working methods" (p. 21).
- "I-labs are typically structurally separated from the rest of the public sector and expected to be able to attract external funding as well as "sell" their ideas and solutions within the public sector" (p. 21).
- "I-labs tend to be small structures, specializing on quick experimentations and usually lack the capabilities and authority to significantly influence upscaling of new solutions or processes" (p. 21).
- "The main capabilities of i-labs are their ability to jump-start or show case user-driven service re-design projects" (p. 21).
- ICT play a central role in i-labs. "Many of the tasks i-labs carry out are directly or indirectly related to developing ICT-based solutions for the citizens as well as public sector" (p. 22).

Living labs are settings or environments for open innovation, which offer a collaborative platform for research, development, and experimentation with product and service innovations in real-life contexts, based on specific methodologies and tools, and implemented through specific innovation projects and community-building activities [38]. In living labs, different stakeholders (firms, public organizations, individual citizens, and researchers, among other) interact and collaborate in innovation processes.

Living labs are therefore conceived as a strategic opportunity to improve the creation of multi-stakeholder partnerships with citizens at the center. As a result, they have often been defined as public, private and people partnerships (PPPP) for user-driven open innovation [36]. Along the same lines, [16] state that living labs are increasingly well-established innovation intermediaries that support the implementation of the quadruple helix model, an innovation approach based on cooperation between firms, universities, public organizations and users [4].

[39] identifies two types of living labs: those focused on supporting companies and creating an ecosystem of innovation that benefits both private companies and public

organizations and those focused on opening innovation processes to citizens (the so-called citizen labs).

Citizen labs, such as the Mexican PIDES Innovación Social and Laboratorio para la Ciudad (LabCdMX), have become particularly popular in Latin America as spaces for citizen innovation that pay special attention to the democratization of innovation [43]. Their exponential growth has come hand in hand with the idea that public innovation has to be social innovation [8], and therefore has to (1) produce long lasting outcomes that are relevant, given the needs and challenges of different groups in society, (2) aim at changing the social relationships and the governance among the involved stakeholders, (3) involve relevant stakeholders in the design, implementation or adoption of an innovation, which corresponds to the notion of open innovation, and (4) see the process of innovation as a learning and reflection process.

Table 1 summarizes the main differences and similarities between i-labs and living labs.

Table 1. Differences and similarities between i-labs and living labs as open innovation intermediaries.

	Innovation labs	Living labs
Operation	Operate autonomously but inside government	Operate autonomously outside government
Funding	Mainly public-funded	Several sources of funding
Type of innovation	Public innovation	Social innovation
Main beneficiary	Government is the main beneficiary	Several beneficiaries: universities, public organizations, private companies, citizens (quadruple helix model)
Methods	Experimentation, co-creation and open innovation methodologies	Experimentation, co-creation and open innovation methodologies

Despite the identification of different open innovation intermediaries in the public sector, many research questions remain unanswered: what is the specific role of these intermediaries in public innovation processes? How do they implement open innovation methodologies? What is the contribution of different public open innovation intermediaries to innovation outcomes? And, what determines these outcomes in the context of organizational intermediaries? It is therefore a necessary and interesting task to understand and compare the dynamics and contribution to public innovation of both i-labs and living labs.

4   Concluding Remarks

The purpose of this paper is to better understand open innovation in the public sector and the role of intermediaries. Based on this, this paper provides the following contributions:

- It collects and organizes the existing research about open innovation and open innovation intermediaries in the private and public sectors.
- It highlights the importance of open innovation intermediaries.
- It proposes a concept of open innovation intermediaries for the public sector.
- It identifies the characteristics of open innovation intermediaries.
- It considers the characteristics and challenges of the public sector context in terms of innovation.

After this review of previous studies, this paper provides a definition and some ideas for future research regarding open innovation in the public sector. Many interesting activities are happening in living labs and innovation labs that could improve our understanding of the role of intermediaries. We recognize that much is still needed in terms of empirical research about this topic. However, our aim with this paper is to start a discussion about this broad theme and call the attention of other researchers interested in open government innovation from multiple disciplines.

As mentioned before, open innovation intermediaries are currently working with governments around the world in diverse projects and through different methodologies and activities. More research is needed to understand this emerging phenomenon that links public and private sector organizations around innovation to generate value for citizens. In addition, open government innovation needs to be studied using different theoretical lenses and disciplinary perspectives. This will help to create an integrated view that helps government and citizens to face, and potentially solve, complex public problems.

References

1. Almirall, E., Wareham, J.: Living labs: arbiters of mid- and ground-level innovation. Technol. Anal. Strateg. Manag. **23**(1), 87–102 (2011)
2. Almirall, E., Wareham, J.: Living labs and open innovation: roles and applicability. Electron. J. Virt. Organ. Netw. **10** (2008)
3. Amico-Roxas, S., Piroli, G., Sorrentino, M.: Efficiency and evaluation analysis of a network of technology transfer brokers. Technol. Anal. Strateg. Manag. **23**(1), 7–24 (2011)
4. Arnkil, R., Järvensivu, A., Koski, P., Piirainen, T.: Exploring quadruple helix. Outlining user-oriented innovation models. University of Tampere – Institute for Social Research – Work Research Centre, Tampere (2010)
5. Baccarne, B., Mechant, P., Schuurman, D.: Empowered cities? An analysis of the structure and generated value of the smart city Ghent. In: Dameri, R.P., Rosenthal-Sabroux, C. (eds.) Smart City. PI, pp. 157–182. Springer, Cham (2014). doi:10.1007/978-3-319-06160-3_8
6. Bakici, T., Almirall, E., Wareham, J.: The role of public open innovation intermediaries in local government and the public sector. Technol. Anal. Strateg. Manag. **25**(3), 311–327 (2013)

7. Bason, C.: Powering European Public Sector Innovation: Towards a New Architecture. Publications Office of the European Union, Luxembourg (2013)

8. Bekers, V., Tummers, L., Voornerg, W.: From public innovation to social innovation in the public sector: a literature review of relevant drivers and barriers. Paper presented at the 2013 EGPA Conference. Edinburgh, 11–13 September 2013

9. Bekkers, V.J.J.M., Edelenbos, J., Steijn, B.: Linking innovation to the public sector: contexts, concepts and challenges. In: Bekkers, V.J.J.M., Edelenbos, J., Steijn, B. (eds.) Innovation in the public sector. Linking capacity and leadership (Governance and Public Management, 6), pp. 3–34. Plagrave McMillan, Houndsmills (2011)

10. Bommert, B.: Collaborative innovation in the public sector. Int. Public Manag. Rev. **11**(1), 15–33 (2010)

11. Chan, C.M.L.: From open data to open innovation strategies: creating e-services using open government data. In: Proceedings of the 46th Hawaii International Conference on System Sciences, pp. 1890–1899. IEEE, Los Alamitos (2013)

12. Chesbrough, H.: Open innovation: the new imperative from creating and profiting from technology. Harvard Business School Press, Boston (2006)

13. Chesbrough, H.: The era of open innovation. MIT Sloan Manag. Rev. **44**(3), 35–41 (2003)

14. Chesbrough, H.W., Bogers, M.: Explicating open innovation: clarifying an emerging paradigm for understanding innovation. In: Chesbrough, H., Vanhaverbeke, W., West, J. (eds.) New Frontiers in Open Innovation, pp. 3–28. Oxford University Press, Oxford (2014)

15. Christiansen, J., Bason, C.: Profile of the public sector lab. Økonomistyring Informatik **26**(4), 323–348 (2011)

16. Cleland, B., Mulvenna, M., Galbraith, B., Wallace, J., Martin, S.: Innovation of e-participation strategies using living labs as intermediaries. Electron. J. e-Government **10**(2), 120–132 (2010)

17. Daglio, M., Gerson, D., Kitchen, H.: Building organisational capacity for public sector innovation. Paper presented at the OECD Conference "Innovating the Public Sector: From Ideas to Impact". Paris, 12–13 November 2014

18. De Vries, H., Bekkers, V., Tummers, L.: Innovation in the public sector: a systematic review and future research agenda. Public Adm. **94**(1), 146–166 (2016)

19. Dias, C., Escoval, A.: The open nature of innovation in the hospital sector: the role of external collaboration networks. Health Policy Technol. **1**(4), 181–186 (2012)

20. Feller, J., Finnegan, P., Nilsson, O.: Open innovation and public administration: transformational typologies and business model impacts. Eur. J. Inf. Syst. **20**, 358–374 (2011)

21. Füzi, A.: Quadruple helix and its types as user-driven innovation models. Paper presented at the Triple Helix International Conference 2013, London, 7–10 July 2013

22. Hennala, L., Parjanen, S., Uotila, T.: Challenges of multi-actor involvement in the public sector front-end innovation processes: constructing an open innovation model for developing well-being services. Eur. J. Innov. Manag. **14**(3), 364–387 (2011)

23. Hilgers, D., Ihl, C.: Applying the concept of open innovation to the public sector. Int. J. Public Participation **4**(1), 67–88 (2010)

24. Hossain, M.: Performance and potential of open innovation intermediaries. Procedia Soc. Behav. Sci. **58**, 754–764 (2012)

25. Howells, J.: Intermediation and role of intermediaries in innovation. Res. Policy **35**, 715–728 (2006)

26. Kattel, R., Karo, E.: Start-up governments, or can bureaucracies innovate? Blog of the Institute for New Economic Thinking. https://www.ineteconomics.org/perspectives/blog/start-up-governments-or-can-bureaucracies-innovate. Accessed 17 May 2017

27. Lakomaa, E., Kalberg, J.: Open data as a foundation for innovation: The enabling effect of free public sector information for entrepreneurs. IEEE Access. **1**, 558–562 (2013)
28. Lee, M., Almirall, E., Wareham, J.: Open data and civic apps: First-generation failures, second-generation improvements. Commun. ACM **59**(1), 82–89 (2016)
29. Lee, S.M., Hwang, T., Choi, D.: Open innovation in the public sector of leading countries. Manag. Decis. **50**(1), 147–162 (2012)
30. López-Vega, H.: Open innovation. Organizational practices and policy implications. ESADE Business & Law School, Barcelona (2012). Unpublished doctoral thesis
31. Louis, C., Mergel, I., Bretschneider, S., Smith, J.: Crowdsourcing policy innovations using Challenge.gov. Paper presented at the Public Management Research Conference, Madison, WI, 20–22 June 2013
32. Mergel, I.: Open innovation in the public sector. Paper presented at the 2015 International Summer School, Snekkersten, 30 June 2015a
33. Mergel, I.: Opening government. Designing open innovation processes to collaborate with external problem solvers. Soc. Sci. Comput. Rev. **33**(5), 599–612 (2015)
34. Mergel, I.: Implementing open innovation in the public sector: the case of Challenge.gov. Public Adm. Rev. **73**(6), 882–890 (2013)
35. Mergel, I., Desouza, K.: Implementing open innovation in the public sector: the case of Challenge.gov. Public Adm. Rev. **73**(6), 882–890 (2013)
36. Nesti, G.: Urban living labs as a new form of co-production. Insights from the European experience. Paper presented at ICPP - International Conference on Public Policy II. Milan, 1–4 July 2015
37. Osborne, S., Strokosch, K.: It takes two to tango? Understanding the co-production of public services by integrating the services management and public administration perspectives. Br. J. Manag. **24**(S1), S31–S47 (2013)
38. Schaffers, H., Turkama, P.: Living labs for cross-border systemic innovation. Technology Innovation Management Review, 25–30 September issue 2012
39. Serra, A.: Tres problemas sobre los laboratorios ciudadanos. Una mirada desde Europa. Revista Iberoamericana de Ciencia, Tecnología y Sociedad **8**(23), 283–298 (2013)
40. Sørensen, E., Torfing, J.: Collaborative innovation in the public sector: an analytical framework. Working paper no. 1/2010. Working Paper Series: Studies in Collaborative Innovation (2010)
41. Tonurist, P., Kattel, R., Lember, V.: Discovering innovation labs in the public sector. Working paper no. 61. Working Papers in Technology Governance and Economic Dynamics 82015
42. Vicini, S., Bellini, S., Sanna, A.: The city of the future living lab. Int. J. Autom. Smart Technol. **2**(3), 201–208 (2012)
43. Von Hippel, E.: Democratizing innovation. The MIT Press, Cambridge (2005)
44. Winch, G., Courtney, R.: The organization of innovation brokers: an international review. Technol. Anal. Strateg. Manag. **19**(6), 747–763 (2007)
45. Zuiderwijk, A., Helbig, N., Gil-Garcia, R., Janssen, M.: Special issue on innovation through open data - a review of the state-of-the-art and an emerging research agenda: guest editors' introduction. J. Theor. Appl. Electron. Commer. Res. **9**(2), 1–8 (2014)

Tensions in Online Communities: The Case of a Mass Size eParticipation Initiative

Alessio Maria Braccini[1], Tommaso Federici[1], and Øystein Sæbø[2(✉)]

[1] Department of Economics and Entrepreneurship,
University of Tuscia, Viterbo, Italy
{abraccini,tfederici}@unitus.it
[2] Department of Information Systems,
University of Agder, Kristiansand, Norway
oystein.sabo@uia.no

Abstract. While Online Communities (OCs) are increasingly used to involve people in organizations and societies, few studies focus on how OC influence political decision making within eParticipation initiatives. This issue is explored through an interpretive case-study of the Italian Five Star Movement (M5S), a mass-size eParticipation political initiative recently founded by private citizens. The use of OCs is a common strategy to involve groups of people to easily connect on-line, cooperating on common and shared interests. We here focus on understanding the internal and external forces influencing on the OCs, to better understand how to manage such OCs within the eParticipation domain. We do so by introducing the concept of tensions, to describe the states that these contrasting forces produce on the OCs, addressing the research question: what tensions occur in OCs for eParticipation? Our work contributes to a deeper understanding of the OCs phenomenon within the eParticipation domain, while also provides avenues for further research.

Keywords: Tensions · Online communities · eParticipation · eGovernment · Five start movement

1 Introduction and Motivation

Information and communication technologies (ICT) are increasingly being adopted to involve citizens in decision-making processes [1, 2] to recapture citizens' declining interest in politics. Research in the eParticipation area focuses on the identification of the processes and structures through which ICT supports the relationship between citizens, governments and public bodies [3, 4]. A vast majority of eParticipation studies focuses on the use of ICT in conjunction with traditional communication channels [5]. Only few of these eParticipation initiatives have achieved their intended aims [6], and many remain local or small-scale [1].

In this landscape, the Italian Five Star Movement's (M5S) uses an OC to encourage direct citizens' participation in politics, and represents an exceptional example for several reasons [7, 8]. First, the daily collective activities and decisions may engage online several thousand participants (even up to 40,000). M5S is hence among the largest

P. Parycek et al. (Eds.): ePart 2017, LNCS 10429, pp. 149–160, 2017.
DOI: 10.1007/978-3-319-64322-9_13

eParticipation projects in Europe. Second, the M5S was initiated from outside of the established elite as a protest organizations by initiators not being part of a traditional political system. Their online activities are really the core of their acting, not only something added on top of a traditional party's activities (like most eParticipation projects are). Third, all their decisions at the national level are made through processes performed online, making the OC's role central and eParticipation real. Finally, their success in attracting a large group of members to actively participate online seems to inspire similar kind of initiatives, in countries like Spain, Greece and Iceland.

The use of OC is a common strategy to involve groups of people to easily connect on-line, cooperating on common and shared interests [9]. However OCs are not stable entities [10]. OCs are under the effect of internal and external forces. The literature uses the concept of tension to describe the unstable conditions that these forces produce into the OCs [9, 11]. Tensions are inevitable for an OC, being produced and reproduced by their very nature [12] through the continuous co-presence of both the individual and the communal dimension [13]. Resources flow discontinuously inside communities, and at any moment there are alternative and competing possibilities for decisions, objectives, aims, and actions in the OC [9, 10].

Being inevitable, tensions cannot be resolved permanently, but should be managed [9] to allow an OC for eParticipation to achieve its aims. Since few researchers have addressed the issue of governing tensions in OC [9, 14], and fewer within the eParticipation domain [8, 15], we identify and discuss in this paper tensions within OCs for eParticipation purposes. Our work is motivated by the following research question: *which tensions occur in OCs for eParticipation?* The main contribution from our work is a better understanding of the role of tension within OCs in eParticipation project. Based on the identification of tensions and the discussion of how they influence an OC for eParticipation, we contribute by suggesting implications for practice and avenues for further research.

The rest of the paper is organised as follows: first, we introduce the theoretical premises for our work: OCs and tensions. Then, before introducing our results, we briefly present the research context and approach. We conclude by discussing our findings and providing implications for practice and trajectories for future research.

2 Theoretical Background

2.1 Online Communities

Internet and ICT are becoming more and more pervasive, reaching an enlarging share of the world population, and continuously providing new opportunities and new challenges to individuals and organizations. ICT make resources sharing, information diffusion, and cooperation among groups of people who have sporadic physical contacts easy [16], giving rise to OCs that affect actions and behaviours of individuals, teams, and organizations [10].

The relevance of OCs is still under dispute. On the one side, we observe OCs being used by individuals, teams and organizations to work and cooperate in a hitherto unseen manner, affording for flexibility, increased absorptive capacity, participated knowledge generation and circulation, empowered capability to pursue communal objectives together. On the other side, OCs form detached virtual worlds where people live in a bubble based on alternative facts and reality.

OCs are persistent collections of people who share common interests and goals, and who mainly communicate through the Internet [17]. In an OC members cooperate on, if, and when, they agree that this is better for them and for the OC itself [18] to solve issues they could otherwise not solve individually [19]. OCs are built for a variety of purposes, such as managing relations with customers and partners [20, 21] cooperating on knowledge generation [9, 10], or sharing information of public interest [22]. The communication flows through digital channels used by the OC to enable the collective action of members [23]. Structuring and managing the community to stimulate group actions and avoid the adverse outcome of independent actions is challenging [24]. Inside the community there is a coexistence of an individual and a collective rationality [12], which poses challenges to the actual realization of a collective action of the community where the communal objective prevails over individual goals.

2.2 Tensions in Online Communities

Few research studied tensions in OCs and how to manage them, as well as the consequences for the survival of the community itself [9, 13, 14, 25]. The concept of tension is used by the literature to define difficulties, internal or external to the community, or unstable conditions, oscillating between two different and competing states that the community should address to ensure community survival over time [9]. The tensions in OCs have been studied mainly at the level of community members' behaviour, possibly discussing the consequences that individual behaviours produce on the community itself.

Communications flow inside the OCs, and the related tensions that they might develop, are relevant for the community survival. Two different souls live in OCs: that of the individual, and that of the group. These two perspectives do not necessarily coincide, as what is good for the individual may not be good for the group. The opposite is also true. This produces consequences on individual and community decisions, generating tensions [12]. One intrinsic consequence to this regard is the tension generated by the conflict of communal versus individual orientation of the community. According to von Krogh et al. [26], the interaction of individuals and institutions inside OCs produce two different kinds of resources: internal and external. Internal resources are property of the individual, while external resources are public goods in the community. The production of internal and external resources always takes place concurrently, hence the tension between the communal versus the individual is unavoidable.

Given the continuously changing state of OCs, due to ebb and flow of resources [9], and to the competition between the communal and the private orientation [12, 26] tensions produce and reproduce continuously in the community. The literature agrees that tensions in OCs are not problems to be avoided, but rather enduring conditions that reproduce continuously. As a consequence, OCs' can only manage these tensions, and not solve them permanently [9, 27]. Such tension management would require the OC to act ambidextrously [14, 28], because not necessarily one aspect of the tension is desirable and the other is not desirable. Moreover, further tensions than those discussed by the literature, might be present in OCs [9]. When used for eParticipation strategies, the openness of OCs frictions with the strictures of institutional participation processes, and specific tensions arise also in such cases [7].

3 Research Design

The empirical setting investigated is that of the M5S, an Italian political movement born from an OC that uses this OC to involve citizens directly in the action of political institutions.

3.1 Case Context

The M5S is an Italian political movement that sharply distinguishes itself from traditional Italian parties. One of the main differences is that most activities related to the dissemination of political information, consultation, and decision-making processes are performed through online tools to promote citizens' involvement and participation in political processes. As an association, the M5S was established in 2009, building upon the community born since 2005 around the blog of Beppe Grillo, one of the founders and prominent member of the movement [29]. The M5S grew up throughout the years connecting an increasing number of people, and at the national elections in 2013 was the second most-voted party.

The OC is formed by people who follow the movement on-line. A subset of them also subscribe to the OC. Subscription is a voluntary process performed online, and is mandatory to fully participate to the collective action of the OC. Applications are evaluated and approved by the M5S staff. Upon approvals, applicants are 'certified' and have full access to the M5S OC. Applicants who are 'not yet certified' have their subscription on a pending status, and have limited access to the community in the form of restricted actions they are entitled to perform online. At the time of the data collection, the M5S OC connected about 100,000 certified subscribers, with 30,000-40,000 on average participating to online activities, and with 700,000 more subscriptions on a pending status.

The M5S OC is double layered: all members share the same tools and rules at the central national level, while at the local level members are organized in groups active across Italian territories, where every group chooses its own tools and adopts its own rules. People continuously interact with representatives, contributing to their work. Representatives are at the same time OC members, and sit it in institutions: since they are strictly obliged to follow OC decisions, they are named internally 'spokespersons'.

3.2 Data Collection and Analysis

The empirical setting was investigated through a qualitative research strategy with semi-structured interviews (approximately 13 h of recorded material) and archival data (internal documents, web pages, and observations of online platforms). We conducted nineteen interviews with different members of the OC. We interviewed members across two different towns' local groups, representatives sitting in the national parliament and in regional councils. Interviewees were distributed among what we identified as the three characteristics figures of stakeholders:

- Nine M5S representatives, among parliamentarians and councillors at regional and municipal level (entitled REP in the empirical section);
- Seven certified subscribers (SUB) of the M5S, from either local group;
- Three voters (VOT), who being non-subscriber declared to have voted for the M5S in the 2013 elections of the national parliament.

Based on a common interview track slightly adapted to meet each figure's point of view, interviewees were asked to report on difficulties within the M5S OC, and in the interplay between such community and the organizational setting of the institutions (e.g. councils of municipalities, regional parliament, and national parliament) in which representatives of the M5S sit and operate. The interviews were recorded, transcribed and analysed individually by the authors, who iteratively discussed the results of their individual analyses to compose a mutually agreed-upon interpretation. Archival data and observations data were also included and triangulated [30] to strengthen the relevance of the knowledge gleaned from interviews, archival data, and used ICT tools.

Following a grounded theory approach [31], the research team identified tensions letting them emerge from the data without adhering to any a priori constructs. The resulting ideas were later analysed considering current related literature to identify how the study added to existing research.

4 Empirical Evidences

We will here report findings related to the overall ideas of how tensions work in the M5S, before we summarize tensions identified through our analyses.

The M5S' main objective is to achieve direct citizen involvement in the decision-making processes of political institutions, to allow them to contribute to the generation of knowledge and decision-making processes. Our interviewees reported difficulties in such interplay, ascribed to OC members' lack of technical expertise in the issues discussed, and in the difference among values, rules, and routines between the community and the organizational setting of the political institution. For example, the M5S uses a system designed to collectively engage citizens in the co-production of law texts that M5S' representatives should propose in the institutions. The representatives reported the difficulties to use direct citizens' input, as the average citizen often lacks contextual and procedural knowledge which are instead required by the formal processes of the institution:

> 'We have many problems with this kind of approach, which is really impacting; it is really creating fights and battles with the traditional system because the rules are not built to bring the people in the institutions directly.' (REP1)

Another consequence concerns the volume of information generated using ICT: the produced pieces of information do not have a proper structure or organization, and this complicates the life of community members to contribute to the discussions and decision making. At the same time, the knowledge generation processes are not strictly focused to support representatives' needs, making it difficult to identify the contents that are useful for their work. Whereas ICT might facilitate a paradigm shift that will make organising collective actions more efficient [32], the example of the M5S illustrates the tension arising from the massive amount of content generated:

'The time constraint restricts my work. I had the ability to vote, but out of 800 candidates, I read about 400 CVs. I couldn't actually read all of them.' (SUB1)
'I cannot read 1,000 suggestions every day and understand which is best.' (REP2)

The M5S OC builds strongly on the potential advantages of reduced transaction costs to connect people and fluidity in team organization, leaving, by intention, groups free to self-organize in the OC. The M5S adopts a flat structure, with a limited set of rules and regulations, allowing members to freely organise in teams. At the same time, this makes the coordination of actions of OC's members more difficult. The structure of the OC follows a double-loop design, consisting of a structured core and a flexible periphery. The organic nature of the periphery is showed by the freedom to choose and change routines, rules, and coordination technologies, to bypass rules, and to change the mind on these aspects several times over time:

'The best tool will survive. We leave really to the activists the freedom to develop the best tool. It is our philosophy.' (REP1)
'When you set a regulation, you do not have to power off your brain. We have this regulation that forces us to rotate regulations but this guy has been working for two years in managing Twitter. Rationally, I would say: ok for the regulation, ok for the rotation, but he can do this and it would be a stupid thing to change this.' (SUB2)

The mechanic structure is at the central level, where the mediating technologies are more enforcing, improvisation is not possible (the technologies common to all OC are designed and deployed by the movement staff, and not by community members), and access is regulated by norms established by the movement.

In the frontier of interaction between the community and the institution, the clash on values, rules, and routines produces tensions. The presence of these tensions is witnessed by the mutual attempt of the OC and of the organizational setting of the institution to impose or extend their values, rules and routines on the other. The working dynamics in institutions rely on the delegations to the representatives, and create a divide with common practices, based on continue interaction with members and the sharing of decision-making of the M5S. They receive pressure from the institution, henceforth they try to impose their view on the organizational setting of the institution:

'We have many pressures [...] and it is not easy to keep our values because we have many bad influences. The political systems are trying to change us, I have many pressures from other parties to become like others, to change our values, to create alliances or collaboration that will change us [...] but at the same time we are trying to change the system from the outside.' (REP1)

The tensions arising between the community and the institutions might be an underpinning cause of the decay of the relationship between these two entities. The difficulties in letting the community easily interoperate with other organizations might influence on the individuals' motivation to stay within the OC, since members may find it difficult to identify how institutions are influenced by their individual contributions within the OC. The same might hold true from the other side, where the value of relying on the OC to reduce the costs of managing the relationships with stakeholders might be lower than the efforts needed to make sense of the contributions from OC.

5 Analysing Evidences

Based on the analysis of the M5S OC, we identified eight tensions. They are briefly introduced in Table 1 and further discussed below.

At any given moment, an OC can be in a state resulting from the tension between *Inertia* and *Action*. People inside the OC might act to achieve the objectives of the community, or they might do nothing, resulting in an OC remaining silent and inactive.

The activity of the community is subject to the influence of the tension between *Content vs Garbage*. OC are goal-oriented entities. When actions take place, they could generate targeted and useful contents in relation to the goal, or a mass of contents (here defined as garbage) not useful or not manageable for the aim of the OC. This condition is enforced in the case of OCs for eParticipation, where members are called to produce content.

An OC for eParticipation is a collection of people using Internet to achieve OC's aims, then sharing with everybody information and processes. While this is an opportunity for OC of showing in detail its action, it is also a way to disclose to other subjects plans and strategies, which may not be always convenient. There is a potential tension in finding the balance between the level of confidentiality in OC actions (*Private*) and the level of openness (*Public*) in the OC actions.

Action takes place in an OC for eParticipation and its sub-groups, which operate at a different level, being oriented to a specific territory or topic. If sub-groups are present, their actions may proceed according to common rules and using the same tools of the entire community, or instead the sub-community may adopt its own rules and tools. To this regard, OCs are subjects to tension between the internal *Groups* and the entire community (*Whole*).

Contents production may be open to all, when everyone may contribute to OC's action. In this case, an OC for eParticipation works just like a speaker's corner: whoever has something to tell may do so. On the contrary, OC may have rigid rules and standard procedures for allowing members to contribute, where members are required to fulfil programs and procedures before their contributions are accepted. OCs are hence impacted by a tension we have named *Speaker's Corner vs Conference*.

Information and procedures involving issues like how to join the OC, which roles and responsibilities are present, and how to contribute may be transparent and clear to all members (and potential members) of the OC. On the contrary, some working dynamics and rules existing in the OC might be (deliberately or not) ambiguous and difficult to identify, making it more demanding for members (and interested persons)

Table 1. Tensions within the OC

	Tension	Definition
1	Inertia vs Action	OC can be in the tension between the inertia (when people are not acting or doing nothing), and action (where people are taking actions in the community)
2	Content vs Garbage	Interaction among members in the OC is targeted to achieve a specific outcome (i.e. a decision, the production of a knowledge asset). In any given moment, the community can rely on useful contents and then it moves towards this target, or be immersed in loads of useless contributes (garbage) and it drifts without a specific route
3	Public vs Private Action	The use of internet technologies may lead the OC to reveal information to the external environment or not. Hence, there is a potential tension related to the level of openness (public actions) and the level of confidentiality (private actions)
4	Groups vs Whole	An OC is not a monolithic entity, but is composed by sub-groups. These sub-groups live inside the community sharing the same environment, but may also create micro-environments. It arises a tension when norms, values, processes or tools of the OC clash with that of the sub-groups
5	Speaker's Corner vs Conference	The tension is about the possibility to allow anybody to participate to the OC, contradicted by the possibility of restricting the participation based on selection processes
6	Transparent vs Obscure	There is a tension between transparency, where information on roles, rules and activities are communicated openly and explicitly to everyone, and obscurity, where such information may be only implicitly, indirectly and vaguely communicated
7	Liquid vs Solid	The tension here arises by the contrasting needs of keeping the OC liquid, by maintaining flexibility to dynamically adapt roles, rules, processes, and allowing exceptions from such if needed, and of reaching a solid state, where such regulations are stable and recognizable over a long period of time
8	Us vs Them	When an OC interacts with external institutions (e.g. other communities, governments, political parties), it either receives or put pressures on the environment, producing a tension, which in the end may make the OC re-ensemble the environment

who do not know exactly what to do and how. OCs may then experience the tension of *Transparency vs Obscurity*.

Internal processes and routines may be rigid and enforcing, leaving OC members with no other alternative than to fulfil them before being able to take actions, then reinforcing processes certainty. On the contrasting side, some (or even all) processes and routines may stay flexible and liquid, allowing for freedom to bypass or dynamically change existing rules, or to create new ones. The OC is therefore under the influence of the *Liquid vs Solid* tension, and it should effectively balance the two states.

An OC has boundaries and an external environment, and works specifically to distinguish between what is part of the OC and what is external to it. The OCs for eParticipation relate to external entities, such as government organisations, political parties and other OCs. These relationships involve exchanges through communication and actions: here, there may be differences in how the OC works in relation to the external entities. An OC for eParticipation needs to communicate externally, with the need for creating and defending its own identity, and to interact with other institutions, with possible great differences in the respective ways of acting. Therefore, an OC is influenced by the tension *Us vs Them*, with regards to how the OC relates with external entities and the environment.

6   Discussing Tensions

The M5S case shows that the interplay of large and complex OCs for eParticipation creates challenges and tensions. These tensions arise from: (i) the differences among values, rules, and routines internal to the community and that of the external environment that in our case is composed by the political institutions (tension 8); (ii) the different alternatives in terms of organizational arrangements of the interior of the OC (tensions 3 to 7); (iii) the different levels of commitment and motivation of OC members on the collective action (tension 1); and (iv) an externality of collective action (tension 2).

In the M5S case, the tension between the OC and the external environment is a consequence of a reciprocal effort to put pressure on each other, to let the other become more similar. The dynamics of this effort is in nature conflictual, up to the point that the isomorphism is seen also as a loss of identity. We assume that this originates in the organization of the political institutions, which includes units and groups in competition among themselves, so the loss of identity is a negative consequence that signals the defeat of the unit succumbing to the other in the competition. It is also important to point out that the M5S was born as a protest movement, and strong opposition to the political establishment is the glue that keeps the OC together. When internal competitions among organizational units is not in place, it should be investigated whether the management of the tensions between the community and the organization will still be conflictual or not.

The internal tensions relate to the different alternatives in terms of organizational arrangements of the OC. The literature stresses the need to structure the online community to have collective action [7, 8, 29]. However, due to the versatility of ICT, this can be realized in various ways. The different alternatives in the structuration of the internal processes supporting collective action (communication, contribution, decision-making models, and repertoire of contestations) give raise to tensions in the community as the results of different groups of members aiming for alternative ways of structuring.

The individual motivation is producing a tension in OC. The individual decision to contribute or not generates a fundamental tension in the OC, that of inertia vs action, which is a direct manifestation of the so called zero contribution thesis [23]. The M5S OC is designed to help citizens influence institutions by collecting ideas that, through the spokespersons, influence the political decision making processes. This depends on action of community member, while the lack of individual motivation may result in the lack of participation, giving rise to tensions among community members. Parties and movements rival to the M5S, take advantage of this by attempting to delegitimize action of the OC, arguing that this is not expression of the voluntary of a community, but the preference of a small number of individuals.

Finally, a tension relates to the externality of the collective action process. The literature on OCs is concerned with studying conditions that stimulates participation. These contributions praiseworthily aim at stimulating engagement by individuals, hence solving the inertia vs action tension. However, even in the presence of engagement, the OC is still under the tension of garbage vs content. In a mass size community like that of the M5S, a high level of engagement is a success indicator of the community. At the same time, a high level of engagement often leads to a high volume of useless actions and garbage, as members fail and producing a convergent result other than that of showing the presence on-line and declaring their support for the OC. Then, particularly in the case of OCs for eParticipation, it arises the need for a citizen-engagement strategy aimed at deriving more value from net-savvy citizens [33].

7 Conclusion and Further Work

The M5S' use of OC is a particularly interesting case to study for understanding eParticipation, because it sheds light on how an OC may address a huge number of citizens to create more participatory, open and transparent political discourses. Our case provides several evidences of the tensions that occur in OCs for eParticipation, because of their nature, their purposes and their organizational choices. Tensions are almost always inevitable for an OC, and often cannot be resolved permanently. Notwithstanding, to achieve its aims, an OC for eParticipation should find solutions to mitigate tensions' negative impact.

From the literature we learned that technologies used on OC have action capabilities that allow to achieve desired objectives [9]. An interesting avenue for further research is to investigate how mechanisms leveraging on such capabilities influence – reduce or increase – tensions within OCs. Issues to explore include how knowledge on tensions are broadening what we already know about dynamics of OC. On the same route, it will be important to raise implications for practice on how to balance these tensions within eParticipation projects. Future studies are needed also to better articulate how tensions may influence on OCs operating in the broader eGovernment area.

Another interesting suggestion for furthering research is the apparent commonality of many identified tensions also with OCs pertaining to domains different to eParticipation. Such suggestion asks for more study in various contexts.

References

1. Medaglia, R.: eParticipation research: moving characterization forward (2006–2011). Gov. Inf. Q. **29**, 346–360 (2012)
2. Sæbø, Ø., Rose, J., Flak, L.: The shape of eParticipation: characterizing an emerging research area. Gov. Inf. Q. (2008)
3. Rahman, M.M., Ahsan Rajoin, S.A.: An effective framework for implementing electronic governance in developing countries: bangladesh perspective. Int. J. Comput. Inf. Technol. **3**, 360–365 (2012)
4. Veit, D., Huntgerburth, J.: Foundations of Digital Government. Leading and Managing in the Digital Era. Springer-Verlag, Berlin, Heidelberg (2014)
5. Criado, J.I., Sandoval-Almazan, R., Gil-Garcia, J.R.: Government innovation through social media. Gov. Inf. Q. **30**, 319–326 (2013)
6. Sæbø, Ø., Flak, L.S., Sein, M.K.: Understanding the dynamics in e-Participation initiatives: looking through the genre and stakeholder lenses. Gov. Inf. Q. **28**, 416–425 (2011)
7. Federici, T., Braccini, A.M., Sæbø, Ø.: "Gentlemen, all aboard!" ICT and party politics: reflections from a Mass-eParticipation experience. Gov. Inf. Q. **32**, 287–298 (2015)
8. Braccini, A.M., Federici, T., Sæbø, Ø.: Exploring collective action dynamics in online communities from a critical realist perspective. In: D'Ascenzo, F., Magni, M., Lazazzara, A., Za, S. (eds.) Blurring the Boundaries Through Digital Innovation. LNISO, vol. 19, pp. 271–282. Springer, Cham (2016). doi:10.1007/978-3-319-38974-5_21
9. Faraj, S., Jarvenpaa, S., Majchrzak, A.: Knowledge collaboration in online communities. Organ. Sci. **22**, 1224–1239 (2011)
10. Majchrzak, A., Faraj, S., Kane, G.C., Azad, B.: The contradictory influence of social media affordances on online communal knowledge sharing. J. Comput. Commun. **19**, 38–55 (2013)
11. Kane, G.C., Johnson, J., Majchrzak, A.: Emergent life cycle: the tension between knowledge change and knowledge retention in open online coproduction communities. Manage. Sci. **60**, 3026–3048 (2014)
12. Kollock, P., Smith, M.: Managing the virtual commons: cooperation and conflict in computer communities. In: Herring, S.C. (ed.) Computer-Mediated Communication: Linguistic, Social, and Cross-Cultural Perspectives, pp. 109–128. John Benjamins Publishing Company, Amsterdam/Philadelphia (1996)
13. Hutter, K., Hautz, J., Füller, J., Mueller, J., Matzler, K.: Communitition: the tension between competition and collaboration in community-based design contests. Creat. Innov. Manag. **20**, 3–21 (2011)
14. Huang, J., Baptista, J., Newell, S.: Communicational ambidexterity as a new capability to manage social media communication within organizations. J. Strateg. Inf. Syst. **24**, 49–64 (2015)
15. Wahid, F., Sæbø, Ø.: affordances and effects of promoting eParticipation through social media. In: Tambouris, E., Panagiotopoulos, P., Sæbø, Ø., Tarabanis, K., Wimmer, Maria A., Milano, M., Pardo, Theresa A. (eds.) ePart 2015. LNCS, vol. 9249, pp. 3–14. Springer, Cham (2015). doi:10.1007/978-3-319-22500-5_1
16. Majchrzak, A., Markus, M.L.: Technology Affordances and Constraints in Management Information Systems (Mis). Encycl. Manag. Theory. **5** (2012)
17. Preece, J.: Online Communities: Designing Usability and Supporting Socialbilty (2000)
18. Olson, M.: The Logic of Collective Action. Harvard University Press, Cambridge (2009)
19. Flanagin, A.J., Stohl, C., Bimber, B.: Modeling the structure of collective action. Commun. Monogr. **73**, 29–54 (2006)

20. Dellarocas, C.: Strategic manipulation of internet opinion forums: implications for consumers and firms. Manage. Sci. **52**, 1577–1593 (2006)
21. Leidner, D.E., Kock, H., Gonzalez, E.: Assimilating generation Y IT new hires into USAA's workforce: the role of an enterprise 2.0 system. MIS Q. Exec. **9**, 229–242 (2010)
22. Wasko, M.M., Faraj, S.: Why should i share? Examining social capital and knowledge contribution in electronic networks of practice. MIS Q. **29**, 35–57 (2005)
23. Ostrom, E.: Collective action and the evolution of social norms. J. Econ. Perspect. **14**, 137–158 (2000)
24. Ostrom, E.: Governing the Commons (1990)
25. Ribes, D., Finholt, T.A.: The long now of technology infrastructure: articulating tensions in development. J. Assoc. Inf. Syst. **10**, 375–398 (2009)
26. von Krogh, G., Haefliger, S., Spaeth, S., Wallin, M.: Carrots and rainbows: Motivation and social practice in open source software development. MIS Q. **36**, 649–676 (2012)
27. Ågerfalk, P.J., Fitzgerald, B.: Outsourcing to an unknown workforce: exploring open-sourcing as a global sourcing strategy. MIS Q. **32**, 385–409 (2008)
28. O'Reilly, C.A.I., Tushman, M.L.: Organizational ambidexterity: past, present, and future. Acad. Manag. Perspect. **27**, 324–338 (2013)
29. Sæbø, Ø., Braccini, A.M., Federici, T.: From the blogosphere into real politics: The use of ICT by the five star movement. In: Mola, L., Pennarola, F., Za, S. (eds.) Lecture Notes in Information Systems and Organisation, pp. 241–250. Springer International Publishing, Cham (2015)
30. Eisenhardt, K.M.: Building theories from case study research. Acad. Manag. Rev. **4**, 532–550 (1989)
31. Corbin, J., Strauss, A.: Basics of Qualitative Research. Techniques and Procedures for Developing Grounded Theory. SAGE Publications Inc., Thousand Oaks (2015)
32. Bekkers, V., Edwards, A., de Kool, D.: Social media monitoring: Responsive governance in the shadow of surveillance? Gov. Inf. Q. **30**, 335–342 (2013)
33. Chatfield, A.T., Scholl, H(., Brajawidagda, U.: Tsunami early warnings via Twitter in government: net-savvy citizens' co-production of time-critical public information services. Gov. Inf. Q. **30**, 377–386 (2013)

Author Index

Printed in the United States
By Bookmasters